Teaching a People's History of Abolition and the Civil War

Edited by Adam Sanchez

A Rethinking Schools Publication

Teaching a People's History of Abolition and the Civil War
Edited by Adam Sanchez

A Rethinking Schools Publication

Rethinking Schools is a nonprofit publisher and advocacy organization dedicated to sustaining and strengthening public education through social justice teaching and education activism. Our magazine, books, and other resources promote equity and racial justice in the classroom. We encourage grassroots efforts in our schools and communities to enhance the learning and well-being of our children, and to build broad democratic movements for social and environmental justice.

Rethinking Schools
6737 West Washington Street, Suite 3249
Milwaukee, Wisconsin 53214
800-669-4192
www.rethinkingschools.org

© 2019 Rethinking Schools, Ltd.
First edition

Cover Design: Nancy Zucker
Book Design: Kate Hawley
Proofreading: Lawrence Sanfilippo
Operations Director: Gina Palazzari
Front cover image: Howard Barry

ISBN: 978-0-942961-05-8

Table of Contents

Acknowledgements

Teaching a People's History of Abolition and the Civil War, like all Rethinking Schools publications, is the result of a collective effort. In addition to Rethinking Schools editors and staff, the Zinn Education Project (ZEP) team played an essential role in overseeing the book from start to finish. Huge thanks to the ZEP and Rethinking Schools family: Wayne Au, Bill Bigelow, Ari Bloomekatz, Lindsay Stevens, Michael Charney, Linda Christensen, Grace Cornell Gonzales, Lauren Cooper, Jesse Hagopian, Bill Holtzman, Stan Karp, David Levine, Deborah Menkart, Larry Miller, Nqobile Mthethwa, Katie Orr, Gina Palazzari, Mykella Palmer, Bob Peterson, Dyan Watson, Ursula Wolfe-Rocca, Moé Yonamine, and Missy Zombor.

Rethinking Schools Curriculum Editor and ZEP Co-Director Bill Bigelow has been my teaching and editing mentor even before this project began. He wrote half of the lessons in this book and provided invaluable support throughout the editorial and production process. Teaching for Change executive director and ZEP co-director Deborah Menkart also provided crucial editorial feedback. Zinn Education Project organizer Victoria Smalls helped collect the images used throughout the book.

Lesson 4 was originally drafted by Portland, Oregon, teachers Brady Bennon and Deb Delman. My colleague Jessica Lovaas also added several roles to that lesson that helped round out the types of abolitionists represented. Linda Christensen's work provided essential inspiration for Lessons 2 and 10. Thanks to Alyss Dixson for allowing us to use her poem, "Write that I . . . (A Frederick Douglass Narrative)" in Lesson 2.

I am grateful for the layout and design work by Kate Hawley and Nancy Zucker as well as the cover art by Howard Barry.

New York City art teachers Caryn Davidson and Brittany Kaiser provided helpful suggestions for Lesson 5. Brian Jones and Leslie Harris gave important feedback on early drafts of the book as a whole.

The students, teachers, and administrators at Harvest Collegiate High School have provided me with the support and rich intellectual environment that have helped hone my craft and shaped many of these lessons over the last few years. Thank you Sally Abdelghafar, Kate Burch, Andrew Del Calvo, Fayette Colon, Liana Donahue, Mike Dunson, Steve Lazar, Jessica Lovaas, Daniel Marshall, Andy Snyder, Joshua Vasquez, and Nitzan Ziv. Special thanks to my students Cassidy Pacheco, Lisa Narinedhat, Jada Vazquez, and Angela Washington for allowing me to quote or photograph them for the book or feature their artwork in Lesson 5.

Finally, my partner Madelynn Katz provided both editorial and pedagogical commentary on several lesson drafts as well as other support that allowed me to work on the book. I could not have completed this project without her. Our new daughter, Yemaya Fae Sanchez, gives me a renewed determination to help provide a people's history to young people who desperately deserve a better world.

Introduction

Why We Need a People's History of Abolition and the Civil War

By Adam Sanchez

EVERY YEAR, I start teaching about slavery and the Civil War by asking my high school students "Who freed the slaves?" Without fail, the vast majority, if not the entire class, answers "Abraham Lincoln." Holding back my desire to immediately puncture this simplistic narrative, I continue questioning: "Well, if Lincoln was the Great Emancipator and freed the slaves, what do you think he said in his first speech as president?" My students throw out various hypotheses that I list on the board: Slavery is evil, immoral, unjust; people should have equal rights regardless of color; it's time to get rid of slavery; slaveholders should be punished; and so on.

We then turn to Lincoln's actual first inaugural address and students are shocked to read that Lincoln

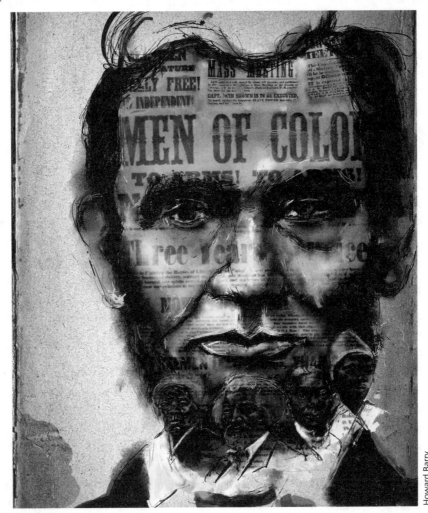

Abolitionists played a key role in pressuring Lincoln toward emancipation.

Howard Barry

stated that he had "no inclination" to "interfere with the institution of slavery in the states where it exists," that he promised to uphold the Fugitive Slave Act, and that he expressed support for the Corwin Amendment, which would have prevented Congress from ever tampering with slavery in any state. For many students, this is a rupture of epic proportions. "Were we lied to?" they ask. "Did Lincoln really free the slaves?" "If he didn't, who did?" "What else have we been lied to about?" These kinds of questions can ignite deep learning and historical engagement.

The real story of slavery's end involves one of the most significant social movements in the history of the United States and the heroic actions of the enslaved themselves. Revealing this history helps students begin to answer fundamental questions that urgently need to be addressed in classrooms across the country: How does major social change occur? What is the relationship between those at the top of society — presidents, Congress, elites — and ordinary citizens? What kind of power do "leaders" have? What kind of power do we have? What role have Black people played in fighting for their own liberation? What role have white people played in maintaining and fighting Black oppression? Can social movements make a difference? How can we learn from the past to influence the future?

Today, hate crimes against Black people and other people of color continue. Police regularly murder Black citizens with impunity. The wealth gap between Black families and white families is staggering and continues to widen. We need to arm a new generation with not just an historical understanding of slavery, racism, and oppression, but also the heroic history of anti-racist struggle. If problematic, simplistic historical narratives — like Lincoln freed the slaves — persist, our students will confront the world without understanding how change happens. What could be more important than learning how one of the country's greatest evils was ended? It's in this spirit that my colleagues and I at the Zinn Education Project have prepared the 10 lessons and materials in *Teaching a People's History of Abolition and the Civil War*.

Rethinking Lincoln, Emancipation, and the Civil War

Of course, Lincoln's views on slavery and Black rights did not start or end with his first speech as president. As an Illinois congressman, Lincoln endorsed state laws barring Blacks from voting, holding office, serving as jurors, and marrying white people. Lincoln strenuously opposed extending slavery into new U.S. states and territories and denounced the institution as a "monstrous injustice," but he also did not believe that the Constitution gave the federal government power to interfere with slavery where it existed. His preferred strategy was one of gradual emancipation, compensating slaveholders for their loss, and sending free Blacks to be colonized outside of the United States.

But by his second inaugural address in 1865, Lincoln had issued the Emancipation Proclamation and campaigned for the 13th Amendment abolishing slavery without compensation or colonization. In this speech, he was much less conciliatory toward the South. He painted an image of divine retribution against slavery's horrors by stating that "every drop of blood drawn with the lash shall be paid by another drawn with the sword." It's the Lincoln of 1865 that has been memorialized as the Great Emancipator. But what prompted Lincoln to change his public position?

To start, in order to demythologize Lincoln, it's necessary to demythologize the North. At the start of the war, Lincoln was under immense pressure from Northern bankers who had financed slavery and from Northern businessmen whose profits depended on their financial ties with the South. The entire U.S. economy — not just Southern plantations — was built on the labor of enslaved Blacks. Although by 1860 enslaved people made up less than 13 percent of the population, their economic worth (in dehumanizing

> *For many students, this is a rupture of epic proportions. "Were we lied to?" they ask. "Did Lincoln really free the slaves?" "If he didn't, who did?" "What else have we been lied to about?"*

capitalist terms) was valued at more than the factories, banks, and railroads combined. This is why in 1861, shortly after the South seceded, Mayor Fernando Wood suggested to the New York City Council that the city should also secede. The Northern financial and industrial elite were determined to keep their profitable relationship with the South. When compromise failed, they turned to war. The 1860 Republican platform recognized that "to the Union of the States this nation owes . . . its rapid augmentation of wealth." Now that wealth was in danger. The new Confederacy nullified $300 million in debt the South owed Northern creditors and Northern elites were determined to recover their losses. As Lincoln asked in a July 1861 message to Congress, justifying waging a war for union, "Is it just . . . that creditors should go unpaid?" When Lincoln insisted repeatedly during the early years of the war that he was fighting the Civil War not to end slavery, but to restore the Union, he was not only worried about the border slave states that had remained in the Union defecting to the Confederacy. He was also signaling to the capitalists of the North that the war would be waged in their interests.

But there were other interests that Lincoln was forced to consider. The abolitionists and, most importantly, the enslaved themselves understood that slavery was so monstrous that it needed to be completely eliminated. For decades prior to the war, abolitionists — Black and white, male and female — petitioned the government, organized rallies and public meetings, produced antislavery pamphlets and books, ran candidates for public office, built new political parties, and created a vast network to harbor runaways and resist slave catchers. By the time of the war, abolitionist ideas had seeped into the new Republican Party. When Republicans swept the 1860 election, antislavery activists nevertheless continued their familiar tactics and criticized Lincoln's and Congress' half-measures. Yet now they reached a new, enlarged audience that included those in the halls of power. Formerly derided as radical extremists, the abolitionists seemed prophetic as it became clear to many that the war could not be won without destroying slavery.

The enslaved, who had fought back in various ways since slavery began, escalated their own resistance during the Civil War. As soon as the Union Army came within reach, enslaved people freed themselves — by the tens of thousands. As historian Vincent Harding wrote:

> This was Black struggle in the South as the guns roared, coming out of loyal and disloyal states, creating their own liberty. . . . Every day they came into the Northern lines, in every condition, in every season of the year, in every state of health. . . . No more auction block, no more driver's lash. This was the river of Black struggle in the South, waiting for no one to declare freedom for them. . . . The rapid flow of Black runaways was a critical part of the challenge to the embattled white rulers of the South; by leaving, they denied slavery's power and its profit.

These runaways also created opportunities for the all-white Union Army, in desperate need of soldiers and laborers. Lincoln realized that the Union needed Black soldiers to win the war. Although it is possible to interpret Lincoln's Emancipation Proclamation as an exceptionally cautious document, declaring the enslaved free in only those parts of the Confederacy where Lincoln had no direct control, and exempting the border slave states and other Union-controlled areas in the South, it was nonetheless an acknowledgement of the changing public opinion in the North and the reality of self-emancipation on the front lines. The proclamation officially opened the army to African Americans for the first time. With Black soldiers now taking up arms against the Confederacy, Lincoln's war for union was transformed into a war for liberation. The emancipation of 4 million people from slavery ushered in a revolutionary transformation of U.S. society led by African Americans.

If problematic, simplistic historical narratives — like Lincoln freed the slaves — persist, our students will confront the world without understanding how change happens.

More than 186,000 Black soldiers fought in the Civil War.

The reason corporate curriculum and conservative textbooks so often hide or distort this history is because truly understanding the causes of the Civil War, and how that war was transformed, requires an approach that questions those in power and emphasizes collective resistance. As Howard Zinn explained:

> When I look at the history of the United States, what I see is that whenever anything good has been accomplished, whenever any injustice has been remedied . . . it has come about only when citizens became aroused. That's how slavery was abolished. Slavery was not abolished because Abraham Lincoln issued the Emancipation Proclamation. Slavery was abolished because slaves, the ex-slaves, the escaped slaves, and some white abolitionists got together and formed a great movement against slavery. That movement grew from a small group of people into a national movement that committed acts of civil disobedience and violated the law, violated the Fugitive Slave Act, which required the government to return escaped slaves to their masters. People broke into courthouses, broke into police stations; they rescued slaves, and all kinds of acts of civil disobedience took place. Only then did Lincoln act, only then did Congress act, to abolish slavery, to pass constitutional amendments. And we see this all through American history.

To understand abolition and the Civil War then, is to understand how ordinary citizens — with ideas that seem radical and idealistic, taking action together, breaking unjust laws, pressuring politicians to act — can fundamentally change society. There is no more important lesson that our students can learn from studying history.

The purpose of this unit is not to simply dethrone Lincoln as the Great Emancipator. There have been many worthwhile defenses of Lincoln's record, his antislavery intentions, and his actions. No doubt, when put into historical context and seen through his point of view, Lincoln can be a sympathetic figure. But the popular narrative that a single white politician ended an institution that formed the economic backbone of U.S. society is simply inaccurate, racist, and dangerous. It took the courageous actions of hundreds of thousands to crush such a profitable system of brutal exploitation. Our job as educators should be to expand the viewpoints through which our students look at history. As Zinn pointed out, "Lincoln was a politician. . . . We are citizens. We must not put ourselves in the position of looking at the world from their eyes and say, 'Well, we have to compromise, we have to do this for political reasons.' We have to speak our minds." I've found that students are capable of complex thinking around the role that Lincoln played in the abolition of slavery. However, students' conclusions about Lincoln are less important than their ability to develop an understanding that the abolitionists and the enslaved fundamentally shifted the political terrain that Lincoln was operating on — in other words, a more complex historical narrative that puts ordinary citizens, like themselves, at the center.

The reason corporate curriculum and conservative textbooks so often hide or distort this history is because truly understanding the causes of the Civil War, and how that war was transformed, requires an approach that questions those in power and emphasizes collective resistance.

Furthermore, it was not simply Lincoln who was transformed during the war. Opening the Union Army to Blacks had profound effects on white soldiers and the Northern white public. In the Freedmen and Southern Society Project's book *Free at Last: A Documentary History of Slavery, Freedom, and the Civil War*, the editors write, "Nothing eradicated the prejudices of white soldiers as effectively as Black soldiers performing well under fire. . . . General James S. Brisbin, who supervised the recruitment of Black soldiers in Kentucky, described to his superiors how the 'jeers and taunts' of white soldiers were silenced by their Black comrades' bravery." And maybe nothing reveals the rapid shift in public opinion more than the warm welcome white New Yorkers gave the 20th U.S. Colored Infantry, the first Black regiment formed in New York City, as they paraded down the city streets in February 1864. Only seven months earlier, Blacks had been brutally beaten and murdered during the draft riots. While racism survived the abolition of slavery, the bold actions of Black men and women in securing and defining freedom, and the changing racial attitudes of white citizens in response, laid the foundation for postwar anti-racist politics. As abolitionist Wendell Phillips wrote to Sen. Charles Sumner, "These are no times for ordinary politics; they are formative hours. The national purpose and thought ripens in 30 days as much as ordinary years bring it forward." This concept — that people's ideas can change, and sometimes change rapidly — is crucial for students who have grown up in a world full of racism, sexism, warmongering, and climate denial.

We need a curriculum that surfaces the moments of solidarity, resistance, and courage that made this a more just, more inclusive society. Students often feel alienated from history and politics because they are told that great (usually white) men make history. Too often, students arrive in my classroom cynical about the possibility for social change. There are countless stories of collective struggle that are antidotes to cynicism. Let's tell them.

A Bottom-Up Pedagogy

As the classroom story beginning this introduction makes clear, one of the aims of this unit is to develop students' ability to pose critical questions about history and rethink narratives they have previously accepted. But in order to develop students' democratic capacities, it's not enough to simply tell them an alternative account. As Rethinking Schools curriculum editor Bill Bigelow puts it, "A people's history requires a people's pedagogy."

Many of the lessons in this collection first appeared on the Zinn Education Project website. The Zinn Education Project, coordinated by Rethinking Schools and Teaching for Change, has promoted and supported the teaching of people's history in classrooms across the country for more than 10 years. In my classrooms, first in Portland, Oregon, and then in New York City, I developed this unit incorporating lessons from the Zinn Education Project and adding others I developed with help from my colleagues. While working as the Zinn Education Project organizer and curriculum writer during the 2017–2018 school year, I began to knit these lessons together into a coherent unit. With the support and advice of the Zinn Education Project staff, the lessons in this unit draw from a variety of pedagogical methods that aim to not just teach content, but also crucial academic and civic skills.

The first two lessons in the unit begin with narrative and poetry in an attempt to nurture empathy with the plight of the enslaved, but also appreciation for the varied ways Black people resisted their enslavement. "Lesson 1: Frederick Douglass Fights for Freedom" attempts to ground what can often seem like distant history in the lives of our students, while "Lesson 2: Poetry of Defiance" culminates in a collective "Write that I" poem that asks students to center and celebrate resistance in telling the history of the enslaved.

The next several lessons attempt to paint a picture of the social movement that developed to combat slavery. Through role play, these lessons ask students to imagine themselves as abolitionists and consider the choices that these activists faced.

"Lesson 3: If There Is No Struggle. . . ," for example, asks students to portray members of the American Anti-Slavery Society. In character, they confront the questions that abolitionist organizers also encountered: Should they support attempts to buy enslaved people and colonize them out of the country? Should they maintain a singular focus on slavery in the South or spend their energies also opposing racism in the North? Should they support the Seneca Falls gathering by women's rights advocates, or do they think this would divide the movement? How should they respond to the 1850 Fugitive Slave Act? Should they support John Brown's daring raid to capture the federal arsenal at Harpers Ferry?

By confronting these questions as abolitionists, students are able to see that people make history. Rather than seen as an inevitable stream of events, students in this lesson encounter history as a series of choices and turning points that either pushed the abolitionist movement forward or held it back. By running their own meeting and making decisions collectively, this lesson also allows students to gain valuable skills they need as engaged citizens, skills too often de-emphasized in the era of high-stakes testing.

Too often, students arrive in my classroom cynical about the possibility for social change. There are countless stories of collective struggle that are antidotes to cynicism. Let's tell them.

"Lesson 4: Who Fought to End Slavery?" introduces students to 28 prominent and lesser-known abolitionists. Through a mixer role play, students confront different tactics used and conflicting ideas held by these individuals in their efforts to abolish slavery. In "Lesson 5: Raising the Voices of Abolitionists Through Art," students read and listen to abolitionist speeches and analyze abolitionist art. Utilizing the powerful words they encounter during the lesson, students then make art of their own.

In "Lesson 6: Mapping the Slave Economy," the focus shifts to the economic roots of the Civil War. This classroom simulation and the accompanying reading challenge another historical fable: the virtuous antislavery North.

"Lesson 7: The Election of 1860 Role Play" gives students a clearer picture of the electoral coalition that brought Lincoln to power. Students take on the roles of different social groups, confront the major issues the different candidates addressed, and ultimately decide who they will vote for.

Armed with a deeper understanding of the economic and political landscape before Lincoln's election, students then analyze some of the main causes of the Civil War and question their prior assumptions. "Lesson 8: A War to Free the

Slaves?" challenges one common misunderstanding: that Lincoln and the North waged war against the South to free the enslaved. Through a close reading of Lincoln's first inaugural address and the Emancipation Proclamation, students are encouraged to rethink the war's initial purpose.

Throughout the unit, we attempt to provide teachers with student-friendly readings that reinforce these main themes often left out of the K–12 curriculum: the resistance of the enslaved, the history of the abolitionist movement, and Northern complicity in slavery. "Lesson 9: 'Who Freed the Slaves?' Civil War Jigsaw" asks students to critically weigh how historians emphasize different historical actors when storying slavery's demise. The final lesson asks students to construct their own argument from the varied perspectives they encounter throughout the unit.

One caveat: Although the first few lessons provide some background, this unit is not directly about the institution of slavery itself. These lessons are an attempt to bring to life in the classroom the rich history of antislavery resistance. The success of that resistance opened up a new set of questions during the Reconstruction era, which are explored in the Afterword and in a subsequent lesson. Around the same time I began to compile this unit, the Zinn Education Project began our Teach Reconstruction campaign because too often Reconstruction is given short shrift in classrooms and history textbooks. We hope this unit can lay the basis for a stronger understanding of Reconstruction by engaging students in looking at the process that began with resistance to slavery, culminated in the Civil War, and subsequently led to some of the most dramatic social and political changes in U.S. history.

As Howard Zinn reminded us, moments like the triumphant struggle against slavery "should be remembered because they suggest to us what is possible for apparently powerless people to accomplish in the face of overwhelming odds." Today, from climate change to mass incarceration, we face overwhelming odds. But this unit aims to help students and teachers across the country envision the possibility of overcoming those odds and building a better world.

Suggestions for Use

If taught in its entirety this curriculum will require at least three weeks, assuming the class meets every day. Furthermore, "Lesson 10: Arguing Abolition: Essay with an Attitude" encourages teachers to not just assign an essay at the end of the unit, but to also teach essay writing, which can take another significant chunk of class time. In other words, it's a long unit but worth it, as the lessons focus on fundamental issues about the nature of today's society, and how we got here.

This brief introduction tries to make the case for why we should devote so much time to the question of how slavery ended in the United States. As a general rule, we encourage schools and social studies teachers to consider the benefits of prioritizing depth over breadth. Nevertheless, we also recognize that many teachers are limited, for various reasons, in how much class time they can allot to a particular subject. Should you find yourself with less time than you would like, we suggest using the following as a guide:

ONE-WEEK CURRICULUM:

Lesson 2: Poetry of Defiance: How the Enslaved Resisted

Lesson 4: Who Fought to End Slavery? Meet the Abolitionists

Lesson 6: Mapping the Slave Economy

Lesson 8: A War to Free the Slaves?

Lesson 9: "Who Freed the Slaves?" Civil War Jigsaw

TWO-WEEK CURRICULUM:

Add: Lesson 3: If There Is No Struggle. . .

Lesson 7: The Election of 1860 Role Play

THREE-WEEK CURRICULUM:

Add: Lesson 1: Frederick Douglas Fights for Freedom

Lesson 5: Raising the Voices of Abolitionists Through Art

One final note: The curriculum in this unit is mostly chronological, focusing primarily on the period between 1830 and 1865. Although for the most part we recommend approaching this history in the order the lessons are laid out, as I mention in the classroom story that begins the introduction, opening the unit with a close reading of Lincoln's first inaugural speech — the first half of "Lesson 8: A War to Free the Slaves?" — can be a powerful way to "hook" students.

Frederick Douglass Fights for Freedom

BY BILL BIGELOW

ANY STUDY OF SLAVERY in the United States should convey its horrors, but also the numerous and varied ways African Americans resisted their enslavement — how they sought to maintain their humanity in a system that regarded them as nothing more than a unique form of property. An important document of resistance is the autobiographical *Narrative of the Life of Frederick Douglass*, published in 1845. In this book, conceived as a tool for the abolition movement, Douglass describes his life from slavery to escape to freedom.

Frederick Douglass was celebrated for his resistance to slavery and his many contributions to the abolitionist movement. Here his picture is used to illustrate the sheet music for an antislavery song.

The lesson described here asks students to empathize with Douglass' desperate confrontation with slave owners and their agents by drawing on their own experiences resisting those who would seek to control them. This is not to suggest any parity of oppression between slavery and students' lack of independence. But our imaginative capacity is limited by our experience, and it's that experience we must use as a resource if we're to attempt to comprehend the lives of others.

As the student handout "Their Lives and Ours" suggests, "It's impossible for us to fully understand the conditions in people's lives that prompted them to rise up against the slave system. As Frederick Douglass himself pointed out, 'He only can understand the deep satisfaction which I experienced, who has himself repelled the bloody arm of slavery.' But by digging into our own experiences, we can try."

This personal storytelling lesson also honors the tradition of narrative writing by formerly enslaved people. Frederick Douglass's *Narrative* may be the most prominent of these, but there were an estimated 150 published testimonies of slavery during the 18th and 19th centuries that made up an essential canon of literary resistance to the slave system.

Materials Needed

- Copies of excerpt from *Narrative of the Life of Frederick Douglass* (Handout 1–A) for every student. Note that some additional paragraph breaks have been added to this excerpt for ease of student reading.

- Copies of "Their Lives and Ours" (Handout 1–B) for every student

- Optional: Copies of "Narrative Criteria Sheet" (Handout 1–C) for every student

Time Required

One class period to read excerpt and begin writing. Another period to share student writing.

Suggested Procedure

1. Generally, I read the excerpt from Frederick Douglass' narrative (p. 13–16) to students. The structure of the language is a bit archaic and, if read haltingly, loses much of its power. An alternative is to ask one or more students to preview and rehearse the reading in advance of the class session. Before reading, ask students what they know about Douglass. The following are some discussion questions for the excerpt:

   - Douglass decides to walk seven miles from Covey's place to his master's. Why might Douglass have felt that his master would be more sympathetic than Covey?

   - How is Douglass affected by Master Thomas' refusal to act on his complaint?

   - Both Covey and Douglass' master use violence and the threat of violence to get what they want. Why was violence so much a part of the slave system?

   - What would you have found most difficult about Douglass' situation? How would you have wanted to respond?

   - In addition to Douglass' fight with Covey, what other acts of resistance do we see in this excerpt? [You might draw students' attention to the fact that Bill refuses to help Covey beat Douglass even though he is ordered to do so.]

   - How does the battle with Covey change Douglass? Why does it have this effect on him?

   - At the beginning of the excerpt, Douglass writes, "You have seen how a man was made a slave; you shall see how a slave was made a man." How was a slave made a man?

   - How might Douglass' defiance have affected other enslaved people?

   - Douglass was a single, young man when he resisted Covey in the passage we read. Can you think of reasons why enslaved people in different circumstances might have chosen not to resist in the way Douglass did?

2. Tell students you want them to reflect on their own lives as a way of empathizing — if only partially — with Frederick Douglass' defiance. As Douglass himself points out, "He only can understand the deep satisfaction which I experienced, who has himself repelled the bloody arm of slavery." But by digging into our own experiences, we can try.

3. Distribute "Their Lives and Ours" (Handout 1–B) to every student. Read this aloud. Ask students to think about a time in their lives that might fall into one of the three categories listed — when they defied unjust authority, acted on behalf of someone else, or worked collectively to make something better, more fair. In the first instance, it could have been a time when, like Douglass, they fought with someone physically, but it could also have been a time when the defiance was not physical, and perhaps even quite subtle. Offer some examples from your life for each of these: when you refused to teach the assigned curriculum because it was insulting to students' intelligence; when you challenged a friend who you felt was mistreating another friend; when you organized with other community people to protest pollution from a coal-fired power plant; when you joined with teachers in the school district to wear Black Lives Matter T-shirts. Give students a few minutes to list some experiences.

4, Ask for several volunteers to offer short, couple-sentence descriptions of incidents from their lists. Write these on the board to preserve as prompts for other students who may have difficulty thinking of appropriate experiences.

5. My wife and former teaching partner, Linda Christensen, frequently begins writing assignments by leading students in a "guided visualization." When she first introduced me to this technique, I thought it sounded hokey, and too "touchy-feely" for my pedagogical tastes. But it clearly made such a difference in the detail and depth of people's writing, as well as in their capacity to begin their stories, that I became a convert. A visualization might proceed something like this: Once you sense that every student has selected an incident to write about, close the blinds in the classroom and turn off the lights. Ask students to put their heads on their desks and to close their eyes. Say, "Recall where you were when this happened. Were you inside or outside? Was it clear or rainy? What was the temperature? . . . [Pause about 30 seconds between your questions, indicated by ellipses.] Who was there? One by one recall the faces of the people involved. . . . Did any of them speak? Did you speak? What was said? . . . Play the whole experience out in your head, as if it was all caught on video. . . . Try to remember how you felt during this experience. Did you feel anger? fear? sadness? . . . What was the straw that broke the camel's back—what triggered your action? . . . How did you feel when you realized that you weren't going to allow yourself to be controlled, to be silent, or to do nothing? . . . How did you feel after this was all over? . . . When I turn the lights on I don't want anyone to talk. Just begin writing." Even in classes that are definitely not listen-to-the-pin-drop groups, the guided visualization seems to enlist students' imaginations in ways that make them want to record their thoughts. Whether or not the guided visualization is used, it's important that students have an opportunity to begin writing before they leave class. In my experience, to finish something as homework, students need to have begun the piece in class.

6. Either in small groups or in a full-class circle, ask students to share their stories. Before they begin, ask them to take notes on the "collective text" that the class read-around creates. Specifically, they might listen for:

   • What made us feel *able* to speak up or to act? [Point out that frequently we want to stand up for ourselves or for others, but don't feel able to do so. What was different about the times described in these stories?]

- How do the feelings that we had after our actions compare with Frederick Douglass' feelings after his fight with Covey?

- What other patterns do we notice in these stories?

Before discussing these questions after the read-around, ask students to take a few minutes to write on one or more of these. The more they've reflected on the broader implications of the stories, the better the discussion will be.

7. This assignment often produces powerful, vivid writing. You might consider asking students to revise and polish these. If you take this route, distribute "Narrative Criteria Sheet" (Handout 1–C), adapted from Linda Christensen's book *Reading, Writing, and Rising Up: Teaching About Social Justice and the Power of the Written Word*. Have them work with color highlighters (if you have them) and go back through their draft, identifying elements of their narratives. This offers students a striking visual image of their writing, and can provide a road map for revision and expansion.

AN EXCERPT FROM

Narrative of the Life of Frederick Douglass

I HAVE ALREADY INTIMATED that my condition was much worse, during the first six months of my stay at Mr. Covey's, than in the last six. The circumstances leading to the change in Mr. Covey's course toward me form an epoch in my humble history. You have seen how a man was made a slave; you shall see how a slave was made a man.

On one of the hottest days of the month of August 1833, Bill Smith, William Hughes, a slave named Eli, and myself were engaged in fanning wheat. Hughes was clearing the fanned wheat from before the fan. Eli was turning, Smith was feeding, and I was carrying wheat to the fan. The work was simple, requiring strength rather than intellect; yet, to one entirely unused to such work, it came very hard. About 3 o'clock of that day, I broke down; my strength failed me; I was seized with a violent aching of the head, attended with extreme dizziness; I trembled in every limb. Finding what was coming, I nerved myself up, feeling it would never do to stop work. I stood as long as I could stagger to the hopper with grain. When I could stand no longer, I fell, and felt as if held down by an immense weight. The fan of course stopped; everyone had his own work to do; and no one could do the work of the other, and have his own go on at the same time.

Mr. Covey was at the house, about 100 yards from the treading yard where we were fanning. On hearing the fan stop, he left immediately, and came to the spot where we were. He hastily inquired what the matter was. Bill answered that I was sick, and there was no one to bring wheat to the fan. I had by this time crawled away under the side of the post and rail fence by which the yard was enclosed, hoping to find relief by getting out of the sun. He then asked where I was. He was told by one of the

hands. He came to the spot, and, after looking at me awhile, asked me what was the matter. I told him as well as I could, for I scarce had strength to speak. He then gave me a savage kick in the side, and told me to get up. I tried to do so, but fell back in the attempt. He gave me another kick, and again told me to rise. I again tried, and succeeded in gaining my feet; but, stooping to get the tub with which I was feeding the fan, I again staggered and fell. While down in this situation, Mr. Covey took up the hickory slat with which Hughes had been striking off the half-bushel measure, and with it gave me a heavy blow upon the head, making a large wound, and the blood ran freely; and with this again told me to get up. I made no effort to comply, having now made up my mind to let him do his worst.

In a short time after receiving this blow, my head grew better. Mr. Covey had now left me to my fate. At this moment I resolved, for the first time, to go to my master, enter a complaint, and ask his protection. In order to do this, I must that afternoon walk seven miles; and this, under the circumstances, was truly a severe undertaking. I was exceedingly feeble; made so as much by the kicks and blows which I received, as by the severe fit of sickness to which I had been subjected. I, however, watched my chance, while Covey was looking in an opposite direction, and started for St. Michael's. I succeeded in getting a considerable distance on my way to the woods, when Covey discovered me, and called after me to come back, threatening what he would do if I did not come. I disregarded both his calls and his threats, and made my way to the woods as fast as my feeble state would allow; and thinking I might be overhauled by him if I kept the road, I walked through the woods, keeping far enough from the road to avoid detection, and near enough to prevent losing my way.

I had not gone far before my little strength again failed me. I could go no farther. I fell down, and lay for a considerable time. The blood was yet oozing from the wound on my head. For a time I thought I should bleed to death; and think now that I should have done so, but that the blood so matted my hair as to stop the wound. After lying there about three quarters of an hour, I nerved myself up again, and started on my way, through bogs and briers, barefooted and bareheaded, tearing my feet sometimes at nearly every step; and after a journey of about seven miles, occupying some five hours to perform it, I arrived at master's store. I then presented an appearance enough to affect any but a heart of iron. From the crown of my head to my feet, I was covered with blood. My hair was all clotted with dust and blood; my shirt was stiff with blood. I suppose I looked like a man who had escaped a den of wild beasts, and barely escaped them.

In this state I appeared before my master, humbly entreating him to interpose his authority for my protection. I told him all the circumstances as well as I could, and it seemed, as I spoke, at times to affect him. He would then walk the floor, and seek to justify Covey by saying he expected I deserved it. He asked me what I wanted. I told him, to let me get a new home; that as sure as I lived with Mr. Covey again, I should live with but to die with him; that Covey would surely kill me; he was in a fair way for it. Master Thomas ridiculed the idea that there was any danger of Mr. Covey's killing me, and said that he knew Mr. Covey; that he was a good man, and that he could not think of taking me from him; that, should he do so, he would lose the whole year's wages; that I belonged to Mr. Covey for one year, and that I must go back to him, come what might; and that I must not trouble him with any more stories, or that he would himself get hold of me. After threatening me thus,

He asked me if I meant to persist in my resistance. I told him I did, come what might; that he had used me like a brute for six months, and that I was determined to be used so no longer.

he gave me a very large dose of salts, telling me that I might remain in St. Michael's that night, (it being quite late,) but that I must be off back to Mr. Covey's early in the morning; and that if I did not, he would get hold of me, which meant that he would whip me.

I remained all night, and, according to his orders, I started off to Covey's in the morning (Saturday morning), wearied in body and broken in spirit. I got no supper that night, or breakfast that morning. I reached Covey's about 9 o'clock; and just as I was getting over the fence that divided Mrs. Kemp's fields from ours, out ran Covey with his cowskin, to give me another whipping. Before he could reach me, I succeeded in getting to the cornfield; and as the corn was very high, it afforded me the means of hiding. He seemed very angry, and searched for me a long time. My behavior was altogether unaccountable. He finally gave up the chase, thinking, I suppose, that I must come home for something to eat; he would give himself no further trouble in looking for me. I spent that day mostly in the woods, having the alternative before me — to go home and be whipped to death, or stay in the woods and be starved to death.

That night, I fell in with Sandy Jenkins, a slave with whom I was somewhat acquainted. Sandy had a free wife who lived about four miles from Mr. Covey's; and it being Saturday, he was on his way to see her. I told him my circumstances, and he very kindly invited me to go home with him. I went home with him, and talked this whole matter over, and got his advice as to what course it was best for me to pursue. I found Sandy an old adviser. He told me, with great solemnity, I must go back to Covey; but that before I went, I must go with him into another part of the woods, where there was a certain root, which, if I would take some of it with me, carrying it always on my right side, would render it impossible for Mr. Covey, or any other white man, to whip me. He said he had carried it for years; and since he had done so, he had never received a blow, and never expected to while he carried it. I at first rejected the idea, that the simple carrying of a root in my pocket would have any such effect as he had said, and was not disposed to take it; but Sandy impressed the necessity with much earnestness, telling me it could do no harm, if it did no good. To please him, I at length took the root, and, according to his direction, carried it upon my right side. This was Sunday morning.

I immediately started for home; and upon entering the yard gate, out came Mr. Covey on his way to meeting. He spoke to me very kindly, bade me drive the pigs from a lot nearby, and passed on towards the church. Now, this singular conduct of Mr. Covey really made me begin to think that there was something in the root which Sandy had given me; and had it been on any other day than Sunday, I could have attributed the conduct to no other cause than the influence of that root; and as it was, I was half inclined to think the root to be something more than I at first had taken it to be.

I now resolved that, however long I might remain a slave in form, the day had passed forever when I could be a slave in fact.

All went well till Monday morning. On this morning, the virtue of the root was fully tested. Long before daylight, I was called to go and rub, curry, and feed the horses. I obeyed, and was glad to obey. But whilst thus engaged, whilst in the act of throwing down some blades from the loft, Mr. Covey entered the stable with a long rope; and just as I was half out of the loft, he caught hold of my legs, and was about tying me. As soon as I found what he was up to, I gave a sudden spring, and as I did so, he holding to my legs, I was brought sprawling on the stable floor. Mr. Covey seemed now to think he had me, and could do what he pleased; but at this moment — from whence came the spirit I don't know — I resolved to fight; and, suiting my action to the resolution, I seized Covey hard by the throat; and as I did so, I rose. He held on to me, and I to him. My resistance was so entirely unexpected that Covey seemed taken all aback. He trembled like a leaf. This gave me assurance, and I held him uneasy, causing the blood to run where I touched him with the ends of my fingers. Mr. Covey soon called out to Hughes for help. Hughes came, and, while Covey held me, attempted to tie my right hand. While he was in the act of doing so, I watched my chance, and gave him a heavy kick close under the ribs. This kick fairly sickened Hughes, so that he left me in the hands of Mr. Covey. This kick had the effect of not only weakening Hughes, but Covey also. When he saw Hughes bending over with pain, his courage quailed. He asked me if I meant to persist in my resistance. I told him I did, come what might; that he had used me like a brute for six months, and that I was determined to be used so no longer. With that, he strove to drag me to a stick that was lying just out of the stable door. He meant to knock me down. But just as he was leaning over to get the stick, I seized him with both hands by his collar, and brought him by a sudden snatch to the ground.

By this time, Bill came. Covey called upon him for assistance. Bill wanted to know what he could do. Covey said, "Take hold of him, take hold of him!" Bill said his master hired him out to work, and not to help to whip me; so he left Covey and myself to fight our own battle out. We were at it for nearly two hours. Covey at length let me go, puffing and blowing at a great rate, saying that if I had not resisted, he would not have whipped me half so much. The truth was, that he had not whipped me at all. I considered him as getting entirely the worst end of the bargain; for he had drawn no blood from me, but I had from him. The whole six months afterwards, that I spent with Mr. Covey, he never laid the weight of his finger upon me in anger. He would occasionally say, he didn't want to get hold of me again. "No," thought I, "you need not; for you will come off worse than you did before."

This battle with Mr. Covey was the turning point in my career as a slave. It rekindled the few expiring embers of freedom, and revived within me a sense of my own manhood. It recalled the departed self-confidence, and inspired me again with a determination to be free. The gratification afforded by the triumph was a full compensation for whatever else might follow, even death itself. He only can understand the deep satisfaction which I experienced, who has himself repelled by force the bloody arm of slavery. I felt as I never felt before. It was a glorious resurrection, from the tomb of slavery, to the heaven of freedom. My long-crushed spirit rose, cowardice departed, bold defiance took its place; and I now resolved that, however long I might remain a slave in form, the day had passed forever when I could be a slave in fact. I did not hesitate to let it be known of me, that the white man who expected to succeed in whipping, must also succeed in killing me.

From this time I was never again what might be called fairly whipped, though I remained a slave four years afterwards. I had several fights, but was never whipped.

It was for a long time a matter of surprise to me why Mr. Covey did not immediately have me taken by the constable to the whipping post, and there regularly whipped for the crime of raising my hand against a white man in defense of myself. And the only explanation I can now think of does not entirely satisfy me; but such as it is, I will give it. Mr. Covey enjoyed the most unbounded reputation for being a first-rate overseer and negro-breaker. It was of considerable importance to him. That reputation was at stake; and had he sent me — a boy about 16 years old — to the public whipping post, his reputation would have been lost; so, to save his reputation, he suffered me to go unpunished.

Their Lives and Ours:
Standing Up for What's Right

U.S. HISTORY IS FULL of cruelty and exploitation. But it's also full of defiance, sacrifice, and solidarity. There were people who profited from slavery. But there were also enslaved people who defied their "owners," ran to freedom, and joined the abolition movement — like Frederick Douglass, Sojourner Truth, and Harriet Tubman. And there were free Blacks and whites who also joined the abolition movement, and worked for the benefit of others when they had nothing to gain for themselves — people like David Walker, William Lloyd Garrison, Sarah and Angelina Grimké, David Ruggles, and John Brown.

It's impossible for us to fully understand the conditions in people's lives that prompted them to rise up against the slave system. As Frederick Douglass himself pointed out, "He only can understand the deep satisfaction which I experienced, who has himself repelled the bloody arm of slavery." But by digging into our own experiences, we can try.

Writing Choices

1. **Defying unjust authority.** Think about a time when you refused to accept someone's authority over you because you felt it was unjust or unfair. As with Frederick Douglass, it could have been a time when you felt that you had to resist the authority physically. But it may be that you resisted in a different, nonviolent way. You might have defied a parent, a teacher, an administrator, an employer, a police officer, store clerk, or even a friend, or simply peer pressure.

2. **Acting on behalf of someone else.** After Douglass ran away, he became an example of this kind of standing up for what's right. When he became an abolitionist — dedicating his life to free others who were still enslaved, he was no longer standing up for himself; he was standing up for others. Think of a time when you defended someone else, worked to support someone else, helped someone who was in need. Perhaps you risked something to do this. This would be a time when you didn't stand to gain anything but the satisfaction of helping someone who needed help.

3. **Working collectively to make things better.** There were lots of individuals, not as prominent as Frederick Douglass, who joined the abolition movement because they knew that to help others would require them not just to work alone, but also to work in a large group. Think of a time when you joined with others to make a change, to help other people, or to defy unjust authority.

Narrative Criteria Sheet

MARK EACH OF THESE ELEMENTS on your draft. If you have a highlighter or colored pencils, color each of the elements with a different color. If not, put the number of the element in the margin of your paper. For example, every time you use dialogue put #1 in the margin next to it. (The elements marked * are not essential, but give your writing more depth.)

___1. Dialogue

- What are the characters saying?
- Do they each have a "voice print"?

___2. Blocking

- What are the characters doing while they are talking? Leaning against a wall? Tossing a ball in the air?
- Where are they located?

___3. Character Description

- Physical description
- Attitude description — how they walk, talk, act.

___4. Setting Description

- Where does the story take place?
- What does it look like?
- What does it smell like?
- What's on the walls?

___5. Figurative Language*

- Did you use metaphors and similes — comparisons?
- Did you use personification — giving human qualities to nonhumans?

___6. Interior monologue*

- What is going on inside your mind, or the mind of one or more of your characters?
- What are you or one or more of the characters thinking while the action is happening?

Adapted from Linda Christensen, *Reading, Writing and Rising Up: Teaching About Social Justice and the Power of the Written Word*, (Rethinking Schools, 2017).

Poetry of Defiance: How the Enslaved Resisted

By Adam Sanchez

"From the beginning, Black men and women resisted their enslavement . . . under the most diffi-cult conditions, under pain of mutilation and death, throughout their 200 years of enslavement in North America, these Afro-Americans continued to rebel. Only occasionally was there an organized insurrection. More often they showed their refusal to submit by running away. Even more often, they engaged in sabotage, slowdowns, and subtle forms of resistance which asserted, if only to themselves and their brothers and sisters, their dignity as human beings."

—**Howard Zinn,** *A People's History of the United States*

FOR TOO LONG historians painted a picture of the idyllic old U.S. South with paternalistic slave owners and docile and content slaves. Though challenged in the 1930s and '40s by historians like W. E. B. Du Bois and Herbert Aptheker, this remained the dominant narrative of slavery until the late 1960s and '70s. Today, any discussion of slavery should be coupled with the myriad and heroic ways enslaved people resisted their enslavement.

It's also important to put this resistance in the broader context of how the U.S. economy was built on the backs of enslaved people. While "Lesson 6: Mapping the Slave Economy" further explores how the cotton trade enriched not just slaveholders but also many Northern capitalists, students should also

Though rare, rebellions like the one led by Nat Turner terrified the slaveholding South and encouraged abolitionists.

grapple with how central the labor, knowledge, and skills of enslaved people were to the entire Southern economy. As historian William Loren Katz argues, "Slave labor did far more than bring in Southern crops." Katz points out that on slaveholders' estates, African Americans also worked as:

tailors, shoemakers, carpenters, smiths, turners, wheelwrights, weavers, [and] tanners. Slaves built George Washington's Mount Vernon and Thomas Jefferson's Monticello. Slaves constructed the famous balconies of New Orleans, built churches, jails, and the beautiful Touro Synagogue in Newport, Rhode Island. Slaves were managers of plantations and rice mills, and a few were architects, civil engineers, and inventors. . . . Slaves were miners, lumber and iron workers. . . . They built Southern canals, railroads, tunnels, ships, turnpikes, and worked for gas and light companies.

Indeed, it is hard to find any part of the economy not somehow connected to the institution of slavery. Therefore, the stakes for maintaining slavery were high and any resistance was often met with brutal retaliation.

Nevertheless, enslaved people, with great courage, engaged in all sorts of resistance. While this pre-Civil War resistance did not ultimately topple the deeply entrenched institution of slavery, it challenged pro-slavery arguments that enslaved people were happy and content and provided fuel for abolitionist denunciations of slavery. Maybe more importantly, it established a tradition of defiance that was built upon during the Civil War and Reconstruction when wider acts of resistance became possible.

The mixer activity, described below, introduces students to several of these concepts, establishes the various ways that enslaved people resisted, and celebrates that resistance, culminating in a collective poem.

Materials Needed

- Copies of "Resisting Slavery Mixer Questions" (Handout 2–A) for every student.

- "Resisting Slavery Quotes" (Handout 2–B), cut up.

- (Optional) Copies of "Write that I" Poem Example (Handout 2–C)

- Copies of "I Freed Myself" (Handout 2–D) for every student.

Time Required

One class period for the mixer and poetry writing. A portion of another class to read and/or discuss "I Freed Myself."

Suggested Procedure

1. Explain to students that they will be participating in an activity to learn about the various ways that enslaved people resisted slavery. Because we are still facing the legacy and reality of racism today, studying slavery can be painful. But for

this same reason it's important we examine how Black people resisted their enslavement and kept the hope for abolition alive.

2. First, to provide some context, place this statement on the board:

   "By 1860, there were more millionaires (slaveholders all) living in the lower Mississippi Valley than anywhere else in the United States. In the same year, the nearly 4 million American slaves were worth some $3.5 billion, making them the largest single financial asset in the entire U.S. economy, worth more than all manufacturing and railroads combined."

   — historian David Blight

3. Ask students to read the statement. Ask for their reactions. Is anything about this quote surprising? After ensuring students understand the statement, lead a discussion on the following questions: Why was the labor of enslaved people so important to the economy? What power did enslaved people have? What could they do to resist? What prevented them from resisting?

4. Depending on your students' prior knowledge, during this discussion you might clarify what a labor strike is and how this type of collective action was a potentially powerful weapon against slavery and therefore dangerous. You might also point out that while most enslaved people worked on plantations as farmworkers, this was not the only place where slave labor was used. The knowledge and skills of enslaved people — and the possibility of withholding knowledge or skills — had a profound impact. The main point of the discussion is to have students anticipate some of the forms of resistance that they will encounter during the subsequent mixer activity and to put that resistance in context.

While the pre-Civil War resistance of the enslaved did not end slavery, it did puncture many of the arguments used to justify slavery, thus providing important ideological weapons for abolitionists.

5. Once you've finished this short discussion, explain that in the following activity students will look at several stories to help them understand the many and varied ways enslaved people resisted their enslavement. Distribute one or two resisting slavery quotes to each student (Handout 2–B). If you give a student more than one quote, make sure both quotes are in the same "group." (Note: Group numbers and themes are listed at the beginning of each quote.) Give students a few minutes to read their quote(s) and help clarify any quote(s) for students who are struggling.

6. Next, distribute "Resisting Slavery Mixer Questions" (Handout 2–A) to each student. Go over the questions as a class and encourage students to note the question or questions their quote(s) answers.

7. Tell students that for this activity they will get up out of their seat and go around the room sharing their quotes with others. They should have one-on-one conversations and aim to fill out the questions on the handout as they go.

8. When it seems like most students have finished answering the questions, ask them to get into their groups. Group numbers are listed on the quote(s) they have.

9. If you have the time, before moving on to the collective poem, this is a good place to have students reflect on how the resistance of enslaved people challenged the ideology that justified slavery. Write this quote from George Fitzhugh on the board: "The negro slaves of the South are the happiest, and in some sense, the freest people in the world. The children and the aged and infirm work not at all, and yet have all the comforts and necessaries of life provided for them. They enjoy liberty, because they are oppressed neither by care or labor. The women do little hard work, and are protected from the despotism of their husbands by their masters." Explain to students that this quote is taken from an 1857 book written to justify slavery and was a typical pro-slavery argument that you would hear in both the South and the North. Ask students to identify how the stories of resistance they just learned about challenge this argument.

    Although the pre-Civil War resistance of the enslaved did not end slavery, it did puncture many of the arguments used to justify slavery, thus providing important ideological weapons for abolitionists. Furthermore, it created a pattern of resistance that enslaved people drew on during the Civil War and Reconstruction when the opportunity for much wider resistance arose.

10. Explain to students that they will now create a collective "Write that I" poem* based on the quotes that they have. You might also share with them the "'Write that I' Poem Example" (Handout 2–C).

11. I start students off by writing the first two lines of the poem on the board for the class:

---

* The idea and the provided example of a "Write that I" poem comes from *Rhythm and Resistance: Teaching Poetry for Social Justice*, edited by Linda Christensen and Dyan Watson (Rethinking Schools, 2015).

When you tell the story of slavery,
Write that I resisted. . .

12. Tell students that a "Write that I" poem, like many other poems, uses repetition to weave the poem together. You might share with them a stanza from the example below. Explain that in this poem, each stanza should start with a phrase that is similar to "Write that I . . ." Give students a few examples of phrases that have a similar meaning — say that I, tell them that I, when you tell my story — and ask them to add phrases to the list. Write all of these phrases on the board so students can access them while writing their portions of the poem.

13. Explain that each group will be tasked with finishing the poem by writing one stanza of the collective "Write that I" poem. Encourage students to begin by reading each other their quotes. When they finish, they should brainstorm ways to express their group's theme poetically and begin writing their stanza. Encourage students to consider how enslaved people's resistance challenged not only the brutality of their enslavement, but also the nationwide institution of slavery and the ideology that supported it.

14. When every group is finished, collect their stanzas and read the collective poem to the class (Note: You may want to edit them together and read the collective poem the following day.)

15. Here are a few stanzas, from one of the collective poems my students wrote:

Write that I broke tools, slowed work,
and plowed his crops too shallow.
When in the fields
I sang slowly and hid messages
in each lyric.
Spiritual words,
with double meanings,
could help you find the way
up North.

Tell how I ran,
By the thousands,
to find loved ones,
to find freedom,
with dogs and hunters behind me.
I would not be stopped.

Tell how I spoke up and stood up
to the white men
who stood over me
with whips and chains.

Write how I trapped their horses,
burned their homes,
defied their curfews,
stole their guns,
protected my people.

Let them know you can't erase the names of
those who were lost
through bloody revolts
against the bloodiest of crimes.

16. As a follow-up, assign David Williams' "I Freed Myself" (Handout 2–D). Another reading to consider using is the beginning portion of Howard Zinn's chapter "Slavery Without Submission, Emancipation Without Freedom," from *A People's History of the United States* (included as Handout 10–A in Lesson 10). The beginning of the chapter until the line "While Southern slaves held on . . . ," like the "I Freed Myself" reading, focuses on the resistance of the enslaved and the brutality of the system of slavery.

17. Ask students to take notes while they complete the Williams reading. Have them draw a line down the center of a piece of paper and list on one side the ways enslaved African Americans resisted their enslavement and on the other the ways slave owners and slave catchers tried to prevent resistance. You might also ask students to find material that can connect with the

collective poem they wrote. If you are planning to finish this unit of study by asking students to write an essay on "who freed the slaves?" you might ask them to highlight any quotes they think they could use as evidence in their essay. Also encourage students to raise at least two questions that they would like to discuss with the rest of the class.

18. In addition to students' own questions, here are some questions for further discussion of or writing about "I Freed Myself" (Handout 2–D):

    • Besides punishment from slave owners or slave catchers, what were other reasons some enslaved people might not want to run away? What were some of the reasons enslaved people did run away?

    • What were some of the ways those enslaved resisted without running away?

    • The author writes, "For some slaves, the ultimate resistance, the only escape, was death." How could suicide be resistance? Why would some enslaved mothers kill their children?

    • What were some of the laws governing what an enslaved person could and could not do?

    • Although enslaved people could not legally marry, why did some slaveholders encourage them to do so at an early age?

    • According to the author, why did slaveholders begin pushing for the expansion of slavery? What evidence does he give for this?

    • The author argues that "collective resistance" was becoming more frequent throughout the 1850s. What evidence does he give for this?

    • According to the author, why did the Southern states secede after Lincoln's election?

    • The last paragraph summarizes the author's main argument. Put this argument in your own words.

Resisting Slavery Mixer Questions

1. Find someone who has a quote or quotes about theft and property destruction. How was theft and property destruction a form of resistance?

2. Find someone who has a quote or quotes about maintaining the family. In what ways did enslaved people maintain families despite hardships? How is this a form of resistance?

3. Find someone who has a quote or quotes about music. How did enslaved people use music as a form of resistance?

4. Find someone who has a quote or quotes about religion and/or education. How did enslaved people use religion and/or education as a form of resistance?

5. Find someone who has a quote or quotes about how enslaved people resisted while working. Why might this kind of resistance have been particularly effective?

6. Find someone who has a quote or quotes about running away. Why and how did enslaved people run away?

7. Find someone who has a quote or quotes about verbal and/or physical confrontation. Why did enslaved people engage in these confrontations despite the risks?

8. Find someone who has information about one of the large slave revolts that took place in the 1800s. Write down information about this revolt.

9. Find someone who has a quote or quotes that discuss the risks enslaved people took when resisting slavery. What were some of those risks?

Resisting Slavery Quotes

Group 1: Theft and Property Destruction

Most of what historians have termed "day to day" resistance involved "crimes" against property. Enslaved people pulled down fences, sabotaged farm equipment, broke implements, damaged boats, vandalized wagons, ruined clothing, and committed various other destructive acts. They set fires to outbuildings, barns, and stables; mistreated horses, mules, cattle, and other livestock. They stole with impunity: sheep, hogs, cattle, poultry, money, watches, produce, liquor, tobacco, flour, cotton, indigo, corn, nearly anything that was not under lock and key — and occasionally found the key.

Adapted from John Hope Franklin and Loren Schweninger's *Runaway Slaves: Rebels on the Plantation*

Group 1: Theft and Property Destruction

Since their labor was stolen, slaves justified, and counted as a form of resistance, stealing from slaveholders. A woman found with her mistress's trinkets said, "Don't say I'm wicked . . . it's all right for us poor colored people to appropriate whatever of the white folks' blessings the Lord puts in our way."

Adapted from William Loren Katz's *Breaking the Chains: African-American Slave Resistance*

Group 1: Theft and Property Destruction

Theft was the main way slaves obtained the goods they needed to survive. They took the food and drink they wanted [and that they had produced with their own skilled labor.] They reasoned that it could not be stealing, because "it belongs to massa, and so do we, and we only use one part of his property to benefit another."

Adapted from Stephanie M. H. Camp's *Closer to Freedom: Enslaved Women and Everyday Resistance in the Plantation South*

Group 1: Theft and Property Destruction

Enslaved people also asked embarrassing questions when they were told not to steal. "Dey allus done tell us it am wrong to lie and steal," exploded Josephine Howard of Texas, "but why did white folks steal my mammy and her mammy? Dey lives clost to some water, somewhere over in Africy. . . . Dat de sinfulles' stealin' dey is." The whites did the first stealing, sneered another ex-slave, when they stole our people from Africa.

Adapted from Eugene D. Genovese's *Roll, Jordan, Roll: The World the Slaves Made*

Group 1: Theft and Property Destruction

Planters also found that almost anything used in production could be ruined. There were mysteriously bent hoes, broken plows, toothless rakes, and injured field animals. Slaves deliberately overworked field animals and plowed too shallow for planting of crops. Sabotage by enslaved people was so widespread that planters invented a thick "slave hoe" that could not easily be broken.

Adapted from William Loren Katz's *Breaking the Chains: African-American Slave Resistance*

Group 1: Theft and Property Destruction

Fires that swept through cotton warehouses and gin presses in the South were blamed on Blacks. In November, fire destroyed $6,000 worth of corn, fodder, and cotton on one Georgia plantation. Another fire burned down a gin house two miles from Columbus. In Virginia, authorities charged two slaves named Jerry and Joe with setting several fires.

Adapted from David Williams' *I Freed Myself*

Group 2: Maintaining the Family

Historians have shown that while separation was devastating to individuals, families, and even communities, the slave family as an institution adapted to, even as it was ravaged by, personal loss. Naming children for absent family members and the orientation toward extended family were but a few practices that enabled the family, as a valued social institution to survive. When the distance was not too far, separated family members sometimes reunited during nighttime visits.

Adapted from Stephanie M. H. Camp's *Closer to Freedom: Enslaved Women and Everyday Resistance in the Plantation South*

Group 2: Maintaining the Family

Frederick Douglass opened his classic 1845 autobiography with the faint memories he still had of his mother, who lived some 12 miles from him in Maryland. "I never saw my mother or knew her as such," Douglass wrote, "more than four or five times in my life; and each of these times was very short in duration and at night." Douglass' mother ran away from her hirer as often as she could, which was not very often, to visit her son "in the night, traveling the whole distance on foot, after the performance of her day's work." She could only stay a short while before returning back to her site of forced labor before daybreak.

Adapted from Stephanie M. H. Camp's *Closer to Freedom: Enslaved Women and Everyday Resistance in the Plantation South*

Group 2: Maintaining the Family

Protecting family unity became the African American community's first line of defense. A strong, united family provided the love, hope, and courage necessary for survival in a hostile land. In fighting for family, each individual knew he or she was not alone and affirmed a vital sense of identity and self-worth. The family unit's strength became the psychological base from which other resistance was launched.

Adapted from William Loren Katz's *Breaking the Chains: African-American Slave Resistance*

Group 2: Maintaining the Family

Often enslaved people tried to handle the visits to wives or loved ones with honest bargaining. In one instance, six men asked for a leave, were turned down, and argued for weeks with the overseer of a river improvement project. When he still refused, they picked up and left. The overseer, to head off a complete breakdown of his authority, hastily decided to let the rest visit their wives.

Adapted from William Loren Katz's *Breaking the Chains: African-American Slave Resistance*

Group 2: Maintaining the Family

Moses Grandy escaped to England and dictated his autobiography. He recalled this scene: "I remember well my mother often hid us all in the woods, to prevent master selling us. When we wanted water, she sought for it in any hole or puddle . . . full of tadpoles and insects: she strained it, and gave it round to each of us in hollow of her hand. For food, she gathered berries in the woods, got potatoes, raw corn, etc. After a time the master would send word to her to come in, promising he would not sell us."

Adapted from William Loren Katz's *Breaking the Chains: African-American Slave Resistance*

Group 2: Maintaining the Family

In Georgia, Aleck was one enslaved man who asked, "Should each man regard only his own children, and forget all the others?" If parents and relatives were traded away or children sold without their parents, men and women without blood ties stepped in to share parenting responsibilities. The practice of taking in children changed the meaning of the word *parents* in the slave community to mean all adults. "Parents means relations in general . . . family," explained Robert Smalls. A Black community expression was "If you hurt one of the family, you hurt them all."

Adapted from William Loren Katz's *Breaking the Chains: African-American Slave Resistance*

Group 3: Culture, Music, Religion, and Education

The oppressor promoted his religion and culture to help instill obedience and conformity. But in the privacy of huts, African traditions and words survived in secret. White owners sought to control the naming process and selected babies' names from Greek or Roman history or folklore. To assert their power, masters denied the enslaved people any last names but the masters' own. But in the slave quarter, people used their original first and last names, said enslaved Robert Smalls, a ship pilot who achieved fame in the Civil War.

Adapted from William Loren Katz's *Breaking the Chains: African-American Slave Resistance*

Group 3: Culture, Music, Religion, and Education

Southern laws imposed harsh penalties for anyone teaching slaves to read or write. Some Black women daringly conducted secret schools. In Natchez, Louisiana, Lilly Ann Granderson, who learned to read from the children of her Kentucky enslaver, ran a "midnight school" of 12 pupils each term that taught reading and writing between 11 p.m. and 2 a.m. She graduated hundreds. Some pupils soon applied their knowledge by writing passes for runaways fleeing to Canada.

Adapted from William Loren Katz's *Breaking the Chains: African-American Slave Resistance*

Group 3: Culture, Music, Religion, and Education

Planters and slaves fought a long tug of war for control of enslaved people's music, its themes, words, and tempo. Fanny Kemble wrote that "many masters and overseers on these plantations prohibit melancholy [sad] tunes or words and encourage nothing but cheerful music." Some banned "any reference to particular hardships." Masters demanded an accelerated beat in the work songs in order to speed up labor in fields or on docks. When whites manipulated the musical tempo to increase production, African American laborers tried to slow the beat to relieve the strain.

Adapted from William Loren Katz's *Breaking the Chains: African-American Slave Resistance*

Group 3: Culture, Music, Religion, and Education

Despite the walls erected by their masters, African Americans creatively employed religion to tear at the chains that bound them. Biblical heroes and a world struggle for liberty masked the real theme of a coming day of liberation. They recast the European's abstract, severe God as one committed to justice, who was willing to drown the pharaoh's army of slaveholders to save the Hebrew children. God and Jesus were portrayed as leaders on freedom's battlefield. As early as 1810, Richard Byrd of Virginia informed the governor that "slave preachers used their religious meetings as veils for revolutionary schemes."

Adapted from William Loren Katz's *Breaking the Chains: African-American Slave Resistance*

Group 3: Culture, Music, Religion, and Education

Sometimes songs spread important news. Some lyrics conveyed hidden messages to enslaved people that whites could not decipher. "Steal away, steal away, steal away to Jesus" encouraged runaways without warning masters. To tell Blacks that one of their number had betrayed them, a song was used: "O Judas he was a 'ceitful man, He went an' betray a most innocent man." "Follow the Drinking Gourd" voiced love for freedom: "The old man is awaiting to carry you to freedom, so follow the drinking gourd." Another stanza detailed directions for runaways, telling them to follow the North Star to Canada.

Adapted from William Loren Katz's *Breaking the Chains: African-American Slave Resistance*

Group 3: Culture, Music, Religion, and Education

Spirituals often had double meanings. The song "O Canaan, sweet Canaan, I am bound for the land of Canaan" often meant that slaves planned to get to the North, their Canaan. During the Civil War, enslaved people began to make up new spirituals with bolder messages: "Before I'd be a slave, I'd be buried in my grave, and go home to my Lord and be saved." And the spiritual "Many Thousand Go":

> *No more peck o' corn for me,*
> *no more, no more,*
> *No more driver's lash for me,*
> *no more, no more.*

Adapted from Howard Zinn's *A People's History of the United States*

Group 4: Resistance at Work

In the cities, some enslaved people refused to handle dangerous factory jobs. Complaining of beatings, lack of food, overwork, and having to wash their own clothes on Sunday, several enslaved people working for a railroad contractor stopped work. In many factories sickness was so common bosses could not tell when men were ill or faking.

Adapted from William Loren Katz's *Breaking the Chains: African-American Slave Resistance*

Group 4: Resistance at Work

Enslaved people pretended to be sick, hid in outbuildings, did not complete their assigned tasks, and refused to perform dangerous work. It was difficult to sneak off for an entire day, but on some plantations slaves did so. An enslaved 18-year-old Louisiana woman managed to slip off and remain in the woods, at least until her overseer found her one morning lying on her stomach. The overseer got off his horse and, holding the reins with his left hand, struck her 30 or 40 stripes across the shoulders. He continued to whip her until she cried for mercy. "She meant to cheat me out of a day's work — and she has done it, too," the overseer complained.

Adapted from John Hope Franklin and Loren Schweninger's *Runaway Slaves: Rebels on the Plantation*

Group 4: Resistance at Work

Enslaved people sometimes refused to work, demanded concessions, rejected orders, threatened whites, and reacted with violence. Verbal and physical confrontations occurred regularly, without regard to time and place. Indeed despite severe punishments — or perhaps because of them — these challenges to white authority remained as much a part of the slavery as the slave trader.

Adapted from John Hope Franklin and Loren Schweninger's *Runaway Slaves: Rebels on the Plantation*

Group 4: Resistance at Work

Production on some plantations varied as much as 100 percent due to slowdowns and sabotage. Enslaved people pretended to be too sick or lame to work, women pretended they were pregnant, and illness soared when work was hardest. In Mississippi, the Wheeles plantation calculated one working day each week was lost by sickness.

Adapted from William Loren Katz's *Breaking the Chains: African-American Slave Resistance*

Group 4: Resistance at Work

Strikes, slowdowns, or what owners called "the danger of a general stampede to the swamp" were common. One manager told reporter Frederick Olmsted that slaves ran away to protest overseers and harsh working conditions: "They hide in the swamp and come into cabins at night to get food." Some lengthy stoppages were only settled when owners agreed to negotiate with the people they enslaved.

Adapted from William Loren Katz's *Breaking the Chains: African-American Slave Resistance*

Group 4: Resistance at Work

While planters dreamed and schemed about the creation of orderly plantations in which the location of enslaved people was neatly determined by laws, curfews, rules, and the demands of crops, enslaved people engaged in truancy, a practice that disturbed and in some cases alarmed slaveholders. When bondspeople engaged in absenteeism, they withdrew their labor, confronting and opposing the authority of their owners and creating a problem of labor discipline in the Old South.

Adapted from Stephanie M. H. Camp's *Closer to Freedom: Enslaved Women and Everyday Resistance in the Plantation South*

Group 5: Running Away

Like enslaved people everywhere, Salli Smith was forbidden to leave her plantation home without a pass. But Smith broke the rules and laws that dictated where she ought to be and when she ought to be there. Smith sometimes ran away to nearby woods, eating what she found, burrowing under the leaves and moss to sleep at night, and sneaking to the quarters on a nearby farm for occasional shelter from the cold. When she returned to her owner, he had her tortured inside of "a big barrel he kept to roll us in, with nails drove all through it." When Smith emerged from the contraption, she "could hardly walk," but she "did not stay more than a month" before she ran away again.

Adapted from Stephanie M. H. Camp's *Closer to Freedom: Enslaved Women and Everyday Resistance in the Plantation South*

Group 5: Running Away

Most runaways abandoned plantation work on the spur of the moment. These men and women were trying to escape a beating, prevent a sale to a new owner, or to search for nearby relatives and loved ones. Many ran to protest work, whippings, or evil overseers — and tried to remain hidden until they won promises of better conditions. Others carefully planned to reach free land, and some tried to establish their own settlements in remote, hard-to-penetrate swamps or mountains.

Adapted from William Loren Katz's *Breaking the Chains: African-American Slave Resistance*

Group 5: Running Away

Running away was much more realistic than armed insurrection. During the 1850s about 1,000 slaves a year escaped into the North, Canada, and Mexico. Thousands ran away for short periods — despite the terror facing the runaway. The dogs used in tracking fugitives "bit, tore, mutilated, and if not pulled off in time, killed their prey."

Adapted from Howard Zinn's *A People's History of the United States*

Group 5: Running Away

Sometimes large numbers fled together. In 1779, the Edings plantation on Edisto Island, South Carolina, lost 36, including 12 women, who left together. In 1826, 27 enslaved people in Kentucky were being transported down the Ohio River by boat when they broke away. Swinging clubs, axes, and knives, they killed five whites, seized and sank the boat, and fled to Indiana. Mass flights to freedom were more common in the border states of Virginia, Kentucky, Tennessee, Maryland, and Delaware than in the Deep South.

Adapted from William Loren Katz's *Breaking the Chains: African-American Slave Resistance*

Group 5: Running Away

Enslaved people found new opportunities for flight in cities, especially ports or rail depots. A great advantage was the number of free Blacks and friendly whites who might write passes and provide cash, directions, or other help. One Black Louisiana carpenter sold forged passes for runaways. Some fugitives took jobs as sailors and then jumped ship at ports in free states.

Adapted from William Loren Katz's *Breaking the Chains: African-American Slave Resistance*

Group 5: Running Away

The dangers that all women and men anticipated if they thought about escape to the North were fearsome: dogs, patrols, unknown directions, cold, heat, lack of food, risk of capture, and in that event, certain horrific punishment. Women, who played a central role in the Black family, typically concluded that permanent escape was impossible or undesirable. Instead, they chose truancy, generally by fleeing to the nearest woods or swamps and occasionally to nearby towns. Women also played an important role by supporting runaways and truants by feeding them meals.

Adapted from Stephanie M. H. Camp's *Closer to Freedom: Enslaved Women and Everyday Resistance in the Plantation South*

Group 6: Verbal and Physical Confrontation

Women were also ready to risk death for their marriages. Jermain Loguen recalled his mother, armed with "all the tiger's blood in her veins" and a heavy stick, striking a knife from her planter's hand, and then knocking him out. An enslaved woman named Clarinda swung a hoe that discouraged her master's interest in her, and Cherry Logue swung a club at a man who made "insulting advances." In Virginia, Sukie punched her owner, who was trying to rip off her dress and throw her to the floor. Sukie managed to push him, seat first, into a pot of boiling soup. He screamed as he ran, but quietly enough so his wife wouldn't hear.

Adapted from William Loren Katz's *Breaking the Chains: African-American Slave Resistance*

Group 6: Verbal and Physical Confrontation

Enslaved people often bore particular resentment toward overseers. Enslaved people resented being chided, scolded, chastised, punished, and whipped; they disliked being supervised during their workday by young inexperienced white men; they bitterly resented threats against their families. On some plantations, Blacks attempted to undermine the overseer's authority by criticizing him openly or complaining to the owner about harsh or unfair treatment. At times, the tensions between enslaved people and overseers erupted into verbal and physical confrontations. On some plantations, such clashes occurred so often that it was difficult for overseers to inflict punishments for every incident and on a few plantations, overseers were even afraid to chastise people under their command.

Adapted from John Hope Franklin and Loren Schweninger's *Runaway Slaves: Rebels on the Plantation*

Group 6: Verbal and Physical Confrontation

Overseers, often known for their abusiveness, sometimes had to fight for their lives. In rural Alabama, reporter Frederick Olmsted was told: "The overseers have to always go about armed; their life wouldn't be safe if they didn't. As it is, they very often get cut pretty bad." Cudjo Lewis was busy working in the field when he saw a group of women overpower and "soundly thrash" an overseer who had insulted one of them.

Adapted from William Loren Katz's *Breaking the Chains: African-American Slave Resistance*

Group 6: Verbal and Physical Confrontation

Whether alone or with others, however, those who challenged the system paid a heavy price. Those who openly defied the owner, plantation manager, or overseer were usually dealt with quickly and ruthlessly. They were whipped, beaten, mutilated, branded, and sometimes tortured. They were sold away from their families or watched as their children were turned over to slave traders. Those found guilty or sometimes merely accused of serious "crimes" were banished or hanged. Despite this, enslaved people confronted overseers with verbal assaults and physical force; they also attempted to intimidate their white managers. While such defiance was more common in some regions than in others, there were few plantations where enslaved people worked diligently and willingly.

Adapted from John Hope Franklin and Loren Schweninger's *Runaway Slaves: Rebels on the Plantation*

Group 6: Verbal and Physical Confrontation

An overseer in a sugar mill so outraged one enslaved person, he tried to push the white man into the boiling juice. As hired workers, enslaved people particularly resented sweating for someone else's gain — a person who was not even their owner. Anthony, told to work on Sunday by a furnace manager, said Sunday was "his day and that he was not going to take it up going to your place," and the two had a fight.

Adapted from William Loren Katz's *Breaking the Chains: African-American Slave Resistance*

Group 6: Verbal and Physical Confrontation

As slaves grew old — if they grew old — they asserted the right to retire. "Just come to tell you, Massa," an old man announced, "that I've labored for you for 40 years now. And I done earned my keep. You can sell me, lash me, or kill me. I ain't caring which but you can't make me work no more." The response of the shocked master was: "All right, Jake. I'm retiring you, but for God's sake, don't say anything to the others."

Adapted from Eugene D. Genovese's *Roll, Jordan, Roll: The World the Slaves Made*

Group 7: Revolt

Four major slave rebellions shook the South during the first half of the 19th century. For African American communities, the leaders became legends. Whites shuddered at the names. The first was in 1800, in Virginia, where Gabriel Prosser plotted for months to capture the capital city of Richmond. With his wife, Nanny, and his brothers, Prosser assembled on his master's estate a force estimated at more than 900. Some carried scythes and clubs, others bayonets, and a few had guns. A sudden storm brought floods that poured over the six miles of roads to Richmond. Convinced heaven had spoken, they went home to wait for a better omen. The conspiracy began to unravel. Prosser and his officers were betrayed, captured, and sentenced to death. One bravely told his captors he had done for African Americans what Washington had done for white Americans: "I have ventured my life . . . to obtain the liberty of my countrymen."

Adapted from William Loren Katz's *Breaking the Chains: African-American Slave Resistance*

Group 7: Revolt

Enslaved people living and working in cities played a leading role in the largest slave plots and rebellions of the 19th century. In 1856, industrial enslaved workers — Louisiana sugar millers, Arkansas salt boilers, Missouri lead and iron miners — were found conspiring for freedom. Scores were arrested and 29 were executed.

Adapted from William Loren Katz's *Breaking the Chains: African-American Slave Resistance*

Group 7: Revolt

Slave revolts in the United States were not as frequent or as large scale as those in the Caribbean islands or in South America. Probably the largest slave revolt in the United States took place near New Orleans in 1811. Led by Haitian Charles Deslondes, many of the participants had participated in the Haitian Revolution. Four hundred to 500 slaves gathered after a rising at the plantation of a Major Andry. Armed with cane knives, axes, and clubs, they wounded Andry, killed his son, and began marching from plantation to plantation, their numbers growing. They were attacked by U.S. Army and militia forces; 66 were killed on the spot, and 16 were tried and shot by a firing squad.

Adapted from Howard Zinn's *A People's History of the United States*

Group 7: Revolt

The conspiracy of Denmark Vesey, himself a free Negro, was thwarted before it could be carried out in 1822. Vesey planned to burn Charleston, South Carolina, then the sixth-largest city in the nation, and to initiate a general revolt of enslaved people in the area. Several witnesses said thousands of Blacks were implicated in one way or another. Blacks had made about 250 pike heads and bayonets and more than 300 daggers. But the plan was betrayed, and 35 Blacks, including Vesey, were hanged. The trial record itself, published in Charleston, was ordered destroyed soon after publication, as too dangerous for slaves to see.

Adapted from Howard Zinn's *A People's History of the United States*

Group 7: Revolt

Nat Turner's rebellion in Southampton County, Virginia, in the summer of 1831, threw the slave-holding South into a panic, and then into a determined effort to bolster the security of the slave system. Turner, claiming religious visions, gathered about 70 enslaved people, who went on a rampage from plantation to plantation, killing at least 55 men, women, and children. They gathered supporters, but were captured as their ammunition ran out. Turner and perhaps 18 others were hanged.

Adapted from Howard Zinn's *A People's History of the United States*

Group 7: Revolt

In 1856, Gov. Henry Wise of Virginia moved arms into Alexandria to head off a feared insurrection. Thirty-two slaves were arrested. In Tennessee, more than 60 slaves belonging to Sen. John Bell were implicated in a rebellion conspiracy. Nine were hanged. In Dover, Tennessee, six slaves were hanged and one was whipped to death on accusations of plotting insurrection.

Adapted from David Williams' *I Freed Myself*

"Write that I" Poem Example
(A Frederick Douglass Narrative)

By Alyss Dixson

Write that I started in Freedom
praising my God
           feet inscribing the circle of my tribe
Tell how I described paradise
in pounding rhythms
           the sting of skin
                       against drum
and the reassuring heat
                       rising from the earth

Write that I grew up   in chains
praising my Master
with the sweat rolling from my back
     humbled by cotton in the field
Tell how I described paradise
in a bowl of rawhide soup
flea-infested hay
and the regular cracks!
                   Rising and falling from the whip of
                       the overseer

Write that I reached   "Manhood"
less than a man
barely stirring in my sleep
at the sound of my master
taking what was "his" to claim
from my Sisters

Tell how I described Freedom
in a chain
wrapped around a pale wrinkled
       neck
the satisfying crunch!
           of bone and
                       the bulging of blue eyes in
                       a moon-shaped face

Tell how
with fevered brain
I ran north
     ran
           from bloodhounds
           and bounty hunters

blood still
wet   upon my fists

I
     ran   streams   forests
           through   and
the words of slave spirituals
                 and
the faint   sounding of   the train whistle
           my only guides

Say I was bitter
and disappointed
knowing my children
and their children
would cry out
       against these silent chains
       another kind of bondage
       restricting their lives
       binding them
                   to poverty

Tell how I described   Freedom
In pounding syllables of   Revolution
                           Education
                           Equality

Write that I died
praising my Lord
           singing
                 of Amazing
                       Grace
and Write
     that I was proud.

I Freed Myself

By David Williams

GENERATIONS OF AMERICANS have grown up believing that Abraham Lincoln freed the slaves with a stroke of his pen. Lost in this simple portrayal is the role that the enslaved played in forcing the issue. Resistance to slavery took many forms, the most celebrated of which were various escape routes popularly called the Underground Railroad.

Harriet Tubman, the most famous of the railroad's "conductors," led hundreds of escapees to freedom. Rewards offered for her capture totaled as much as $40,000 but she was never caught. Neither was Arnold Gragston, an enslaved Kentuckian who ferried hundreds of fellow slaves across the Ohio River before making his own escape. Peter, a "tall, black African" in Petersburg, sheltered escaping slaves. When his home was searched for refugees, he proclaimed that he "would harbor as many negroes as he d—d well pleased." A local court sentenced him to 20 lashes. Jacob Dill, a Richmond slave, was also whipped for sheltering refugees. Thanks to these men and women, and many others like them, perhaps 100,000 enslaved people escaped north in the first half of the 19th century.

Escaping slavery was dangerous work. Slave catchers and bloodhounds were hot on the heels of nearly every escapee. Captured refugees could have toes or even half a foot cut off to discourage further escapes. Death could also result. One slave was whipped so badly after a failed attempt that he died three days later. For most enslaved people, the

Enslaved people escaping — a key form of resistance to slavery.

Special Collections, University of Maryland Libraries

greatest deterrent to escape was the near certainty that they would never see loved ones again. "My pappy tried to get away," recalled Mary Ella Grandberry, whose family was held in Alabama, "but he couldn't see how to take all us children with him, so he had to stay with us."

Those torn between the burdens of slavery and the love of family often resorted to local escapes. Local escapes were more often temporary affairs lasting days or weeks. It was not unusual for slaves to absent themselves overnight, especially on weekends, to visit friends or family, to attend dances or prayer meetings, or simply to get some rest. Slaves caught without a written pass from their owners could be severely whipped by the "paddyrollers," as the slaves called them. "But us was young and spry," recalled Virginia freedwoman Sis Shackleford, "an' could outrun 'em."

They had to balance their efforts, resisting enough to ease their burden but not so much as to bring on punishment. They organized work slowdowns. They played sick. They sabotaged or destroyed equipment to slow the pace of work. They pretended not to understand instructions.

Whipping and other physical abuse was often a reason for temporary escapes. "If they were treated too cruelly," Virginia Shepard recalled, "our folks would always run and hide in the woods." Delicia Patterson told of running off after being mistreated by her owner. "He sent everybody he thought knew where I was after me, and told them to tell me if I would only come on home, no one would ever bother me anymore. . . . So I went back home . . . and no one ever bothered me anymore." Such bargaining was not uncommon. Other reasons slaves might escape temporarily included bargaining for better food, clothing, working conditions, housing, or visiting rights.

Slaves who bargained in such a way walked a fine line. Punishments for unsuccessful attempts, or for other conduct the owner disliked, could be severe. Slaves were defined as property by slave state courts and, in the *Dred Scott* case of 1857, by the U.S. Supreme Court. As such, slaves were subject to the absolute authority of slaveholders and to whatever controls they chose to employ. W. B. Allen, a former Alabama slave, personally knew some in bondage who were beaten, sometimes to death, for nothing more than being off the plantation without written permission. Other offenses that might result in extreme punishment were lying, loitering, stealing, and talking back to — "sassing" — a white person.

Still, slaves resisted, most often cooperating with each other to do so. They had to balance their efforts, resisting enough to ease their burden but not so much as to bring on punishment. They organized work slowdowns. They played sick. They sabotaged or destroyed equipment to slow the pace of work. They pretended not to understand instructions. Slaves on one plantation rid themselves of an especially cruel overseer by slipping a snake into his cabin. "Put in a snake and out went the overseer," as Mattie Logan recalled. "Never no more did he whip the slaves on that plantation. . . . He was gone!"

Unfortunately, mitigating cruel treatment was rarely so simple. Slavery itself was the greatest cruelty of all, and, for some slaves, the ultimate resistance, the only escape, was death. One Georgia slave took her own life by swallowing strychnine. In Covington, Kentucky, two enslaved parents "sent the souls of their children to heaven rather than have them descend to the hell of slavery." After releasing their children's souls, they released their own. Another enslaved mother killed all 13 of her children in infancy to spare them a life of suffering as slaves.

Sometimes slaves killed their oppressors instead. Most famous for its violence was Nat Turner's 1831 Virginia rebellion, in which more than 50 whites died. There were many others who fought back or conspired to do so. In 1800, more than 1,000 slaves marched on Richmond. The governor called out armed militiamen to turn them back. There were similar efforts to gain liberty in Petersburg and Norfolk. When one slave conspirator was asked what he had to say in his defense, he calmly replied, "I have nothing more to offer than what General Washington would have had to offer, had he been taken by the British officers and put on trial by them. I have ventured my life in endeavoring to obtain liberty of my countrymen, and am a willing sacrifice to their cause." In 1811, 400 Louisiana slaves rose up for freedom. A year later there was a rebellion in New Orleans. In 1837, slaves near that city formed a rebel band and killed several whites before being captured.

Slaves fought back individually too. In 1849, a slave in Chambers County, Alabama, shot his owner. In Macon County, another slave "violently attacked with a knife and cut to pieces" his overseer. After one overseer whipped her, an enslaved Florida woman took a hoe and chopped the man "to a bloody death." Most who resisted violently were either shot or lynched. Some were burned alive. What laws there were restraining whites from murdering slaves for whatever reason were in fact no restraint at all. State slave codes prevented slaves from testifying against whites in court, and few whites would testify against each other.

Aside from the brutality they sanctioned, slave codes defined legal limits for the late-antebellum South's 4 million enslaved people far beyond their status as property. No enslaved person could lawfully carry a gun, own property, travel without a written pass, or learn to read and write. Slave gatherings, even for religious services, were forbidden without a white person present.

Slave codes also prevented local governments from issuing marriage licenses. To do so would have established a legally sanctioned bond between members of slave families, implicitly infringing on the "property rights" of slaveholders. Nevertheless, slaveholders allowed and even encouraged slaves to marry at an early age and have many children. This not only increased the slaveholder's "property" but also provided additional means of control. Besides the constant threat of physical violence, slaveholders found the institution of the family to be an effective means of intimidation. Any slave might be pushed to the point of disregard for his or her own safety and attempt to fight back or escape. But when slaveholders threatened family members, slaves were more likely to hold their anger in check. It was another way to drive home the point that slaveholder was master. Some did not even allow parents to name their own children, reserving that privilege for themselves.

In naming the children of slave women, some slaveholders were actually exercising their own parental rights. For a planter to have any number of mistresses among his slaves was quite common. Slaveholders typically viewed rape as another method of enforcing psychological dominance within the slave community. Others simply viewed slaves as property to be used at their pleasure. The first sexual experience a planter's son had was usually with a female slave. Pregnancy often followed and more children meant more control.

Not only did slaves fear for family members, there was the additional terror that they might be sold off at any time. That fear helped keep overt resistance in check. Slaves with families were less likely to escape since that would mean permanent separation from their loved ones. Of the many thousands who did escape bondage, most were young, single, and childless.

As slave resistance increased, slaveholders pushed harder for the expansion of slavery to the West. Some did so as part of a wider demand for slavery's security, others as a means of giving slaves less free territory into which they might escape. Slave escapes — distant and local, temporary and permanent — were on the rise throughout the late antebellum period, reaching perhaps 50,000 annually during the 1850s. To slaveholders, it was clear that slavery must expand or die.

Rising resistance stoked slaveholder fears and pressed the slavery issue to a breaking point. "It is useless to disguise the fact, its truth is undeniable," wrote a Virginia newspaper editor in 1852, "that a greater degree of insubordination has been manifested by the negro population, within the last few months, than any previous period in our history." A year later, one observer noticed that newspapers throughout the

As slave resistance increased, slaveholders pushed harder for the expansion of slavery to the West. Some did so as part of a wider demand for slavery's security, others as a means of giving slaves less free territory into which they might escape.

Enslaved people fought to maintain family ties in the midst of a system that tore them apart.

South were reporting "complaints of growing insolence and insubordination among the negroes."

Reports of rising resistance, up to and including murder, became more and more common throughout the 1850s. A Missouri slave stabbed his owner to death in 1853 and escaped to Canada. In 1855, another slave from Missouri slashed his owner nearly in half and fled to Iowa. An Alabama bondsman killed his owner and boasted of the murder. A Georgia slave named Lash, after some "rough handling," murdered his owner. A Florida woman chopped her overseer's head off with a hoe. In Maryland, a slave killed his owner with a knife, took flight, and was never seen again. After seeing his sister whipped, a Kentucky slave beat the overseer to death with a club and escaped on the Underground Railroad.

In July 1859, the *Liberator* reported a rash of violence occurring in the spring and early summer. A slave near Grand Cone, Texas, bashed his owner's brains out with an axe, then burned his body. Another slave in Union County, Kentucky, used an axe to kill an overseer who was trying to whip him. A slaveholder in Spencer County, Kentucky, was clubbed to death after whipping two of his slaves. In Lincoln County, Missouri, an enslaved man stabbed his owner to death. Commenting on one murder, a St. Louis paper remarked that reports of slaves killing whites had become "alarmingly frequent."

Collective resistance was also becoming more frequent. In 1856, Gov. Henry Wise of Virginia moved arms into Alexandria to head off a feared insurrection. Thirty-two slaves were arrested. In Tennessee, more than 60 slaves belonging to Sen. John Bell were implicated in a rebellion conspiracy. Nine were hanged. In Dover, Tennessee, six slaves were hanged and one was whipped to death on accusations of plotting insurrection. A newspaper editor in Galveston, Texas, wrote in 1856 that "never has there been a time in our recollection when so many insurrections, or attempts at insurrection, have transpired in rapid succession as during the past six months."

In 1857, a group of Carter County, Kentucky, slaves were tried on suspicion for plotting insurrection. February 1858 saw a "fearful insurrection" in Arkansas. Blacks were said to have attacked two settlements and killed 23 whites. A newspaper editor in Franklin, Louisiana, reporting the murders of two slaveholders by their slaves, noted that there were "more cases of insubordination among the negro population . . . than ever known before." In August, more than 50 slaves on a Mississippi plantation declared that "they would die to a man before one of their party should be whipped." It took 75 armed whites to put down the resistance.

The tide of resistance continued to swell in the winter of 1859–60. Fires that swept through cotton warehouses and gin presses were blamed on Blacks and Northern abolition agents. In November, fire destroyed $6,000 worth of corn, fodder, and cotton on one Georgia plantation. Another fire razed a gin house two miles from Columbus. In Virginia, authorities charged two slaves named Jerry and Joe with setting several fires. December found Blacks in Bolivar, Missouri, attacking whites with stones and threatening to burn the town.

This volatile atmosphere framed the 1860 presidential campaign. Although Lincoln was no threat to slavery where it existed, and said so often during the campaign, the secessionists rallied against him as a radical abolitionist with a secret agenda to foment slave rebellion. Such overheated rhetoric was intended to stir up support for secession among Southern whites, but Southern Blacks heard the message too. What Blacks heard was what slaveholders generally feared — that Lincoln was a direct threat to slavery.

Slaves increasingly acted on their hopes for freedom in the summer and fall of 1860. Resistance and rumors of resistance pervaded the South that year and drove slaveholder fears to a fever pitch. Slave control had never been easy. By the 1850s, it was getting more difficult. A Lincoln presidency could only make it harder. If the slave states remained in the Union, most slaveholders feared that their "property" would be nearly impossible to control. Slaveholders' fear of their slaves was a primary force driving secession during the weeks after Lincoln's election.

South Carolina was the first to go on Dec. 20, 1860. In its "Declaration of Immediate Causes" justifying its move, the state's secession convention frankly admitted its fear of "servile insurrection." Everywhere justifications for secession were much the same. Mississippi blamed Northerners for promoting "insurrection and incendiarism in our midst." Georgia's excuse was that Northerners were trying to "excite insurrection and servile war among us." Underlying slaveholders' fear was the certain knowledge that slaves wanted freedom. It was that certainty, born of many decades of slave resistance that led to secession, war, and slavery's downfall.

Slaveholders' doubts about their ability to maintain slavery indefinitely had a long history. The need to justify slavery had for decades occupied their brightest minds. Blacks had never submitted to slavery willingly or completely. They did little more than what they had to do and took liberties where they could. They resisted in so many ways that the slaveholders' need to exercise control was constant and all-consuming. Had Blacks been content to remain enslaved, slaveholders would have had no cause for alarm. Nor would abolitionist arguments have inspired such panic among them. As it was, slaveholder fears of threats to slavery led them to insist on guarantees for slavery's future and the means to control that future. And that fear led them to secede when those guarantees seemed at risk. It was then, at the heart of it all, the unrelenting resistance to slavery among slaves themselves that was the essential condition, the one thing without which the sectional crisis, secession, and the Civil War would not have happened.

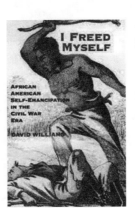

Adapted from David Williams, *I Freed Myself* (New York: Cambridge University Press, 2014).

David Williams is a professor at Valdosta State University in Georgia, and the author of several books on slavery and the Civil War.

"If There Is No Struggle. . ."

Teaching a people's history of the abolition movement

By Bill Bigelow

"WHO HERE WOULD HAVE BEEN AGAINST slavery if you suddenly found yourself living in those times?"

I've asked a version of this question to many U.S. history classes over the years. Every student raises a hand.

"So what exactly would you have done to end slavery?"

Puzzled looks are generally the response to this question. What *should* we do, what *can* we do, when we are confronted by the enormity of an injustice like slavery? It's not an easy question for my students, and it wasn't an easy question for the people who opposed slavery in those times. The answers were struggled over in the abolition movement, one of the most significant social movements in U.S. history, but underappreciated in today's history curriculum.

A few summers ago, my wife, Linda, and I vacationed in upstate New York. We went to visit John Brown's grave site at North Elba, near Lake Placid. Brown was executed Dec. 2, 1859, by the state of Virginia shortly after leading a raid on the Harpers Ferry arsenal, hoping to trigger an antislavery rebellion.

In a nearby town, we went to a talk, part of a lecture series on abolitionism, by scholar Eric Foner. Foner's thesis was that the

Frederick Douglass escaped slavery and became a prominent leader in the abolition movement.

abolition movement was the foundation of virtually all social justice movements in the United States. It led to the first antiwar movement, against the U.S. invasion and occupation of Mexico (1846–48), which abolitionists saw as a land grab to expand slavery. (Henry David Thoreau coined the term "civil disobedience" in defending his willingness to go to jail for his refusal to pay taxes to support the war.) The abolition movement seeded the movement for women's rights in the United States: The leaders of the first gathering of women to demand rights *as* women, at Seneca Falls, New York, in 1848, were abolitionists like Lucretia Mott and Elizabeth Cady Stanton. For all its imperfections, the abolition movement was this country's first multiracial movement. And it was the first anti-racist movement in U.S. history, demanding an end not only to slavery but also to racial segregation and discrimination in the North. As Foner writes in *The Story of American Freedom*, "The origin of an American people unbounded by race lies not with the founders, who by and large made their peace with slavery, but with the abolitionists. . . . [A]bolitionists invented the concept of equality before the law regardless of race, one all but unknown in American jurisprudence before the Civil War."

U.S. history textbooks and curricula tend to marginalize the abolition movement. For example, Oregon's state social studies standards mention "abolitionists" only once in the 8th-grade benchmarks, and not at all in the high school standards. One of my favorite quotes is from Amy Goodman, host of the radio/TV program *Democracy Now!* Goodman says that journalism needs to go where the silences are. The same can be said of the school curriculum. And one of the greatest silences is about the fact that social movements have transformed the United States — that everything good and decent about our society is the product of people working together to make things better.

But like so much other media, textbooks prefer to regard social progress as the product of great individuals. Ask a typical group of students "Who freed the slaves?" and they'll say Abraham Lincoln. Yet Lincoln was never an abolitionist. In fact, the Great Emancipator was not even an abolitionist when he signed the Emancipation Proclamation — a document that carefully listed the regions, county by county, where enslaved people were to remain enslaved, "as if this proclamation were not issued." Earlier, in March 1861, during his first inaugural address, Lincoln had not been president for five minutes before he quoted one of his own pro-slavery speeches: "I have no purpose, directly or indirectly, to interfere with the institution of slavery in the states where it exists. I believe I have no lawful right to do so, and I have no inclination to do so. . . ." He then promised to enforce the Fugitive Slave Act

and to support a constitutional amendment "to the effect that the federal government shall never interfere with the domestic institutions of the states, including that of persons held to service." Lincoln left a complicated legacy — and no doubt, through the course of the Civil War he came to espouse positions held by white and Black abolitionists — but he began his presidency by promising slave owners that they could keep people enslaved forever.

Foner's talk about the significance of the abolition movement inspired me to rethink how I had been approaching the antislavery struggle in my classes. First, I realized that I needed to spend more time teaching it. I wanted to find teaching strategies that would underscore the difficult choices that confronted the abolition movement. Instead of having students simply read about the abolition movement or listen to me talk, I wanted to engage them as movement participants, so that the strategic dilemmas of ending slavery would unfold in class. In other words, I wanted a *people's* pedagogy to match the bottom-up *people's* history I hoped to impart to my students.

I created a role play in which every student in class portrayed a member of the American Anti-Slavery Society (AASS). As the AASS, the class would encounter some of the difficult strategic choices that confronted the actual organization throughout its history. My hope was that students would taste a bit of the uncertainty but also the exhilaration that actual antislavery organizers experienced as they sought to abolish the greatest injustice of their time.

Materials Needed

- Copies of "Member, American Anti-Slavery Society; on the reverse side, "Autobiography of an Abolitionist" (Handout 3–A), enough for every student in the class.

- Copies of "Role Play: Ending Slavery — American Anti-Slavery Society Choices" (Handout 3–B) for every student.

Time Required

At least three class periods.

Suggested Procedure

1. Before beginning the role play, it's helpful if students have background knowledge on slavery and the slave trade.

2. Tell the class that they are going to do a role play on the movement to end slavery in the United States, and that each of them will become a member of the American Anti-Slavery Society, the most significant abolition organization in the country.

3. Distribute a role sheet — "Member, American Anti-Slavery Society" (Handout 3–A)

— and read it aloud.

The role begins:

You are a member of the American Anti-Slavery Society, an organization founded in 1833 to end slavery in the United States. Your members include both Blacks and whites. To you, slavery is the central evil in American life. Of all the injustices, this one — that allows human beings to own other human beings and to treat them purely as property — is far and away the worst.

The role sheet goes on to describe aspects of slavery and some of the first actions against slavery, and concludes by reminding the students-as-abolitionists that "it's one thing to oppose slavery and quite another thing to know what to do about it. There is sharp debate among abolitionists — people who want to end slavery. How can we end this enormous evil? That is the question we face."

4. To encourage students to connect more personally to their role as abolitionists, ask them to write their autobiography, to imagine the experiences that led them to dedicate their lives to the fight against slavery. Emphasize to them what a remarkable thing it was for someone to become an abolitionist — slavery was the dominant institution in the United States. It had existed here for more than 200 years, was protected by the Constitution and U.S. Supreme Court rulings, and was the single most profitable "industry" in the country. By the birth of the abolition movement, most U.S. presidents had enslaved people. Ask students: "What motivates you to work against your

Sojourner Truth was an abolitionist and a women's rights activist.

government and for equality? How did you come to think that you could make a difference in the world?"

Tell students that they are free to choose their gender, age, race, social class, and region of the country. To help them find a route into their autobiographies, the handout on the reverse of their role, "Autobiography of an Abolitionist," offers a number of general scenarios. Students need not be limited to these, but a couple of the choices include:

- You escaped from slavery. You know from your own experience the horrors of being enslaved. Every day of your life you can't stand the fact that people just like you are still being whipped, still being sold apart from their families, still being abused — just because of the color of their skin.

- Your father was a slave owner. You witnessed firsthand the conditions of enslaved African Americans.

The intent of the autobiography writing assignment is to help students imagine lives of commitment, to consider experiences that might lead a person to dedicate one's life to something beyond simply making a living, enjoying one's family, and having a good time. Of course, an assignment like this also invites stereotype — that despite previous lessons, students may not have enough background to plausibly describe someone's transformation into an abolitionist. That's OK. As you read students' writing and hear their discussion, you'll become alert to areas that need to be taught in greater depth, and the objective is less exact historical accuracy than it is for students to spend time "inside" an individual committed to racial justice and to radically changing the society. We want students to try on the personas of individuals who had created lives of activism and defiance.

5. This assignment can produce wonderful writing. It is helpful to share examples with students to show what you're looking for. Here are a couple pieces from students I worked with at Franklin High School, in Portland, Oregon. This first is from Nicole McDonald, a kind, quiet, and bookish student who fired to life when we talked about women's issues in class. Nicole's character is a young white woman raised in the North:

I was brought up in a staunch Christian home by my father and elder brothers, my mother having passed away giving birth to my brother a year younger than me. Living without a woman, none of us were quite sure how a girl was supposed to act. I'm sure I had the queerest upbringing in all of New England. I didn't start wearing skirts until I was 10 because my father did not want to spend the money on an entire wardrobe just for myself when my brothers' hand-me-downs were as good as anything. I worked with the boys in the barn and in the fields. I had to — they needed my help. I was always big for my age, and never had a problem with physical labor.

But none of this tells how I entered the antislavery movement. All I can say is that I know what it feels like. No, I have never been whipped. I have never been forced to pick cotton in the fields, torn from my family and all that I know. But as I entered society, I realized, really, I do not have much freedom either. I cannot get a job besides being a teacher, and even then only if I do not date or am not married. My shackles are invisible. I am given the illusion of freedom, but not the reality. In reality, I am as much a slave as anybody. My situation is immovable except into marriage. And then I will be like a servant.

Mariya Koroteyev, a big-hearted, religious, Russian immigrant, took her autobiographical story in a different direction. She imagined herself enslaved as "Maggie":

I leaned against the tree with closed eyes. I took a moment to catch my breath. "You!" I heard the watcher yell. "Get moving. Don't waste precious time." So once more I took my heavy basket and began to pick. Row by row, basket by basket, under the burning sun, I picked cotton and so did the other slaves. When the day came to an end and the sun, understanding our pain, hid behind the mountain, I heard the whistle ordering us to go back to our cabins, for the day's work was over.

Mariya's character, Maggie, learns that a friend has been killed for stealing food. Distraught, she decides to run away and is joined by two other friends:

As we crossed the border of Canada, I was filled with joy. "Larrie!" I shouted. "We are free!" "Free, free," my words echoed through the cave where we stopped to make our new home. Then it was quiet. We each thought of the horrible place we had escaped, and Matt was first to reply: "We are," he said. "But I think about the millions of others." And so did I. I thought of the four girls in my cabin, and the hundreds of slaves who were beaten in the fields, and my eyes filled with tears. "I wish I could help," I whispered. "I wish I could."

Ultimately, Maggie begins attending antislavery meetings, joins the abolition movement, and volunteers her house as a stop on the Underground Railroad.

Students will create a great diversity of abolitionists in their autobiographies. Here are a few from that year: a dockworker who encounters slave auctions where he sees "how carelessly families are torn apart"; an enslaved woman who cannot bring herself to raise her daughter to be a slave, and remembers her own mother's stories of Africa retold through the years; a white worker disgusted by parasitic slave owners

— "Where I come from, no matter who you are, you take care of and clean up after yourself"; and a young white woman from a tight-knit, devoutly Christian family, frustrated by her parents' inability to "take their devotion one step further" to become abolitionists: "I have no patience for anyone who is too self-absorbed to care about the suffering of others simply because of their skin color."

6. Ask students to form a circle to read these aloud and to appreciate them, one by one. It is worth spending a substantial amount of class time listening to these stories, both because a read-around in which students express such humanity is a great community builder, but also because a successful abolition role play depends on students steeped in their collective anti-racist imagination.

7. The day following the conclusion of the read-around, distribute the "Role Play: Ending Slavery — American Anti-Slavery Society Choices, 1833" (Handout 3–B) with five strategic dilemmas that faced the AASS at different points from its founding in 1833 until 1858:

- Should the AASS support "colonization" schemes to send people freed from slavery to Africa?

- Should the AASS spend time and money opposing racial discrimination in the North as well as attempting to end slavery in the South?

- Should the AASS support efforts to gain greater equality for women?

- Should the AASS support armed attempts to resist enforcement of the Fugitive Slave Act?

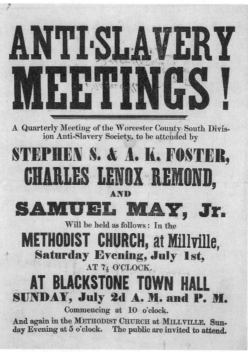

ANTI-SLAVERY MEETINGS !

A Quarterly Meeting of the Worcester County South Division Anti-Slavery Society, to be attended by

STEPHEN S. & A. K. FOSTER,
CHARLES LENOX REMOND,
AND
SAMUEL MAY, Jr.

Will be held as follows : In the
METHODIST CHURCH, at Millville,
Saturday Evening, July 1st,
AT 7½ O'CLOCK.
AT BLACKSTONE TOWN HALL
SUNDAY, July 2d A. M. and P. M.
Commencing at 10 o'clock.
And again in the METHODIST CHURCH at MILLVILLE, Sunday Evening at 5 o'clock. The public are invited to attend.

- Should the AASS support John Brown either with guns or money?

These were actual historical dilemmas, although the activity takes the liberty of suggesting that they were each debated in an assembly of AASS members. Here's an example from the handout:

Situation: It's 1848. Many of the people in the abolition movement are white women. As they worked against slavery, many women began to feel that they too were heavily discriminated against. Even in some antislavery gatherings, women are not allowed to speak or to be leaders. In almost every state, married women cannot own property. Women's husbands even own the wages that women earn. In almost every state, the father can legally make a will appointing a guardian for his children in the event of his death. Should the husband die, a mother can have her children taken away from her. In most states, it is legal for a man to beat his wife. New York courts have ruled that, in order to keep his wife from nagging, a man can beat her with a horsewhip every few weeks! Women are not allowed to vote in any state.

A number of prominent white women — many of them, perhaps most, active in the abolition movement — have organized a women's rights convention for Seneca Falls, New York, in July of this year. Some of the organizers would like the American Anti-Slavery Society to endorse this gathering. This will be the first time that women in the United States have organized a meeting to discuss the condition of women.

Question: Should the American Anti-Slavery Society publicly endorse this gathering?

Arguments: Those in favor argue that the abolition movement should stand against all oppression, including the oppression of women. They argue that women abolitionists would be more effective if they were allowed to speak publicly. Some supporters also believe that the women's rights movement would bring in many people who have not been active in abolitionist work, and that this could ultimately strengthen the movement against slavery. And besides, they argue, we're trying to build a society based on equality and freedom from all oppression.

Others argue that this is nonsense, that this threatens to divide antislavery forces. They argue that without question, the greatest evil of our time is the enslavement of Black human beings by white human beings, and that as bad off as some white women have it, this discrimination cannot be compared to slavery. Opponents argue that associating the American Anti-Slavery Society with women's rights will confuse and divide our supporters — and will weaken the antislavery movement.

8. With the entire class, review one of the questions as an example. Tell students: "These were real issues that antislavery activists faced. I want you to think about each of these questions as if you're a member of the American Anti-Slavery Society." Tell them they will be discussing and making decisions about these questions in a large AASS meeting, but first they should discuss the dilemmas in small groups. Divide students into groups of four or five and urge them to stay in the "roles" that they created through their autobiographies, and ask them to try to reach agreement about the best course of action for their organization. These are tough questions, and the premise of asking students to first answer these questions in small groups is that their whole-class discussion will be richer and more democratic

if students have thought about the issues beforehand. Although, if pressed for time, it works simply to move directly into the whole-class role play.

As students talk about the thorny questions that the abolition movement faced, some will continue to represent the individual they'd created in their autobiography, and some will abandon their character in favor of trying to figure out what they personally think is the best course of action. Either is fine; the autobiographies will have served their purpose by getting students into an abolitionist mind-set.

9. Give the small groups about 50 minutes or so to talk through the issues and to write down preliminary thoughts on what they feel is the best course of action for each strategic choice. Circulate through the classroom, and get a sense for how they are answering these. It is fine if they can't agree, because students will be talking about these issues as a whole class following the small-group work, but encourage them to make their best attempt to reach consensus.

10. Arrange students' desks in a circle. Explain: "The real abolitionists didn't have a teacher there to guide their discussion. They were on their own. That's how it's going to be in here, too. I'll take notes on your discussion, but how you run your discussion and the decisions you make about each question will be up to you. The only requirements are that you do your best to take this seriously, and that you *discuss* the questions and don't simply bring them to a vote." In watching students do whole-group role plays over the years, I've found that the best route is for students to raise hands and have each speaker call on the next speaker. Tell them to be sure to decide on a process to carry on their conversation before they begin, or people will just start calling things out, and it can get chaotic.

The most recent time I led this activity with high school students — I've also used it in preservice teacher education programs and in workshops with teachers — one of my two classes doing this activity decided to choose a trusted student to chair the proceedings; the other class followed my suggestion and called on each other. Neither was problem-free, but by and large both worked fine. In whole-group role plays, there is almost always a rough period that can try a teacher's patience, but the students' struggle to do this *together* without an adult leader is itself a key piece of the lesson.

Immediately prior to students' deliberation, emphasize that, even though we may now think the end of slavery was inevitable, there was no way abolitionists could have known with certainty that it would end. In fact, territories open to slavery had spread, and slavery became more legally entrenched between the founding of the AASS in 1833 and 1858 (the year the AASS debated the final question in the role play). Urge them to approach each question thoughtfully and seriously. In real life, these decisions had life-and-death consequences.

11. Tell them to begin. At first, class discussion may be a bit halting. But the first question, about whether the AASS would support sending people who had been freed from slavery to Africa, is the easiest, both for students and for the real AASS. As the African American abolitionist Maria W. Stewart said: Before she would go to a strange land, "the bayonet shall pierce me through." (Stewart was the first U.S.-born woman to speak in public and leave written texts of speeches.)

In teaching this activity, I have been delighted by the seriousness and passion that students bring to these discussions. These often go on much longer than I'd planned, but I promise students that as long as they are engaged in discussing the issues, I won't interrupt or hurry them. I sit at my desk and take careful notes on their arguments. Here is a sampling of one class's discussion about whether they should consider armed resistance to oppose enforcement of the 1850 Fugitive Slave Act:

Austin: *There are so many other ways to make our point other than with violence.*

Luke: *Austin said that there are so many non-violent things to do. Name one.*

Tim: *Think of when you walk by a house and there is a little yapping dog tied on a leash. You walk by day after day. You don't pay any attention to the dog. You know that it can't hurt you. That's who we are. The abolitionists are that yapping dog, and we're not making any difference at all. We have to unleash the dog and it has to bite the slave owners on the butt.*

Tiffany: *Well, if we're that dog, and that dog does bite, then we're going to get put to sleep. The whole government and army is going to come down on us and we'll be destroyed.*

Eron: *People keep saying that we need to find other ways besides violence. Fine. What other ways? The bounty hunters are rounding up Blacks. What if the bounty hunters started rounding up white people in the North? Would we still urge nonviolence then? Would we just sit back and say let's stay nonviolent and continue to publish our pamphlets and speak in churches as they are destroying our lives?*

Alex: *I like the yapping dog analogy. We need to go after them. We can't just look at the legalities. They'll just change the law anytime they feel like it.*

Tiffany: *People are saying that the law is unimportant. It's not unimportant. If it were unimportant, then why are we trying to pass a law outlawing slavery? It's not like the choice is to be violent or to do nothing. We could develop a strategy to help freed Blacks. We could establish communities of armed Blacks for self-defense. We don't have to attack people but we can help people defend themselves.*

Eron: *If we are going to abide by this fugitive slave law, we can't win. We have to fight this law.*

In that particular class, the students voted 15 to 11, with several abstentions, to reaffirm their commitment not to attack bounty hunters first, but decided to help communities of freed African Americans arm themselves for self-defense. Students' discussion often mirrors the frustration and disagreement within the abolition movement about what to do in the face of the increasingly aggressive measures by pro-slavery forces. Eron was becoming the John Brown of the class, even if he wrongly assumed that the "we" of the abolition movement was all white. Others refused to waver from a strict adherence to nonviolence.

12. It's typical for students to take most of two 50-minute class periods, or one block period to discuss the issues. If the role play continues over from the previous day, you might begin class by reading to them notes you've taken, like those included above. This honors students' intensity and thoughtfulness, and communicates your appreciation for them as

intellectuals. When I have read students' comments back to the class, students are rapt as they listen to me recount the back-and-forth of their arguments. This reading helps students re-enter their roles, and reminds them where they left off. It's also a good idea to talk with students about their decision-making process and to analyze with them when they made progress and when they tended to spin their wheels.

13. Following the role play, ask students to predict how they think the abolition movement resolved these questions. Not surprisingly, students' curiosity to know what "really happened" is much greater because they have tried to figure out the same questions themselves. ("A People's History of the Abolition Movement" by William Loren Katz and James Brewer Stewart, included in Lesson 4, goes through how these debates played out historically.)

14. I hope a number of things will come out of the post-role play discussion. I want them to appreciate the growing militancy of the abolition movement. I also hope the lesson will teach students that the abolition movement, by and large, *did* see racism as the enemy, and not only slavery. In his first speech as an abolitionist, Frederick Douglass argued that "Prejudice against color is stronger North than South; it hangs around my neck like a heavy weight. It presses me out from my fellow men. . . . I have met it every step the three years I have been out of slavery."

John Brown. The artist writes: "I set the portrait of him, based on his time in Kansas, when he was carrying on a running battle with pro-slavery forces there. The house on fire is America, built on the foundation of slavery."

There are important facts that I want students to know and historical figures I want to introduce. But the main aim of this activity is to show students that the movement for racial justice wasn't simply a matter of one thing happening after another — it wasn't the smooth unfolding of History leading to Freedom. The structure of this activity lends itself to students recognizing that history is a series of choice points and there is nothing inevitable about the direction of society, that where things move depends on how we analyze the world and how we act on that analysis. People like them — not only famous leaders — make history.

Alec "Icky" Dunn

Member, American Anti-Slavery Society

YOU ARE A MEMBER of the American Anti-Slavery Society (AASS), an organization founded in 1833 to end slavery in the United States. Your members include both Blacks and whites. To you, slavery is the central evil in American life. Of all the injustices, this one — that allows human beings to own other human beings and to treat them purely as property — is far and away the worst.

David Walker, the son of an enslaved father and a free mother, wrote a pamphlet in 1829 denouncing slavery, *Walker's Appeal.* You were especially influenced by this pamphlet. Walker condemned the idea that somehow whites were inherently superior and had the right to control Blacks: "God has been pleased to give us two eyes, two hands, two feet, and some sense in our heads as well as they. They have no more right to hold us in slavery than we have to hold them." Walker insisted that slavery could not last forever: "Our sufferings will come to an end, in spite of all the Americans this side of eternity." But the year after these words were published, Walker was found dead in Boston. Some think he was poisoned, as slave owners had put a bounty on his head.

In 1831, there was an incident that shocked the nation and forced everyone to think about slavery. Nat Turner was an enslaved man who was a preacher. He led an uprising against whites in Southampton County, Virginia. About 70 enslaved people went from plantation to plantation killing whites — men, women, and children. In the end, more than 50 whites and more than 100 Blacks were killed. For slave owners, the lesson was that they needed to crack down, and pass more laws restricting the freedom of slaves. For people like you, Turner's revolt was just another piece of evidence that slavery is an evil that must be abolished.

But you know that slavery won't disappear on its own. Slavery is a huge industry in the United States — indirectly in the North as well as directly in the South. Obviously, the people who benefit the most are the slave owners, who get free labor to pick their cotton and do countless other tasks on their plantations. But there are others who benefit: textile manufacturers in the North who get cheap cotton, bankers, railroad companies, insurance people, owners of the ships that bring goods to and from the South. There is more money invested in slavery in the United States than in any other industry.

However, it's one thing to oppose slavery and quite another thing to know what to do about it. There is sharp debate among abolitionists — people who want to end slavery. How can we end this enormous evil? That is the question we face.

Autobiography
of an Abolitionist

HOW DID YOU BECOME an abolitionist? Write an autobiography describing the experiences that led you to dedicate your life to the fight against slavery. You can choose your gender, your age, your race, your social class, the region where you live. Give yourself a name and a history. Be imaginative and very detailed in your descriptions. Give yourself a history. Tell the story of the events that made you who you are: an antislavery activist.

Here are some possible general scenarios, but feel free to invent your own:

- You are an escaped slave. You know from your own experience the horrors of slavery. Every day of your life you can't stand the fact that people just like you are still in slavery, still being whipped, still being sold away from their families, still being abused — just because of the color of their skin.

- You are a free Black living in the North. Although you personally have never been enslaved, you are mistreated in the North because of your race. This has sensitized you to the conditions of Black people everywhere, especially those living in the South.

- Your father was a slave owner. You witnessed firsthand the conditions of enslaved African Americans.

- Your parents were strong Christians. You absorbed their religious commitments, but were frustrated by the fact that they didn't act on their religious values when it came to the most important moral concern of our age: slavery.

- You worked on the docks in New Orleans, and witnessed slave ships coming into port. You watched slave auctions, saw families sold apart. Slowly you began to change.

- You are a white woman. You can relate to the conditions of slaves in America, because as a woman, even a white woman, you sometimes feel yourself to be a kind of slave: you can't own property, you can't vote, you can't speak in public, you are not allowed to attend any college in America. According to one court of law, you may be legally whipped by your husband to stop you from "nagging."

Role Play: Ending Slavery
American Anti-Slavery Society Choices, 1833

1. SITUATION: Earlier this century an organization formed called the American Colonization Society. The aim of this group is to free slaves and to pay for them to be relocated in Africa. Recently, people favoring colonization approached your organization. They have asked you to contribute funds to support buying some people out of slavery and sending them to Africa. They also would like to use your organization's name in their publicity.

QUESTION: Will the American Anti-Slavery Society contribute funds for colonization and allow its name to be used in this effort?

ARGUMENTS: Some people believe that because slavery will not end on its own, we'll need to end slavery one person at a time, by buying their freedom. True, this won't end slavery as an institution, but it will end slavery permanently for those people who are freed and allowed to return to Africa. They also argue that because of all the racism in the North and the South, it will be important that freed Black slaves have their own homeland in Africa. American prejudice is so deep that it will never be possible for Blacks to live freely in the United States. Others disagree. They argue that "colonization" is ridiculous and a waste of time — that your organization needs to end slavery forever, not buy just a few people's freedom. Besides, if this plan "worked" and began to buy substantial numbers of people their freedom, the price of enslaved people would simply increase. Finally, they argue that most enslaved Americans were born here, not in Africa, and that people who are enslaved deserve their freedom here in the land that they worked so hard to build. And if there is discrimination here, then we must work to change it.

American Anti-Slavery Society Choices, 1833

2. SITUATION: In addition to the horrors of slavery in the South, racial discrimination in the North is also a huge problem. There is segregation in the North, especially in schools and transportation. There are laws in the North against intermarriage. There are even some Northern churches that oppose slavery but don't allow Blacks as members. Blacks are discriminated against throughout the North. Not a single state in the country treats people equally regardless of one's race.

Recently, in Massachusetts, Black abolitionist David Ruggles was removed from a steamboat for refusing to sit in the "colored-only" section. In response, some abolitionists have proposed leading a struggle to fight segregation in the North.

QUESTION: Should the American Anti-Slavery Society spend time and money opposing racial discrimination in the North as well as slavery in the South?

ARGUMENTS: People in favor of the AASS working to oppose racism in the North argue that our aim should be to fight racial prejudice wherever it occurs — that our deepest aim is not just to end slavery, but to end mistreatment based on race as well. They also argue that the more freedom our Black members have, the more effectively they'll be able to oppose slavery. Furthermore, why fight to free enslaved Blacks just to send them into a deeply racist society that will continue to discriminate against them? Others say: Yes, prejudice in the North is a problem. But it is a separate issue and could divide the antislavery movement. They argue that there are people in the North who oppose slavery but don't yet believe in equality for Blacks, and that we need to keep the movement as broad as possible. People will change slowly, and we must allow that slow change to occur. One fight at a time, these people urge — first we get rid of slavery, then we deal with racial discrimination in the North.

American Anti-Slavery Society Choices, 1848

3. SITUATION: Many of the people in the abolition movement are white women. As they work against slavery, they've come to realize how much they are discriminated against. Even in some antislavery gatherings, women are not allowed to speak or to be leaders. In almost every state, married women cannot own property. Husbands even control the wages earned by women outside the home. In almost every state, the father can legally make a will appointing a guardian for his children in the event of his death. Should the husband die, a mother can have her children taken away from her. In most states, it is legal for a man to beat his wife. New York courts have ruled that in order to keep his wife from nagging, a man can beat her with a horsewhip every few weeks! Women are not allowed to vote in any state.

A number of prominent white women — many of them active in the abolition movement — have organized a women's rights convention for Seneca Falls, New York, in July of this year. This will be the first time that women in the United States have organized a meeting to discuss the condition of women. Some of the organizers would like the American Anti-Slavery Society to endorse this gathering.

QUESTION: Should the American Anti-Slavery Society publicly endorse this gathering?

ARGUMENTS: Those in favor argue that the abolition movement should stand against all oppression, including the oppression of women. They argue that women abolitionists would be more effective if they were allowed to speak publicly. Some supporters also believe that the women's rights movement would bring in many people who have not been active in abolitionist work, and that this could ultimately strengthen the movement against slavery. And besides, they argue, we're trying to build a society based on equality and free from all oppression. Others argue that this is nonsense, that this threatens to divide antislavery forces. They argue that without question, the greatest evil of our time is the enslavement of Black human beings by white human beings, and that as bad off as some white women have it, this discrimination cannot be compared with slavery. Opponents argue that associating the American Anti-Slavery Society with women's rights will confuse and divide our supporters — and will weaken the antislavery movement.

American Anti-Slavery Society Choices, 1850

4. SITUATION: In 1850, the U.S. Congress passed the Fugitive Slave Act and President Millard Fillmore signed it into law. The law made it much easier for slave owners to recapture slaves who had escaped into free Northern states. In fact, it made it easier for slave owners to capture free Blacks and to claim that they are escaped slaves. The law denies a jury trial to anyone accused of escaping. The law requires the national government to prosecute any Northern whites who help slaves escape to freedom, or who harbor them. This is going to lead to a bunch of bounty hunters running around the North, looking for people who have escaped from slavery. And it will make all free Blacks in the North more insecure. In short, this is a terrible new law that puts the U.S. government even more clearly on the side of the slave owners. There is now no doubt: The slave owners are determined to keep slavery forever, and to strengthen it.

In response, many people active in the American Anti-Slavery Society believe that we must also step up our efforts. Some of our members want to organize armed groups to protect escaped slaves and to prevent slave catchers and government officials from re-enslaving people. One strategy would be to organize — and to arm — large groups of people to resist the bounty hunters, and to attack the courts and jails where fugitives from slavery are being held.

QUESTION: Should we support armed attempts to stop the enforcement of the Fugitive Slave Act? If not, how should we respond to this new law?

ARGUMENTS: Those in favor of using force to stop this new law from being enacted insist that we have no choice; we can't allow the slave owners to come into our communities and harm free people. Nonviolence won't work, they argue, because the law and the government is on the side of the enslavers, and their side is more than willing to use violence. It's suicidal to urge nonviolence when the people against us are armed to the teeth. This law is a potential disaster for the antislavery cause, and we need to become even more militant. These people also argue that even if we fail to stop escaped slaves from being captured, our resistance will inspire others, and our resistance may also discourage the enforcement of the law. Those who oppose this strategy argue that whatever we do, we must not use violence. We can continue our educational work — writing, speaking out, and building opposition to slavery. True, slavery has not ended, but there are more people than ever before who agree that slavery is evil. We risk turning these people against our cause if we use violence. We need to do what we do best: educate against slavery. These people argue that if we were to use violence, this would actually play into the hands of the government and slave owners. If the game is violence, the government is sure to win.

American Anti-Slavery Society Choices, 1858

5. SITUATION: Last year, in 1857, the Supreme Court ruled in the *Dred Scott* case that the Western territories of the United States may not prohibit slavery. Chief Justice Roger Taney wrote for the majority of the court that no Black person in the United States had "any rights that the white man is bound to respect." To many people in the abolition movement, this means that slavery cannot be ended with laws or through nonviolence. There are more enslaved people in the United States than ever before — more than 4 million of them. And slavery is the country's biggest business — yes, business — with slaves valued at more than $4 billion. Slaves in the United States are worth more than all the banks, railroads, and factories put together. To think that slavery can be argued away seems more and more ridiculous.

There is one man in particular who argues for action, not talk. His name is John Brown. He led the fight to have Kansas admitted to the United States as a free state rather than a slave state — and he killed pro-slavery people in the process. Brown is now raising money — as much as $25,000 — to "continue my efforts in the cause of freedom." You know that Brown intends to physically confront the forces of slavery, although you're not sure exactly how. Privately, Brown has been asking AASS members to donate guns if they have them. You know that Brown has approached antislavery blacksmiths, asking them to make pikes — ferocious-looking double-edged blades attached to long poles. He also is raising money to hire a military instructor.

QUESTION: Should you and other members of the American Anti-Slavery Society support John Brown with either money or guns? If not, what's your alternative?

ARGUMENTS: People who support Brown argue that despite all the nonviolent work for almost 30 years, slavery is more entrenched than ever. They argue that the traditional tactics of the AASS have failed — that pamphlets, newspapers, speaking, and organizing meetings may have increased the number of Northerners opposed to slavery, but so what? You can win public opinion, but not end slavery. These people argue that slavery must be ended with force, and that Brown has the credentials from his time in Kansas to do the job. Well-targeted raids into the South could encourage slaves to abandon the plantations and run away, or even spark slave rebellions. These people argue that we can't turn our backs on one of the bravest and most determined antislavery activists in the United States. Those opposed to Brown argue that it is foolish to think that a few armed opponents of slavery — even a small army — could go up against the U.S. Army and hope to succeed. What would this accomplish? It would be crushed by the military, and if the government discovered any links between Brown and the AASS, then it could lead to your organization being attacked by the government or even outlawed. No, they argue, we may not be sure what will end slavery, but we know that this won't end slavery. Brown may be committed and brave, but that doesn't make him right.

Who Fought to End Slavery? Meet the Abolitionists

By Adam Sanchez, Brady Bennon, Deb Delman, and Jessica Lovaas

FOR ALL ITS WEAKNESSES and divisions, the abolition movement was perhaps the most significant social movement in U.S. history: an anti-racist movement, a labor movement, a feminist movement, a free speech movement, an antiwar movement. The secession of Southern states in response to Abraham Lincoln's election, which triggered the Civil War, is inexplicable without the fear — and sometimes paranoia — the abolition movement kindled in the Southern imagination. And yet our textbooks cover this essential social movement in a few cursory pages, at best. In curricula and mainstream media, social progress is assigned to Great Men. Young people fail to learn the lesson they need so desperately in order to recognize their own potential power today: Throughout history, social movements have made the world a better place — more democratic, more equal, more just.

The purpose of the abolitionist mixer is to familiarize students with the stories of famous and lesser-known abolitionists and introduce them to a number of the individuals and themes they encounter both in the role play "'If There Is No Struggle...': Teaching a People's History of the Abolition Movement" and the reading "A People's History of the Abolition Movement."

Materials Needed

- Copies of "Abolitionist Mixer: Questions" (Handout 4-A) for every student.

- "Mixer Roles" (Handout 4–B), cut up. One for every student in the class.*

- Blank nametags. Enough for every student in the class.

- Copies of "A People's History of the Abolition Movement" (Handout 4–C) for every student.

William Cooper Nell, William Lloyd Garrison, and Harriet Forten Purvis are a few of the abolitionists featured in the role play.

Time Required

One class period for the mixer. Additional time to discuss "A People's History of the Abolition Movement."

Suggested Procedure

1. Explain to students that they are going to do an activity about the abolitionist movement — one of the largest social movements in the history of the United States. Distribute one mixer role and a blank nametag to each student in the class. There are 28 roles, so in some classes some students will be assigned the same historical characters. In smaller classes, you do not have to use all the roles in order to have a successful mixer. The roles are ordered so including at least the first eight will allow any small class to have a diverse group of abolitionists.

2. Have students fill out their nametags using the name of the individual they are assigned. Tell students that in this activity you would like each of them to attempt to become these people from history. Ask students to read their roles several times and to memorize as much of the information as possible. Encourage them to underline key points. Sometimes it helps if students turn over their roles and list three or four facts about their characters that they think are most important.

3. Distribute a copy of the "Abolitionist Mixer: Questions" (Handout 4–A) to every student. Explain their assignment: Students should circulate through the classroom, meeting other abolitionists. They should use the questions on the sheet as a guide to talk with others about their lives and to complete the questions as fully as possible. They must use a different individual to answer each of the eight questions. Ask students to read these and to check those questions that they might be able to help answer in the mixer.

4. It's helpful to lay out a few rules for the mixer: 1) Students assigned the same person may not meet themselves. 2) No to beehives, yes to speed dating — in other words we want students to engage with each other one on one

and spend some time getting to know the person they are with before moving on to the next. We don't want them to clump together, which can be intimidating for some students to enter. 3) Tell students that it's not a race — the aim is for students to spend time hearing each other's stories, not just hurriedly scribbling down answers to the different questions. Students may also not show their roles to anyone; this is a conversation-based activity. Sometimes students will try to adopt accents, in an attempt to sound like the individual they are portraying. Encourage them not to do this, as it can end up promoting stereotypes.

5. Ask students to stand up and begin to circulate throughout the class to meet one another and to fill out responses. Sometimes to get them out of their seat it's helpful to require that the first person they talk to is sitting across the room from them.

6. Before discussing the mixer as a class, it's helpful to ask students to write answers to a few reflection questions to help them collect their thoughts and calm things down a bit. Here are some possible questions:

   • Out of all the people you met, whose story did you find most interesting. Why?

   • Why do you think that you have not heard of more of these individuals?

   • How much credit should these individuals get for ending slavery?

7. Afterward, ask students to share some of their findings with the whole class. This needn't be exhaustive, as students will learn a lot more about these issues when they read about the abolitionists later on. Beyond the reflection questions students wrote on, here are a few questions to extend the discussion:

   • Beyond your own character, whose story stuck out to you the most? Why?

   • What were some of the different ways abolitionists attempted to end slavery?

   • What were some of the different points of view you encountered for how to end slavery?

8. If students have gone through Lesson 3 ("If There Is No Struggle. . .") you might ask them to recall some of the major divisions in the abolitionist movement. Write these on the board. Afterward, ask them:

- What abolitionists in the mixer fell on different sides of these debates? (Write their names on the board.)

- Do you notice any trends?

- Are there certain debates that Black abolitionists fell mostly to one side of?

- What about male or female abolitionists? Why do they think that this would be the case?

A People's History of the Abolition Movement

9. As a follow-up, assign "A People's History of the Abolition Movement" (Handout 4–C) by William Loren Katz and James Brewer Stewart. The reading is long, which can be difficult for some students, but it is a crucial primer on the movement. Depending on your student population, you may want to modify the suggestions below and jigsaw the six sections of the reading.

10. Ask students to complete a "talk-back" journal with the reading. They should locate at least five passages from the reading that they found interesting, important, surprising, moving, confusing, or outrageous. They should write out each quote and their detailed reaction to it. If you are planning to finish this unit of study by asking students to write an essay on "who freed the slaves?" you might ask them to look for passages that they could use as evidence for their essay. If not, you might ask students to find material that they can connect with information they learned in the mixer, events that relate somehow to their own lives or events going on today. Also encourage students to raise at least two questions that they would like to discuss with the rest of the class.

11. In addition to students' own questions, here are some questions for further discussion or writing:

- What effect did David Walker's *Appeal* have on enslaved people, slave owners, and on white abolitionists?

- What were some of the early campaigns and strategies the abolitionists used to fight slavery? How effective were these campaigns?

- How did people — particularly people in positions of power — respond to the early abolitionist campaigns?

- How did the violence of the late 1830s challenge the abolitionists' early ideas? What were the different ideas and strategies that the abolitionist movement adopted after the 1830s?

- What were the different ways that Black abolitionists pushed the movement further in the 1840s?

- What were the Kansas-Nebraska Act and the *Dred Scott* decision? Why were they important turning points for the movement?

- Who was John Brown? What did he do? Do you agree with his actions?

In addition, if students have completed Lesson 3 ("If There Is No Struggle. . .") this reading will tell them how the debates they simulated in the classroom played out in real life. You might ask them to compare the decisions that they made as a class to the decisions of actual abolitionists. Students should note that some of these decisions split the movement and write down the names and reasons of abolitionists who fell on either side. It's particularly useful to have students think about and discuss times when their class came to a different conclusion from the real abolitionists and why they think that was.

---

* Some of the roles have been adapted from the "Unsung Heroes" teaching activity by Bill Bigelow (https://www.zinnedproject.org/materials/teaching-about-unsung-heroes/)

Abolitionist Mixer: Questions

1. Find someone who has an opinion about whether the abolitionist movement should support women's rights. Who are they? Why do they think this?

2. Find someone who supports the use of violence in self-defense or to end slavery. Who are they? Why do they think violence is necessary or what actions did they take?

3. Find someone who does not support the use of violence to end slavery. Who are they? What nonviolent actions did they take?

4. Find someone who took part in the Underground Railroad. Who are they? What actions did they take to end slavery?

5. Find someone who escaped slavery. What is their story?

6. Find someone who was threatened, imprisoned, injured, or murdered for their attempts to end slavery or fight racism. What is their story?

7. Find someone who wrote an influential book, essay, or published a newspaper. What was the name of the publication? Why was it influential?

8. Find someone who played a role in the Civil War. Who are they? What was their experience?

Mixer Roles

Angelina Grimké

I was the daughter of a South Carolina plantation owner who enslaved people. I saw firsthand the horrors of slavery. As I grew older and more involved in the Presbyterian Church, I began questioning how such a system could exist under God's great banner of heaven. My sister, Sarah, introduced me to the ideas of Quakerism, and I began talking to others in the Presbyterian Church about nonviolence, peace, and abolition. They responded by expelling me from the church. So I left South Carolina. I left my only home and moved to Pennsylvania, where I converted to Quakerism, a religion that believes in peace and nonviolence. As an abolitionist, I questioned why many Northerners continued to buy products made with raw materials from the South — all with the labor of people who were enslaved. I toured throughout the North giving speeches against slavery and eventually for women's rights. Ministers in Massachusetts tried to bar women from speaking from their pulpits and I urged abolitionists to fight against this ban. I knew that if we surrendered the right to speak in public, women would be shamed into silence and would not be able to fight for any cause.

John Brown

People have called me crazy because I, a white man, gave up my life in the cause to free Black slaves. Unlike most Northern abolitionists, who advocated a peaceful resistance to slavery, I believed that the only way to defeat this oppressive system was through violent insurrection. I was fed up with the talk of antislavery when what was really needed was action. I fought in what was known as "Bloody Kansas," to make sure that Kansas did not enter the United States as a state that allowed slavery. And it's true: I killed many people there. But it was a just cause, and I took no pleasure in killing. I'm most famous for leading 22 men, Black and white, to attack the U.S. arsenal at Harpers Ferry, Virginia. Utilizing the vast knowledge of abolitionist Harriet Tubman, I developed a plan to capture 100,000 muskets and rifles and distribute them to local people held in slavery. In one sense, my mission failed, because we were captured, I was imprisoned, and finally executed. But I am convinced that my actions hastened the day of freedom for Black people suffering in slavery.

David Ruggles

When I was 17, I moved to New York City from Connecticut. Six years later, in 1834, I opened my own bookshop. I was the first Black bookseller and operated the first Black lending library in the nation. My magazine, the *Mirror of Liberty*, was the first periodical published by an African American. I used my bookstore and my magazine to promote abolitionism. But I wasn't just a bookseller — I also took action. From 1835 to 1838, I was active in the Underground Railroad. I helped form the New York Committee of Vigilance that helped escaped slaves who had fled the South. We were involved in more than 300 cases in 1836 alone and later took on the case of Frederick Douglass. I also sparked one of the first interracial "sit-ins" in history when in 1841 I refused to sit in the "colored-only" sections of steamboats and railway cars operating in Massachusetts. Because New York's economy depended directly or indirectly on slavery, I was often the target of mob violence. My store was burned down three times; I was beaten in jail twice and once nearly kidnapped to be sold into slavery. Yet I remained a committed fighter for racial justice.

William Lloyd Garrison

I joined the antislavery movement at the age of 25. You may have heard about me because I was the editor of the most widely read abolitionist newspaper, the *Liberator*. In 1833, I helped found the American Anti-Slavery Society, a coalition of abolitionists from 10 states that demanded "immediate emancipation" of enslaved people in the United States. Because slavery was so violent, I felt that we should remain nonviolent and advocated passive resistance to slavery. I also argued that we should not align ourselves with any political party and that we should champion women's rights. An injustice to one person is an injustice to all people. On July 4, 1844, I publicly burned a copy of the U.S. Constitution. Referring to its compromises on slavery, I declared it "a Covenant with Death, an Agreement with Hell." As our movement grew in size, the reaction from supporters of slavery in both the Southern and Northern states was increasingly violent. I woke one morning to find a noose on my front lawn. Later, I was almost killed when a racist mob attacked me. Some Southern states even offered a reward for my capture "dead or alive." But I refused to give up.

Harriet Forten Purvis

I've been praised for being exceptionally lady-like with manners like a "Southern belle," but don't let that description fool you. I have enough spirit to tackle a dozen men. I was raised in a wealthy free Black family in Philadelphia. My dad helped found a private school that I attended with my siblings. I learned foreign languages, music, literature, and many other subjects. My parents were active abolitionists and I continued in their footsteps. My home was a hot spot on the Underground Railroad, and my husband and I helped more than 9,000 enslaved Blacks make their way to freedom. I regularly threw dinner parties and fundraisers at our home to raise money for abolitionist causes. I also helped run a sewing school to help poorer Black women earn income. In addition, with my mom and my sister, I helped found the first biracial women's abolition group, the Philadelphia Female Anti-Slavery Society, with white abolitionists such as Lucretia Mott. A white mob burned down our meeting place, but we persevered. Together we helped launch a citywide boycott of goods such as cotton and food products that had been farmed using enslaved labor. I worked not just for abolition, but also for desegregation in Philadelphia, and for women's voting rights, but faced regular violence and threats because of it.

Harriet Tubman

As a child living in slavery in Maryland, I was beaten and whipped by many enslavers. I was religious at an early age and I began experiencing visions that guided me throughout my life, which I considered signs from God. I had determined that it was not God's will for me to live out my life in slavery, and so I decided that I would escape to freedom, no matter what it took. In 1849, I finally escaped to Philadelphia. After that, I returned to free my family, and other enslaved people seeking freedom. I made 19 trips on the Underground Railroad and rescued more than 70 enslaved people, earning me the nickname Moses. There are other things about me that you may not have heard. I worked with the radical abolitionist John Brown, helping him recruit men to fight during his raid on Harpers Ferry. I was not troubled by his use of violence to end the violent institution of slavery. In fact, during the Civil War I served as an armed scout and a spy and I was the first woman to lead an armed expedition, which burned down plantations and liberated more than 700 people from slavery.

Harry Jarvis

When the Civil War started, I managed to sneak away from my so-called master. He was well known as the meanest man on the entire Eastern Shore. I hid in forests and walked many miles until I found "Fortress Monroe," which the Union soldiers had taken over. I went straight up to General Butler and asked him to let me enlist, but he said it wasn't a Black man's war. I told him it would be a Black man's war before they got through. Two years later, I successfully enlisted in the 54th Regiment Massachusetts Volunteer Infantry, one of the Union Army's first Black regiments. Yes, I know that Lincoln said it wasn't a war to free people who were enslaved. But that's why we fought. And in the end the war did free enslaved people, despite what Lincoln said. When the 54th fought courageously at Fort Wagner, we were praised for our bravery during battle. Our actions encouraged further enlistment and mobilization of Black troops. Although half of our regiment died, we died heroes. No one drafted us. We didn't have to go like lots of white people. We chose to risk our lives for the freedom of others.

Lucretia Mott

As a teacher in New York, I was shocked to find out that male teachers were paid three times more than women. I met my husband, who was also a teacher, and we moved to Philadelphia. In 1811, I joined the Quaker ministry. The Quakers fought slavery nonviolently. We boycotted products made with the labor of enslaved people. I brought together Black and white women to form the Philadelphia Female Anti-Slavery Society and increasingly played a prominent role in the national organization, the American Anti-Slavery Society. I also opened my home to runaways escaping on the Underground Railroad. In 1840, I was sent as a delegate to the World Anti-Slavery Convention in London and was appalled when I, and other female delegates, were not allowed to participate because we were women. But there I met Elizabeth Cady Stanton and together we made plans to hold the first gathering for women's rights in Seneca Falls, New York, in 1848. When slavery was abolished, African American men were granted the rights of citizenship, but women were not. This led some white women, like Stanton, to oppose the granting of these rights to Black men. I grew increasingly uncomfortable with the racist rhetoric Stanton used to justify her positions and resigned from the National Woman Suffrage Association in 1868.

Elizabeth Cady Stanton

Although I am mostly known for supporting women's suffrage, early in my career I fought against slavery. I helped organize the gathering of more than 400,000 signatures asking for legislation to end slavery — half of the signatures were by women. But I became frustrated by the way even abolitionists treated women. In 1840, at the World Anti-Slavery Convention in London, male delegates voted that women should not be allowed to participate, even though we had come as the elected delegates of abolitionist societies in the United States. I came to see that white women in America were themselves treated like we were enslaved. And I began to work for women's rights as well. With Lucretia Mott, I organized the Seneca Falls Conference, the first gathering of women in the United States to demand rights for women. We produced the Declaration of Sentiments expressing our grievances as women and urging needed social changes: guaranteeing women's right to vote, the right to own property, and the right to get a divorce. After the Civil War, I hoped that the government would extend the rights of citizenship to both African Americans and white women, but when it became clear that in the 14th and 15th amendments only Black men would be granted those rights, I opposed their passage.

Sojourner Truth

My name is one that I chose for myself, because I declared that I would travel in truth for the rest of my days on this Earth. In 1806, when I was 9 years old, I was sold at an auction with a flock of sheep for $100. The man who bought me was awful. He raped and beat me daily. In 1826, at age 29, I finally escaped to freedom but had to leave my children behind. I later went to court to recover my son and became one of the first Black women ever to go to court against a white man and win. I became a Methodist and traveled around preaching about abolition, women's rights, religious tolerance, and nonviolence. 1850 was a big year for me. My book, *The Narrative of Sojourner Truth: A Northern Slave*, was published; I purchased a home; and I spoke at the first National Women's Rights Convention. That speech became known as "Ain't I a Woman?" and launched me even further into my lifelong devotion to end both slavery and the mistreatment of women. Over the next decade, I spoke before hundreds of audiences about these issues. During the Civil War, I helped recruit Black troops for the Union Army.

David Walker

I was born in North Carolina to a free mother and an enslaved father. There is no way to describe the horrors that I witnessed as a young boy, but it is those memories that made me decide to devote my life to ending slavery. I quickly became known as an outspoken Black activist who demanded the immediate and unconditional end of slavery. Being an Evangelical Christian gave me the power to call out the hypocrisy of white Christians who justified "owning" other human beings. I became a leader in the Black community of Boston, partly because I wrote what became one of the most radical and influential anti-slavery documents, *An Appeal to the Coloured Citizens of the World*. The goal of the *Appeal* was to instill pride in Black readers and give hope that change would come someday. My *Appeal* also changed the view of many white abolitionists who thought slavery should end gradually. However, I began receiving death threats shortly after the *Appeal* was published. I died in Boston the next year and many people believe that I was poisoned.

Frederick Douglass

I was born into a life of slavery. Separated from my mother, I was raised by my grandparents. The wife of my enslaver broke the rules and taught me how to read and write. At the age of 16, I was sent to work for Edward Covey, a poor farmer known as a "slave breaker." He whipped me regularly. Eventually, I fought back and Covey never whipped me again. In 1838, I escaped to freedom by pretending to be a sailor. I settled in Massachusetts, where I joined a Black church and began attending abolitionist meetings. At those meetings, other activists encouraged me to tell my story. In 1845, my autobiography, *Narrative of the Life of Frederick Douglass, an American Slave*, was published and became an international best seller. I also published my own newspaper, the *North Star*. I rejected the pacifism of many white abolitionists and called on Blacks to defend themselves with guns if necessary against slave catchers. Throughout my life, I fought for equal treatment of all people, including women. I was the only African American at the first women's rights convention in Seneca Falls. I would unite with anybody for justice. Without struggle, there can be no progress.

William Wells Brown

I was born in bondage in Lexington, Kentucky. While still a boy, I was hired out to the captain of a St. Louis steamboat in the booming Mississippi River trade. I tried many times to escape with my mother, but we were caught. She was shipped south to New Orleans and I never saw her again. I kept trying, though, and eventually escaped. I adopted the name of a Quaker, Wells Brown, who aided me when I was a runaway. I moved to Buffalo and joined the American Anti-Slavery Society in 1836. I gave lectures at my home, spoke at abolitionist gatherings, and traveled to Cuba and Haiti to investigate the possibility of emigrating there with other formerly enslaved people. In the 1840s I used my skills as a steamboat operator as a conductor for the Underground Railroad. I also participated in armed attempts to prevent slave catchers from collecting their "property" in the North. Some abolitionists opposed this, saying we must remain nonviolent. Although I was a longtime supporter of nonviolent tactics, I felt like the new Fugitive Slave Law gave us no choice; we couldn't allow the slave owners to come into our communities and harm free people.

Elijah Lovejoy

I opposed slavery on moral and religious grounds. I became the pastor of the Presbyterian Church in St. Louis in 1834. I started a religious newspaper, the *St. Louis Observer*. After being converted to abolitionism through conversations with a local Anti-Slavery Society organizer I started to use my newspaper to advocate against slavery. In 1836, I published a full account of the lynching of an African American in St. Louis and the subsequent trial that acquitted the mob leaders. This critical report enraged some of the locals and an angry mob destroyed my printing press. Unable to publish my newspaper in St. Louis, I moved to Alton, Illinois. I began editing the *Alton Observer* and continued to advocate the end of slavery. Three times my printing press was seized by pro-slavery mobs and thrown into the Mississippi River. Despite repeated threats on my life I continued the fight to spread the word of abolition. Eventually, a mob burned down my office. They brought guns and killed me as I tried to escape the burning building. I was shot dead trying to protect my printing press and the rights of all human beings.

Jermain Wesley Loguen

I was the son of a white slave owner and a woman he enslaved named Cherry, born into slavery in Tennessee. In 1834, I stole my master's horse and escaped to Canada. I moved with my family to Syracuse in 1841, where I taught school and became a licensed preacher of the African Methodist Episcopal Zion Church. I became active in the abolitionist movement and used my house as a major station for the Underground Railroad. I wrote letters to the press openly discussing my activities and asking for donations to assist fugitives. I aided more than 1,500 freedom seekers. The most dramatic case involved a runaway named Jerry, who was arrested under the Fugitive Slave Law. I joined a committee of abolitionists, Black and white, that rescued Jerry and assisted him in escaping to Canada. We used crowbars and a battering ram to break into the jail where Jerry was held. Deputy marshals shot out the window at us, but eventually they realized that the crowd was so large and was so determined that they relented and released Jerry. If the government was willing to use force to capture Black people, it was right for us to use force in response.

Wendell Phillips

As the son of a wealthy white lawyer, I led a relatively privileged life. I graduated from Harvard Law School in 1833. But in 1835, I witnessed abolitionist William Lloyd Garrison being attacked by a mob of several thousand. They stormed the Anti-Slavery office, dragged out Garrison, tied him up and came very close to hanging him. A few men eventually saved Garrison and I became good friends with him. He convinced me to devote my skills to the abolitionist cause. I soon became known as "abolition's Golden Trumpet" because of my skills as a speaker. But public speaking also put me in danger. When I spoke in Cincinnati, a mob threw eggs and charged at me from the audience, and a bottle of explosives was later found in the lobby. I always believed abolitionists should shape politics through public opinion, not violence, but I defended those in the movement like John Brown who chose a different path. During the Civil War, I criticized Lincoln for not committing himself to the abolition of slavery and in 1865 I replaced Garrison as president of the American Anti-Slavery Society. Although I supported women's rights, I believed we needed to fight one war at a time and urged abolitionists to focus on ending slavery first.

Harriet Beecher Stowe

I was born in Connecticut in 1811. My father, Lyman Beecher, was a preacher and a leader in the antislavery movement. My father taught me to hate slavery. In 1836, I married Calvin Stowe. Calvin was a professor who hated slavery as much as I did. We would provide shelter to people who had run away from slavery and who had escaped north to freedom along the Underground Railroad. At the age of 41, I wrote my most famous book, *Uncle Tom's Cabin*. The book followed the lives of people as they were sold into slavery, beaten to death, or separated from their families at slave auctions. My book sold 3,000 copies the first day it was published and there were more copies sold than any other book except the Bible. *Uncle Tom's Cabin* was read by so many people that it even scared slave owners. Later on in life, when I met President Lincoln, he said, "So you are the little woman who wrote the book that started this great war." I also campaigned for the expansion of women's rights, arguing, "the position of a married woman . . . is, in many respects, precisely similar to that of the Negro slave."

Solomon Northup

I was born free in upstate New York in 1808, but was captured by slave traders and taken to Louisiana. My book, *12 Years a Slave*, tells the story of my enslavement, but many people don't know about my abolitionist activity after I was freed. I wrote my book to expose the brutal conditions of enslavement. It became so popular — second only to Frederick Douglass' *Narrative* — that I was able to speak across the United States against the horrors of slavery. I also became active in the Underground Railroad, assisting people who had run away from slavery. Moved by the troubling content of my lectures and autobiography, abolitionists in upstate New York and elsewhere began a campaign asking Congress to compensate me for my years in slavery. Abolitionists argued, and I agreed, that my time away from my family and the loss of my liberty was worth many times my "value" as slave property. Later, in the 1850s, other abolitionists broadened the campaign to call for reparations — some form of payment for all people who had once been enslaved. I'm proud of my role in the first campaign for federal reparations.

Thaddeus Stevens

I grew up in poverty but rose to become a lawyer and in 1858 was elected as a representative to the U.S. Congress. I was one of the most powerful congressional representatives in the country, and I never took that power for granted. I use it on behalf of those whose rights have been trampled, those whose hands built this country but remained in shackles. I always fought for the rights of the oppressed, and slavery is the most oppressive part of this society. That's why before becoming a congressman, I built a secret hidden room at my law office where people who escaped slavery could sleep as part of the Underground Railroad. I knew that slave states would never be able to coexist with free states and that to end slavery, it would take a war or revolution across the South. During the Civil War I was the first in Congress to call for arming people who had escaped slavery, arguing they should be welcomed into the Union Army. And after the war, I called for destroying the power of the slave-owning class, stripping them of their estates, and maintaining troops in the South to guarantee real freedom for formerly enslaved people.

Charles Sumner

I was known for my powerful public speaking. In my first major speech as a senator, I spoke for three hours denouncing the Fugitive Slave Law as fundamentally unconstitutional and immoral. In 1854, Congress passed the Kansas-Nebraska Act, which allowed the Kansas and Nebraska territories to vote to allow slavery. I was furious at this power grab by Southern politicians, so I gave a speech and insulted two of the act's sponsors. The cousin of one of the sponsors came into the Senate and beat me over the head with a metal cane. It took me three years to recover. I became a hero to many Northern abolitionists, who saw the violence as a symbol of how out of control Southerners had become. Later, when enslaved people in Haiti kicked out the French, I led the push to have the United States recognize the new country. During the Civil War, I was a leader of the Radical Republican faction that criticized Lincoln for not making it a war to end slavery. Specializing in foreign affairs, I also worked to ensure the British and the French did not side with the Confederacy.

Robert Smalls

I always loved the water, and Henry McKee, my enslaver, had me work as a dockworker. I learned how to make sails and rig up the ships. During the Civil War I was forced to work on a Confederate military ship. On May 12, 1862, while the white crew went ashore I dressed in a captain's uniform and, with the help of three other enslaved people, steered the ship toward where I knew the Union Navy was. On the way, we stopped nearby to pick up our families. When we finally made it to the Union blockade ship, *USS Onward*, we declared ourselves free and gave the Union soldiers the ship and all that was on board, including six large expensive artillery guns, explosives, and a code book that revealed the Confederacy's secret signals and placement of mines and torpedoes in Charleston Harbor. I was given a reward of $1,500 and given an officer's commission in the Union Army. After the war, when enslaved people were emancipated, I served five terms in the U.S. Congress, and was, for a time, one of the most powerful political leaders in South Carolina.

William Walker

I was one of the 186,017 Black soldiers who fought in the Civil War after President Lincoln finally opened the Union Army to Blacks in 1863. But Black soldiers were not treated equally. We were used for the heaviest and dirtiest work, digging trenches, hauling logs, loading ammunition, and digging wells for white regiments. On top of that, we were paid less. White privates received $13 a month while Black privates received only $10. After being named sergeant of the 3rd South Carolina Volunteer Infantry Regiment, I decided I had had enough of this inequality. I was fighting for freedom and equality and I thought that's what the Union was fighting for, too. I marched my company to my captain's tent and we stacked our guns out in front. We told him that the pay disparity was a breach of our Army contract, and we would lay down our arms until it was rectified. Instead of giving us equal pay, I was court-martialed, tried, convicted, and executed by a firing squad for what they considered "mutiny."

Elizabeth Gloucester

I am a Black woman, born free in Virginia around 1817. When I married Presbyterian minister James Gloucester, we moved to Brooklyn, New York, where I was heavily involved in fundraising for Siloam Presbyterian Church. Our church hosted many abolitionist speakers, such as Frederick Douglass and Henry Highland Garnet. John Brown spoke at our church and even stayed at our home. While many of New York's white abolitionists refused to support Brown's efforts to bring armed men into the South to free enslaved people, we gave Brown funds and encouraged him to "do battle with that ugly foe, slavery." Our home and church were also key stops on the Underground Railroad. During the Civil War, I led fundraising efforts for freedmen and Union soldiers. I also helped mobilize other philanthropists to fund the Colored Orphan Asylum in Manhattan and create a new Colored Orphan's Asylum in the free Black community of Weeksville, in Brooklyn. I did all this while raising six children. I was an astute businesswoman. At my death I was estimated to be worth at least $200,000; the *Brooklyn Daily Eagle* stated I was one of the richest women in the world.

Lewis Hayden

I was born in slavery in 1811 in Lexington, Kentucky. In the mid-1830s my first wife and son were sold to U.S. Senator Henry Clay, who then sold them into the Deep South and I never saw them again. I married a second time in 1842 to Harriet Bell. We escaped together on the Underground Railroad in 1844, fleeing to Canada before making our way to Boston. In Massachusetts, our family ran a clothing store where we also held abolitionist meetings and provided refuge for people escaping from slavery as part of the Underground Railroad. I served on the executive board of the Boston Vigilance Committee and worked closely with William Lloyd Garrison. I stored two kegs of gunpowder in our home in case slave catchers ever attempted to capture the people we sheltered. I also raised funds for John Brown's raid on Harpers Ferry where he attempted to steal guns and distribute them to nearby slaves. During the Civil War I helped recruit Black soldiers and later served a term in the Massachusetts House of Representatives. As a congressman, I worked to erect a monument to honor Crispus Attucks, a Black man who was the first casualty of the American Revolutionary War.

William Cooper Nell

I was the son of a Massachusetts tailor and Black activist. I thought I was lucky to be born in the North. But as a high school student in Boston, I experienced discrimination when the mayor refused to invite me — the only Black honors student — to a banquet recognizing outstanding seniors. Shortly after, I became politically active and was mentored by abolitionist William Lloyd Garrison. In the 1840s, while working as the office manager for Garrison's newspaper, I worked to desegregate the Boston railroad and Boston performance halls. But my biggest campaign was a successful decades-long effort to end segregation in Massachusetts public schools. I created the Boston Vigilance Committee to defend fugitive slaves from slave catchers and I was a part of the Underground Railroad, helping to secure clothing, food, money, and transportation for fugitive slaves. As his publisher, I helped Frederick Douglass start his own newspaper, the *North Star*, from 1847 to 1851, and after the Civil War I wrote two of the earliest histories of African Americans, *Services of Colored Americans in the Wars of 1776 and 1812* and *The Colored Patriots of the American Revolution*.

Harriet Jacobs

From an early age, my life was tough. Born into slavery in North Carolina, my early years were filled with fear and pain, which all enslaved people endure, but enslaved women often bear the additional brutality of sexual assault. In 1835, I escaped and hid in the home of another slave owner, took refuge in a swamp, and then spent seven years in my grandmother's crawl space above her barn. In that tiny space, I could not even sit up straight. Once I finally escaped and made it to the North, I spoke for the antislavery movement, criticizing the Christian Church of the South because of its support of such a horrific institution and its focus on money, as opposed to equality for all people. While working as an abolitionist, I wrote a book with the help of white abolitionist Lydia Maria Child called *Incidents in the Life of a Slave Girl*. This book was published in 1852 and became widely known because it was the first account of the particular horrors of the sexual abuse and terror that young enslaved girls go through.

Sarah Parker Redmond

I was born into a family of Black abolitionists. Our home served as a stop on the Underground Railroad for those fleeing slavery. I gave my first abolitionist speech at the age of 16. This was a radical action at the time, not just because I was young and Black, but also because I was a woman; women were expected to stay out of politics and remain in the home. I was a member of the Salem Female Anti-Slavery Society in Massachusetts. In addition to advocating against slavery and for women's rights, I also fought racial discrimination in the North. When I was 27 I refused to accept segregated seating at an event at Boston's Howard Athenaeum. I was forcibly removed, and then pushed down a flight of stairs by a police officer. I took the city of Boston to court, and several prominent white feminists, such as Lucy Stone, attended my trial. I was awarded a settlement of $500, which was a big win and drew national attention. I traveled across the country as an abolitionist lecturer. Eventually, I went to England and stayed in Europe during the Civil War. I gave lectures urging Europeans to pressure their governments to support the North in the war.

Maria Stewart

I was one of the first prominent Black female abolitionists, born free in 1803. I spent my early career working closely with Black abolitionist David Walker and white abolitionist William Lloyd Garrison in Boston. My writings were published in his newspaper *The Liberator*, and I regularly gave political lectures in Boston. "Ye daughters of Africa, Awake! Arise!" I told my fellow women. "Distinguish yourself and show the world that ye are endowed with noble and exalted faculties." I was the first woman to speak publicly about political issues, and to mixed audiences of men and women, which was considered "promiscuous." Sometimes men harassed me at these speeches, but I refused to be silent just because I was a woman. "What if I am a woman?" I asked my detractors. Women are "martyrs, apostles, warriors, [and] scholars." I received criticism not just for being a woman, but also for being openly critical of men for vices such as drinking and dancing. I believed there was very little time for such things when there was so much work to be done to achieve freedom for Black people, women, and Native Americans. During the Civil War I moved to Washington, D.C., where I worked at the Freedmen's Hospital treating many formerly enslaved people who fled to freedom during the war.

A People's History of the Abolition Movement

By James Brewer Stewart and William Loren Katz

DAVID WALKER WAS A SLIM, 6-foot Black man who made his living running a secondhand clothing store in Boston. His life's goal was to unite African Americans and overthrow slavery. In a few short years he changed the debate over slavery.

In the 1830s, Walker brilliantly and sharply voiced the anguish and aspirations that more than 2 million enslaved people shared with their 320,000 free brothers and sisters. Walker knew from his own family that slave and free were as close as husband and wife. He was born in 1785 in Wilmington, North Carolina, to a free Black woman married to an enslaved man. His father died before David was born. Slaveholder rules assigned the mother's status to the child, so Walker was born free.

In his 20s, Walker said farewell to his mother and began to travel. Soon he left the South: "If I remain in this bloody land, I will not live long," he said. "I cannot remain where I must hear the chains." By the time he arrived in Boston in 1827, he had a purpose: "As true as God reigns, I will be avenged for the sorrows which my people have suffered." In 1829, he published his *Appeal to the Coloured Citizens of the World*.

Whites enslaved Blacks out of greed, Walker argued, but God had ordained freedom. He condemned the U.S. government, Northern discrimination, and advised his people to prepare "to govern ourselves." Walker's booklet rang with passionate threats and warnings: "I speak Americans for your own good. We must and shall be free . . . in spite of you." To his people he wrote: "The entire emancipation of your enslaved brethren all over the world" depended on unity among African peoples.

He wished to avoid bloodshed, but at times he coldly calculated a path forward: "Never make an attempt to gain our freedom, or natural right, from under our cruel oppressors and murdered, until you see your way clear — when that hour arrives and you move, be not afraid." "If you commence, make sure work — do not trifle, for they will not trifle with you . . . kill or be killed." He agreed with Jefferson that people had the right of revolution.

Walker's *Appeal* had an electrifying effect in the South, where distribution was probably speeded by sailors Walker had met through his clothing business. In New Orleans, Richmond, and Savannah, African Americans were arrested for owning copies. Legislatures in Georgia, North Carolina, Mississippi, Virginia, and Louisiana imposed a death penalty on anyone circulating materials encouraging slave rebellion. The governor of North Carolina condemned it as "totally subversive . . . an open appeal to natural love of liberty." The Virginia Legislature met in secret session to deal with the *Appeal*. Rewards of $1,000 or more for Walker's capture or death were offered in Georgia. The mayor of Savannah asked the mayor of Boston to arrest Walker.

On the morning of June 28, 1830, Walker was found dead near his home. His friends believed he had been poisoned. That same year, as if in response to Walker's writings, Southampton County, Virginia, erupted in the largest slave revolt in antebellum [pre-Civil War] America. Nat Turner led an uprising that took the lives of 55 whites. Within days of the rebellion, the government and local militias responded by killing an estimated 200 Blacks, most of whom were not involved in the rebellion.

The white foes of slavery learned from Walker's *Appeal* and Turner's rebellion. William Lloyd

Garrison and other white leaders had previously urged caution and moderation. They believed that emancipation must be slow, owners should be compensated financially for their loss, and those freed shipped to Africa. Many white antislavery activists were members of the American Colonization Society founded in 1816. The Colonization Society encouraged slave owners to voluntarily free their slaves and proposed to resettle U.S. free Blacks in Africa. Most Black leaders rejected colonization as a racist insult.

Abolitionists Get Organized

David Walker's bold language and Nat Turner's bold actions changed the argument. By Jan. 1, 1831, when William Lloyd Garrison began his antislavery newspaper *The Liberator*, he had rejected his own earlier, gradual approach and demanded immediate emancipation without any compensation. His words rang with the indignation of a David Walker: "I will not equivocate — I will not excuse — I will not retreat a single inch — AND I WILL BE HEARD."

In December 1833, Garrison helped launch the American Anti-Slavery Society, a national organization devoted to immediate emancipation. Members of the American Anti-Slavery Society pledged to begin organizing antislavery societies in every city, town, and village.

In May 1835, the society began its first major project, the "Great Postal Campaign." Its aim was to flood every town and village, North and South, with mailings of abolitionist literature. Ministers, elected officials, and newspaper editors in every state were placed on the mailing lists. Organizers assumed that this early campaign would overthrow slavery by building overwhelming moral pressure against the slave owners. One by one, slaveholders would repent, the abolitionists expected, because they would realize that hostile world opinion was "a feeling against which they cannot stand."

The following year, the American Anti-Slavery Society launched the "Great Petition Campaign," sending to the U.S. House of Representatives a tidal wave of citizen requests that Congress pass laws against slavery. Abolitionist women, such as Elizabeth Cady Stanton and Lucretia Mott, took the lead in circulating petitions, signing them, and sending out the forms. Over half the petitions bore women's signatures. By 1838, the campaigns had mailed more than a million pieces of antislavery literature and forwarded more than 415,000 petitions to Washington. The organization had also grown dramatically. They claimed 1,346 clubs and a quarter of a million members.

These efforts set off a huge reaction of mob activity across the country, brutal repression in the South, and controversy in Congress. In the slave states, mobs urged on by elected officials invaded post offices and burned abolitionist mailings, while state legislatures voted to give out cash bounties for the capture of leading abolitionists, including Garrison. White Southerners suspected of "abolitionist sympathies" faced harassment and sometimes the whip or the tar bucket.

The Liberator, *largely supported by African American subscribers, became the most popular abolitionist newspaper.*

The Liberator Files

Meanwhile, in Washington, D.C., Whigs and Democrats joined in 1836 to pass a "gag rule" that prohibited all discussion of abolitionists' petitions to the House of Representatives, an unprecedented restriction of citizens' freedom of political expression. The postmaster general used "states' rights" to justify Southern postmasters' refusal to deliver abolitionist mail. In elections across the nation both parties competed for white male votes by stressing anti-abolitionism and white supremacy. Meanwhile, mayhem erupted in cities and towns throughout the free states. Boston; Philadelphia; Pittsburgh; and Utica, Rochester, and Syracuse, New York, witnessed unruly gangs that disrupted abolitionists' meetings and threatened Black citizens with rocks, garbage, and fists. In New York City and Cincinnati, sheriffs looked unconcerned as buildings in Black neighborhoods and abolitionist offices were burned and looted.

The most frightening scenes were in Alton, a small river town in southern Illinois. In 1836, Elijah P. Lovejoy, a minister and editor of the *Observer*, fled with his family from St. Louis to Alton after a pro-slavery mob destroyed his presses. In St. Louis, Lovejoy had converted to abolitionism through conversations with a local organizer of the American Anti-Slavery Society. He began to use his newspaper to attack slavery as a national sin. After five months in Alton, Lovejoy's *Observer* was again rolling off the presses. Its circulation jumped from 1,000 to 1,700 copies.

Then, in August 1837, a white mob destroyed Lovejoy's press, and later, when another press arrived, they returned to throw it in the river. Meetings denounced the minister, but he remained defiant. "I dare not flee away from Alton," he said; "the contest has commenced here,

Every attempt to silence the abolitionists only drew attention to the movement, publicized its principles, and spread concern about civil liberties. Furthermore, riot and repression showed how much power the Southern planter class exercised in the North, deeply disturbing those who already had some reservations about slavery.

and here it must be finished. . . . If I fall, my grave shall be made in Alton."

In November when another mob assembled, Lovejoy — gun in hand and younger brother Owen at his side — made his stand. The mob set the *Observer*'s building on fire, destroyed the press, and killed Elijah Lovejoy. A grand jury failed to indict any members of the mob.

Lovejoy's death inspired Wendell Phillips, who would later be named "abolition's Golden Trumpet" for his incredible speaking ability, to join the movement. Phillips would always remember Lovejoy's death as the inspiration for his commitment to the cause: "The gun that aimed at the breast of Lovejoy brought me to my feet. I can never forget the agony of that moment."

By the end of the decade, the abolitionists' initial campaigns and, ironically, the repressive acts of their opponents had converted many sympathizers into antislavery activists. Every attempt to silence the abolitionists only drew attention to the movement, publicized its principles, and spread concern about civil liberties. Furthermore, riot and repression showed how much power the Southern planter class exercised in the North, deeply disturbing those who already had some reservations about slavery.

A Movement Divided

But the violent reaction of the late 1830s also challenged abolitionists' early idea that emancipation could be won through moral persuasion. It was now clear that slavery was protected by the federal government, the courts, the two political parties, the bigoted opinions of most white Americans, and even vigilante violence. In the wake of Lovejoy's murder, Garrison captured perfectly the shocked realization sweeping through the movement that abolitionists needed to rethink and revise their fundamental principles:

> *When we first unfurled the banner of the Liberator . . . we did not anticipate that, in order to protect Southern slavery, the free states would voluntarily trample under foot all order, law, and government, or brand the advocates of universal liberty as incendiaries and outlaws. . . . It did not occur to us that almost every religious sect, and every political party would side with the oppressor.*

Garrison concluded that every part of U.S. society was infected by a deep moral disease. He condemned politics as pro-slavery and encouraged abolitionists not to vote. In Garrison's opinion, Northern Whigs and Democrats had reacted much as mobs had, "striving to see who will show the most hatred toward us . . . in order to win Southern votes."

Opponents of Garrison felt strongly that the battle for abolition was being waged within a healthy but seriously flawed society. They pointed to the thousands of ordinary Northerners, who responded to abolitionist attacks on the "slave power" by signing petitions. They insisted that abolitionists had a moral duty to vote for candidates sympathetic to the cause and that abolitionists' main priority should be to win political power. The anti-Garrisonians began to plan a formal political organization, the Liberty Party, to offer abolitionist alternatives in the election of 1840. Over the next two decades, the Liberty Party built coalitions with other new political formations that were not against slavery, but were concerned by the expanding power of the slave states. These coalitions culminated in the formation of the Republican Party in 1854.

Another split occurred in the abolitionist movement over the role of women and women's rights. More than anyone else, Angelina Grimké, supported by William Lloyd Garrison, provoked this debate by refusing to remain in her "appointed female sphere." Born to a wealthy slaveholding family in Charleston, South Carolina, Angelina could have led a life of luxury and ease. But witnessing firsthand the abuses slaves endured deeply disturbed her. After unsuccessfully trying to convince her family to abandon their acceptance of slavery, Grimké moved to Philadelphia where her older sister Sarah lived. By 1835, the Grimké sisters had joined Philadelphia's budding abolitionist movement and two years later left on their first speaking tour. Sarah became well known as a writer, while Angelina quickly became acknowledged as a powerful and persuasive speaker. The Grimkés confronted the deeply ingrained idea that women should not speak in public and pushed the boundaries even further by speaking before "promiscuous assemblies" — mixed groups of men and women.

Angelina Grimké played a key role in pushing for abolitionists to take up the cause of women's rights.

The Liberator Files

When, in 1837, the General Association of Congregational Ministers of Massachusetts told ministers in the state to refuse to allow female speakers from their pulpit, it pushed the Grimkés to advocate for women's rights in addition to abolition. Some abolitionists agreed with the ministers and argued that the increasing role women were playing in the movement hurt the campaign to abolish slavery by alienating potential allies. Angelina responded, "We cannot push abolitionism forward with all our might until we take up the stumbling block out of the road. . . . If we surrender the right to speak in public this year, we must surrender the right to petition next year, and the right to write the year after, and so on. What then can woman do for the slave, when she herself is under the feet of man and shamed into silence?"

Garrison's supporters maintained control over the American Anti-Slavery Society and women's power grew within the organization. As a result, in 1839 opponents of women's rights split to form the American and Foreign Anti-Slavery Society, excluding women from membership. Women also were pushed to the sidelines in the Liberty Party since they could not vote.

African Americans Drive the Antislavery Cause Forward

The impact of these divisions in the abolitionist movement was lessened, however, because a new generation of African American men and women joined the movement. Drawing on lifetimes of discrimination through exclusion from juries, elections, decent schools, and gainful employment, Northern Blacks were painfully aware that complete freedom and formal enslavement represented extremes. For African Americans, far more than for whites, bondage in the South and discrimination in the North were two aspects of the single national problem of white supremacy. Black abolitionists quickly began involving white abolitionists in struggles to resist segregation.

It was Black David Ruggles, for example, who refused in 1841 to sit in the "colored-only" sections of steamboats and railway cars operating in Massachusetts. After being physically ejected, he filed a series of antidiscrimination lawsuits and invited Wendell Phillips and other leading white abolitionists to join him in campaigns of civil disobedience. On a warm August day that same year, Phillips thus found himself on the open air "Negro deck" of a steamer bound to New Bedford, Massachusetts, defying segregation by mingling with 40 Black and white abolitionists, William Lloyd Garrison and Frederick Douglass among them. Soon thereafter, individual acts of civil disobedience and concerted efforts by integrated groups against segregated transportation systems spread throughout New England and quickly expanded to address the issue of segregation in the public schools.

In the early 1840s Black abolitionists launched successful efforts to boycott segregated schools throughout the Northeast. The most significant struggle took place in Boston led by William Cooper Nell. Nell grew up in Boston and as a high school student experienced discrimination when the mayor refused to invite him — the only Black honors student — to a banquet recognizing outstanding seniors. He went on to study law, but was not admitted to the bar because he would not swear allegiance to the pro-slavery Constitution. While working as the office manager for Garrison's *Liberator*, Nell started a petition campaign to desegregate Boston's schools. When petitions failed, boycotts began, sparked by the fact that one of the white teachers in an all-Black school administered excessive punishments and was regularly absent from class. Horace Mann, secretary of the Massachusetts Board of Education, tried without success to work out a compromise, while school authorities continued to reject the petitions. When Mann tried to ease the situation by appointing a new Black principal in one of the segregated schools, Nell called forth the parents, who surrounded the school and attempted to prevent students from registering. Police drove them away from the schoolyard and the African American principal took office, but the boycott remained strong until April 1855, when the Massachusetts Legislature finally outlawed segregation in public schools across the state.

Escaped slaves who became public speakers made perhaps the most effective contribution to the crusade against slavery. By the 1840s, Frederick Douglass, William Wells Brown, Harriet Tubman, Sojourner Truth, and many other people who had escaped slavery had taken to lecturing throughout the North. Their stories of physical abuse and hardship, of separation from loved ones, and of emotional distress forced whites to remember the conditions faced daily by those still enslaved. Slave narratives gave Northern whites a comprehensive picture of life in slavery, countering easy stereotype with brutal reality.

But more than anything else, abolitionist efforts to aid runaway slaves undermined the political harmony between the North and South. African Americans involved in the Underground Railroad usually relied on one another and distrusted whites' involvement. They set up "vigilance groups," like one led by David Ruggles in New York, to prevent slave catchers from capturing fugitives. Starting in the 1840s, more and more white abolitionists joined with Black abolitionists to not just persuade Northerners through antislavery speeches, but also to take direct action by encouraging enslaved Blacks to escape and protecting them once in the North. Most famously, Harriet Tubman, herself a fugitive who operated from Canada, made more than 19 trips into the South and brought back more than 300 people.

"It Outlaws Me and I Outlaw It!": Abolitionists Fight New Laws

Worried Southern planters began to demand new federal legislation to prevent "slave-stealing." Pro-slavery politicians obtained what they wanted in the Compromise of 1850, which included a harsh new Fugitive Slave Law. It imposed severe penalties for aiding runaways, denied the accused the right to testify, and required citizens to help catch runaways. Free Blacks found themselves in jeopardy of being claimed as escapees, seized, and shipped South without so much as a hearing. Whites who had believed that slavery would not touch them now faced jail and fines if they refused to follow the commands of slave hunters. As slavery's violence spilled into Northern streets, many abolitionists abandoned their commitments to nonviolence.

Black communities prepared for battle. Jermain Wesley Loguen, who once had been enslaved, announced: "I don't respect this law — I don't fear it — I won't obey it! It outlaws me and I outlaw it!" Fugitive Lewis Hayden, who hid runaways in his Boston home, announced he had placed two kegs

Black communities prepared for battle. Jermain Loguen, who once had been enslaved, announced, "I don't respect this law — I don't fear it — I won't obey it! It outlaws me and I outlaw it!"

of explosives in his basement and would blow up the house rather than surrender to anyone.

Abolitionists of both races throughout the North announced that they would militantly oppose the new Fugitive Slave Law. "The only way to make the Fugitive Slave Law a dead letter," Frederick Douglass vowed, "is to make half a dozen dead kidnappers." Douglass' words reflected the growing support for direct action. On several occasions well-organized groups of abolitionists overwhelmed federal marshals and helped fugitives to safety. As Blacks and whites united in defying the Fugitive Slave Law, resistance sometimes turned violent, as in Christiana, Pennsylvania, where in 1851 an abolitionist shot a slaveholder, or in Boston in 1854, when an attempt to free a fugitive by storming the courthouse and overpowering guards led to a fatality. And even when physical violence did not occur, speakers such as Wendell Phillips increasingly urged their audiences to physically obstruct federal slave catchers if more peaceable means failed. Most agreed with Phillips when he declared that any Black American "should feel justified in using the law of God and man in shooting [any] officer" attempting to enforce the law.

The Fugitive Slave Law set North against South. It made some Northern whites wonder if owners of slaves might be trying to control all of the United States. By sending Southern posses racing through the streets of Northern cities and towns, slaveholders triggered anger from those who thought they were untouched by slavery. Of course in reality, the Northern economy was always tied to slave labor, but the increased presence of slave catchers made this harder to ignore. As the decade progressed, two more decisions in Washington — the Kansas-Nebraska Act and the *Dred Scott* decision — reinforced the growing divisions between the North and the South and fueled abolitionists' growing militancy.

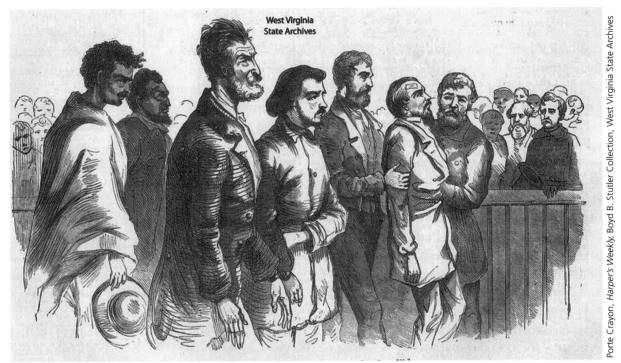

West Virginia State Archives

Porte Crayon, *Harper's Weekly*, Boyd B. Stutler Collection, West Virginia State Archives

John Brown and his multiracial group of fighters proved that white and Black abolitionists were willing to die to end slavery.

In 1854, Congress passed a bill that allowed the voters in the Kansas and Nebraska territories to decide whether slavery would be legal, opening territories previously declared free to slavery. Once passed, the Kansas-Nebraska Act provoked a race to the territories as free-staters and pro-slavery supporters sought to control the elections. In Kansas, the political struggle soon turned into guerilla warfare. Among the abolitionists who went to Kansas to fight against slavery's expansion was John Brown. Before leaving for Kansas, Brown campaigned in the abolitionist strongholds of the North for financial and moral support. With few exceptions, like William Lloyd Garrison who clung to nonviolence, abolitionists supported John Brown's crusade.

Then in 1857, the U.S. Supreme Court declared in *Dred Scott v. Sandford* that slavery would be fully protected by the federal government throughout the United States. Scott, who was enslaved, had been taken by his "owner" into territory declared free and sued for his freedom. Chief Justice Roger B. Taney not only denied Scott's suit, but in a set of sweeping

pronouncements also gave legal justification to the institution of slavery. Taney declared that the Constitution did not give Congress the power to legislate the limits of slavery's expansion. He added that according to the Founding Fathers, Blacks possessed no rights before the law that whites were "bound to respect." Slavery, in short, was a national institution and white supremacy was the law of the land.

Determined to end the system despite the political gains of the slaveholders, abolitionists became increasingly revolutionary. By the 1850s, thousands of its Black and white men and women members were helping runaways escape, challenging federal efforts to return fugitives, and discussing slavery's violent overthrow in the South.

"The Lesson of the Hour Is Insurrection": John Brown's Daring Raid

On abolition's cutting edge was John Brown. In 1858, Brown led a group of 18 armed men into Missouri, liberating five slaves and escorting them to freedom in Canada. While slave catchers were *legally* capturing Blacks in the North and selling them into slavery, Brown *illegally* invaded a slave state and directly freed slaves. In October 1859, John Brown and a multiracial group of devoted fighters were captured while raiding Harpers Ferry, Virginia, in an attempt to provoke rebellion among the slaves. Some of abolitionism's most militant figures such as Frederick Douglass had helped finance Brown's attack. Others had known what Brown was planning. Some activists like Harriet Tubman had even helped Brown recruit supporters for the raid. John Brown's raid was the dramatic example of direct action many abolitionists were hoping for. After weeks of preparation, Brown and his multiracial band of 22 descended on Harpers Ferry, seized the federal arsenal, and took several hostages, hoping to incite insurrection among the enslaved and free Blacks. But enslaved African Americans, who were startled by John Brown's raid, did not join Brown's army of liberation and he and his men were captured by troops commanded by Colonel Robert E. Lee.

Most abolitionists supported Brown's insurrectionary deeds. Brown was jailed, given a quick trial, then sentenced and hanged by Virginia authorities in December of 1859. In Brooklyn, Wendell Phillips electrified an immense audience with his pronouncement that "the lesson of the hour is insurrection." Brown, Phillips declared, "has twice as much right to hang Governor Wise [of Virginia] as Governor Wise has to hang him." For most Blacks, Brown was a hero. His assault proved that some whites were willing to die fighting slavery.

Some abolitionists, Garrison included, clung to nonviolence and hurried to separate their belief in the slaves' inherent right to rebel from what they saw as Brown's terrorism. Yet the whites most anxious to disassociate themselves from Brown were the leaders of the new Republican Party, including Abraham Lincoln. Hoping to distance themselves from "Black abolitionism," Republicans organized anti-Brown protest meetings in major cities. Lincoln explained Brown to slaveholders as the lone, mad assassin who appeared from time to time in world history.

Yet Lincoln's reassurances to the slaveholders did not convince them. The slaveholding South saw the increasing radicalism of the abolitionists as representing the North's true intentions. Nevertheless, the quiet courage and thoughtful words of Brown during the 40 days before his execution stirred the world and placed emancipation on the national agenda. In his final note, handed to a guard just before his execution, Brown predicted the coming Civil War. He declared "that the crimes of this guilty land can never be purged away, but with blood."

Adapted from James Brewer Stewart, *Holy Warriors: The Abolitionists and American Slavery* (New York: Hill and Wang, 1996) and William Loren Katz, *Breaking the Chains: African-American Slave Resistance* (New York: Aladdin Paperbacks, 1990).

James Brewer Stewart *is the James Wallace Professor Emeritus at Macalester College, founder of Historians Against Slavery, and author of a dozen books on the history of the abolition movement in the United States.*

William Loren Katz *is a retired high school and college teacher and the author of more than 40 books on African American history.*

Raising the Voices of Abolitionists Through Art

By Adam Sanchez

GIVING STUDENTS TIME in the social studies classroom to work on art projects can feel frivolous in the era of high-stakes testing. But it's important to carve out time for art in the classroom and push back against the idea that anything that isn't tested shouldn't be taught. Students can come alive and become engaged while working on art projects in ways they might not through reading and writing. Furthermore, art has been an essential tool of social movements throughout history — including the abolitionists.

Abolitionist artists used a variety of mediums to try to turn the public against slavery. One of the most powerful art forms the abolitionists cultivated was public speaking. Through lecture tours and public meetings abolitionists created some of the most powerful speeches in U.S. history. In addition, abolitionist artists created paintings, illustrations, and engravings that appeared in antislavery newspapers, pamphlets, novels, and the personal narratives of formerly enslaved people. These images of slavery were crucial to the antislavery cause. As abolitionist Angelina Grimké explained, "Until the pictures of the slave's sufferings were drawn and held up to public gaze, no Northerner had any idea of the cruelty of the system. It never entered their minds that such abominations could exist."

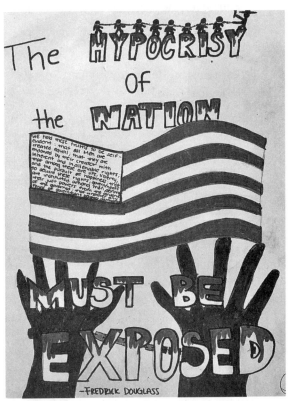

Student Poster: Cassidy Pacheco, 11th Grade

Student Poster: Lisa Narinedhat, 11th Grade

In this lesson, students examine some of the most famous abolitionist speeches and use these powerful words to create their own abolitionist posters. By hearing abolitionists in their own words, students can get a sense of the power and persuasiveness of the movement that can't be obtained through reading secondary sources. Through creating their own art and examining how abolitionists used art to promote their cause, students begin to explore the connection between art and social movements.

Materials Needed

- Copies of "Speech by John Rock" (Handout 5-A) for every student.

- Enough copies of Handouts 5–B, 5–C, 5–D, 5–E, and 5–F so every student in the class has one of the handouts.

- Five computers or tablets — one for each station, each loaded with a video performance of one of the abolitionist speeches (all videos can be found here: https://www.zinnedproject. org/raising-voices-abolitionists-through-art-videos/)

  - David Walker's *Appeal* (Handout 5–B)

  - Jermaine Wesley Loguen, Letter to Sarah Logue (Handout 5–C)

  - Frederick Douglass, "The Meaning of July Fourth for the Negro" (Handout 5–D)

  - Sojourner Truth, "Ain't I a Woman?" (Handout 5–E)

  - John Brown, "John Brown's Last Speech" (Handout 5–F)

- Poster paper and art supplies (colored pencils and markers).

- Copies of "Abolitionist Art" (Handout 5–G) for every student (alternatively, you could put the art on digital slides).

Time Required

One class period to listen to the speeches and for students to begin work on their art. Additional time to discuss abolitionist art.

Suggested Procedure

1. Before students enter the room, set up the desks in five distinct stations. Also set up a computer or tablet at each station loaded with one of the videos of actors' dramatic readings of the abolitionist speeches. Place the copies of the handout that correspond to each video under the computer or tablet for students to use later in the lesson.

2. After students enter, ask them to brainstorm various ways that the abolitionists might have used to get out their message. After discussing students' ideas, explain that two of the most important ways abolitionists publicized their antislavery message was through public speeches and posters. Let them know that in this lesson they are going to hear some powerful abolitionist speeches and then draw words from those speeches to create their own abolitionist posters. Before jumping into the speeches, it's useful to provide one or two contemporary political posters that combine text and art as examples so students have a sense of the kind of quotes they should be looking for. Ricardo Levins Morales has several posters available on his website that incorporate quotes from famous social justice icons. Molly Crabapple's PEN America Protest Posters offer other good examples.

3. After sharing poster examples, start to delve into the abolitionist speeches by reading through "Speech by John Rock" (Handout 5-A) together. You may want to stage a dramatic reading of the speech where you or a student read Rock's fiery words and invite the rest of the class to act as audience members — clapping or cheering for parts they enjoy. In addition, ask students to highlight phrases or sentences that stand out to them and that they think would work well quoted on a poster. When you finish reading, have students share with a partner the phrases or sentences they chose, and explain to a partner why those parts stood out to them. Afterward,

select a few students to share their phrases and responses with the whole class. You might also ask students how the speech made them feel or what images it brought to mind. What metaphors did they notice? If you are planning to finish this unit of study by asking students to write an essay on "Who freed the slaves?" you might also ask them to pull out quotes from the speech to use in their essay.

4. After discussing John Rock's speech, tell students that in small groups they will be reading and listening to some of the most famous speeches by those who fought against slavery. Explain to them that at each station they should have the text of the speech to look at, along with a video of an actor performing that speech. They should watch the video and follow along in the text. While they are reading and listening, in their notebook they should copy down any phrase or sentence that stands out to them, and keep an eye out for phrases they think would make a good quote for their poster. When they finish, they should discuss with their group what stood out to them and why, how it made them feel, what images came to mind while listening, and what metaphors and similes they noticed, just like they did as a class with the John Rock speech.

5. Each video is between three and five minutes long. Sometimes students will want to rewatch a video, and they will also need time to discuss. Depending on your students and how long your classes are, you will want to give students somewhere between seven and 12 minutes at each station. Students do not need to listen to every speech.

6. When it feels like students have listened to enough of the speeches, pause and briefly discuss with them the themes they noticed. Did anything come up repeatedly in the speeches? Next, ask them to look through their notes and choose a line, a metaphor or a simile that they found powerful. Alternatively, students could describe an image that one of the speeches evoked. If time permits, you may have a few students share these out.

7. Explain to students that they will now create a poster. When I describe this assignment to students, I point to the posters on my classroom walls and give several examples from various contemporary social movement posters to provide inspiration. In addition to the examples provided at the beginning of the lesson, the art of Melanie Cervantes, Ernesto Yerena Montejano, Favianna Rodriguez, Jess X Snow, and Sue Simensky Bietila can all provide good inspiration. It's also good to provide at least one example that is metaphorical — for example, Abigail Gray Swartz's "Me Too" bowling ball. As students look at the examples, ask someone in the back of the room if they can read the text on the poster and discuss why that is. Also ask how many colors are utilized in the posters. You want students to notice that the text is almost always big, bold, and often outlined and that many protest posters only use a few colors.

In the past, I've had students create a poster announcing a meeting to protest the execution of John Brown using words from his last speech. I've also had several students simply draw a picture of the abolitionist next to their words commemorating the person and their ideas. Some students have paired the words of an abolitionist with images representing a contemporary issue to show the relevance their words still have to today's injustices. Others have used the imagery in the speeches to guide their artwork. If students do not finish their poster in class, they should be allowed to finish at home, as students invest varying amounts of time and energy into art projects. I've found, however, the more time I give students in class, the better artwork they produce.

8. Either at the end of the class, or at the beginning of the following class, facilitate a discussion around "Abolitionist Art" (Handout 5–G). Here are some questions for discussion or writing:

- How effective do you think this antislavery art was?

- Who were the artists appealing to?

- What emotions were the artists trying to elicit in viewers?

- What is the portrayal of slavery and enslaved African Americans?

- Why should people oppose slavery, according to the artists?

- What should they do to end slavery, according to the artists?

- How do the artists portray resistance to slavery?

- Do you see any racial biases in this art?

- What are the key similarities you see in this art and the posters you made?

- What are the key differences? How would you account for these differences?

I've found that the art students produce through this activity tends to be powerful, and, like many of the speeches they listened to, full of righteous anger.

I've found that the art students produce through this activity tends to be powerful, and, like many of the speeches they listened to, full of righteous anger. Yet, with few exceptions, the historical abolitionist art seems aimed at eliciting mostly pity for enslaved people who appear helpless. The contrast between the two can generate a robust discussion. You might point out to students that most of the speeches were written by Black abolitionists, several of whom had previously been enslaved, whereas most abolitionist painters, illustrators, and engravers were white. As Howard Zinn notes, "Blacks had to struggle constantly with the unconscious racism of white abolitionists." Though this unit does not delve deeply into this point, this discussion could be a starting point for further student research on the topic.

Speech by John Rock

(Printed in *The Liberator*, Aug. 15, 1862)

In July 1862, two years into the Civil War, Congress released and Lincoln approved the second Confiscation Act and the Militia Act. Enslaved people "belonging" to disloyal slaveholders were declared "forever free" and Black men were allowed and encouraged to join the military for the first time. Congress also authorized Lincoln to colonize all Blacks willing to emigrate to "some tropical country" and provided $600,000 to deport them. Furthermore, after the war all the property confiscated by the Union military would revert to the Confederate owners or their heirs. Later, Lincoln proposed an amendment to the Constitution that would compensate all loyal slave owners for slaves they lost as a result of the war. Although Lincoln quickly abandoned this proposal, it outraged Black and abolitionist communities. On Aug. 1, 1862, at a gathering in Massachusetts to celebrate the anniversary of emancipation in Britain, John Rock — abolitionist, teacher, doctor, lawyer, and first African American to practice law before the U.S. Supreme Court — challenged the policies of Lincoln and Congress. Here is an excerpt of that speech.

Mr. President, Ladies and Gentlemen,
Twenty-four years ago, the friends of freedom in Great Britain and in her Colonies held grand jubilees, and thanked God and their rulers that 800,000 human chattels were that day transformed into men, and that the slave could never again clank his chains on British soil.

The British Government has, by this act, set us an example that I think hundreds within the sound of my voice would rejoice to see imitated by the United States. What our President means to do in *this* direction, God only knows. I confess I do not understand how it is, that he has not broken every yoke, and let the oppressed go free. . .

It is indeed humiliating to this civilization of the 19th century that today there exists a "peculiar" and popular "institution," which robs men not only of their earnings, but of themselves and their families, and makes woman the hapless victim of the most depraved wretches, and inflicts upon all who resist its progress tortures which the most barbarous savages of the most barbarous age would have scorned to have inflicted upon their bitterest enemies. . .

[And] why talk about compensating masters? Compensate them for what? What do you owe them? What does the slave owe them? What does society owe them? Compensate the master? No, never. It is the slave who ought to be compensated. The property of the South is by right the property of the slave. You talk of compensating the master who has stolen enough to sink 10 generations, and yet you do not propose to restore even a part of that which has been plundered. This is rewarding the thief. Have you forgotten that the wealth of the South is the property of the slave? Will you keep back the price of his blood, which is upon you and upon your children? Restore to him the wealth of the South. This you owe to the slave; and if you do your duty, posterity will give you the honor of being the first nation that dared to deal justly by the oppressed. . .

The present position of the colored man is a trying one; trying because the whole nation seems to have entered into a conspiracy to crush him. But few people comprehend our position in the free States. The masses seem to think that we are oppressed only in the South. This is a mistake; we are oppressed everywhere in this slavery-cursed land. While colored men have many rights, they have few privileges here. The colored man who educates his son, educates him to suffer. You can hardly imagine the humiliation and contempt a colored lad must feel in graduating the first in his class, and then being rejected everywhere else because of his color. Who is taking our boys in their stores and giving them a chance to rise? Who is admitting them into their workshops, or into their counting room?

And when our Government shall see the necessity of using the loyal Blacks of the free States, I hope it will have the courage to recognize their manhood. It certainly will not be mean enough to force us to fight for your liberty and then leave us when we go home to our respective States to be told that we cannot ride in the cars, that our children cannot go to the public schools, that we cannot vote; and if we don't like that state of things, there is an appropriation to colonize us. We ask for our rights. Hardships and dangers are household words with us. We are not afraid to dig or to fight. A few Black acclimated regiments would shake the Old Dominion. When will there be light enough in the Cabinet to see this!

David Walker's *Appeal* (1830)

In 1829, David Walker, a son of an enslaved father and a free mother, born free in North Carolina, moved to Boston. The next year he published a pamphlet, Walker's Appeal to the Coloured Citizens of the World, *which became widely read and infuriated Southern slaveholders. The state of Georgia offered a reward of $10,000 to anyone who would deliver Walker alive, and $1,000 to anyone who would kill him. Here is an excerpt from his* Appeal.

—From *Voices of a People's History of the United States*,
edited by Howard Zinn and Anthony Arnove

I ASK THE CANDID and unprejudiced of the whole world, to search the pages of historians diligently, and see if [anyone] ever treated a set of human beings, as the white Christians of America do us, the Blacks. I also ask the attention of the world of mankind to the declaration of these very American people, of the United States. A declaration made July 4, 1776.

It says,

We hold these truths to be self-evident — that all men are created equal, that they are endowed by their Creator with certain unalienable rights; that among these, are life, liberty, and the pursuit of happiness; that, to secure these rights, governments are instituted among men, deriving their just powers from the consent of the governed; that whenever any form of government becomes destructive of these ends, it is the right of the people to alter or to abolish it. . .

See your declaration, Americans!!! Do you understand your own language? Hear your language, proclaimed to the world, July 4, 1776 —

We hold these truths to be self-evident — that ALL MEN ARE CREATED EQUAL!! that they are endowed by their Creator with certain unalienable rights; that among these are life, liberty, and the pursuit of happiness!!

Compare your own language above, extracted from your Declaration of Independence, with your cruelties and murders inflicted by your cruel and unmerciful fathers on ourselves on our fathers and on us, men who have never given your fathers or you the least provocation!!!!!!

Now, Americans! I ask you candidly, was your sufferings under Great Britain one hundredth part as cruel and tyrannical as you have rendered ours under you? Some of the whites are ignorant enough to tell us that we ought to be submissive to them, that they may keep their feet on our throats. And if we do not submit to be beaten to death by them, we are bad creatures and of course must be damned, etc.

If any man wishes to hear this doctrine openly preached to us by the American preachers, let him go into the Southern and Western sections of this country — I do not speak from hear say — what I have written, is what I have seen and heard myself.

The Americans may be as vigilant as they please, but they cannot be vigilant enough for the Lord, neither can they hide themselves, where he will not find and bring them out.

Jermain Wesley Loguen, Letter to Sarah Logue
(March 28, 1860)

People who were freed from slavery and people who had escaped from slavery played a vital role in building the Underground Railroad and organizing for abolition. As formerly enslaved people began to tell their stories, some wrote private, or in some cases public, letters to their former owners, defying their attempt to return them to slavery. When Jermain Wesley Loguen, who was pivotal to the Underground Railroad in Syracuse, New York, published his memoir of slavery, it came to the attention of his former enslavers. She wrote to him, asking him to return or to send her $1,000 in compensation. Loguen's reply to her was printed in the abolitionist newspaper The Liberator.*

—From *Voices of a People's History of the United States*,
edited by Howard Zinn and Anthony Arnove

Mrs. Sarah Logue:

Yours of the 20th of February is duly received. It is a long time since I heard from my poor old mother, and I am glad to know that she is yet alive.

You sold my brother and sister, and 12 acres of land, you say, because I ran away. Now you have the unutterable meanness to ask me to return and be your miserable chattel, or in lieu thereof, send you $1,000 to enable you to redeem the land, but not to redeem my poor brother and sister! If I were to send you money, it would be to get my brother and sister, and not that you should get land. I am indignant beyond the power of words to express, that you should be so sunken and cruel as to tear the hearts I love so much all in pieces. Wretched woman! Be it known to you that I value my freedom, to say nothing of my mother, brothers, and sisters, more than your whole body; more, indeed, than my own life; more than all the lives of all the slaveholders and tyrants under heaven.

You say you have offers to buy me, and that you shall sell me if I do not send you $1,000, and in the same breath and almost in the same sentence, you say, "You know we raised you as we did our own children." Woman, did you raise your own children for the market? Did you raise them

for the whipping post? Did you raise them to be driven off, bound in chains? Where are my poor bleeding brothers and sisters? Who was it that sent them off into sugar and cotton fields, to be kicked and cuffed, and whipped, and to groan and die. Wretched woman! Do you say you did not do it? Then I reply, your husband did, and you approved the deed — and the very letter you sent me shows that your heart approves it all. Shame on you! . . .

But you say I am a thief, because I took the old mare along with me. Have you got to learn that I had a better right to the old mare, than Mannasseth Logue had to me? Is it a greater sin for me to steal his horse, than it was for him to rob my mother's cradle, and steal me? Have you got to learn that human rights are mutual and reciprocal, and if you take my liberty and life, you forfeit your own liberty and life? Before God and high heaven, is there a law for one man which is not a law for every other man?

If you or any other speculator on my body and rights, wish to know how I regard my rights, they need but come here, and lay their hands on me to enslave me. I stand among a free people, who, I thank God, sympathize with my rights, and the rights of mankind.

Frederick Douglass, "The Meaning of July Fourth for the Negro"
(July 5, 1852)

July Fourth is held up as a day to celebrate the struggle for freedom and independence. But the great abolitionist Frederick Douglass, himself a former slave and the editor of the abolitionist newspaper the North Star, *dared to challenge the exaltation of the holiday. Here is part of his address to the Rochester (New York) Ladies' Anti-Slavery Society.*

—From *Voices of a People's History of the United States,*
edited by Howard Zinn and Anthony Arnove

Mr. President, Friends, and Fellow Citizens:

He who could address this audience without a quailing sensation, has stronger nerves than I have. I do not remember ever to have appeared as a speaker before any assembly more shrinkingly, nor with greater distrust of my ability, than I do this day. A feeling has crept over me quite unfavorable to the exercise of my limited powers of speech.

The papers and placards say that I am to deliver a Fourth of July Oration. Fellow citizens, pardon me, allow me to ask, why am I called upon to speak here today? What have I, or those I represent, to do with your national independence? Are the great principles of political freedom and of natural justice, embodied in that Declaration of Independence, extended to us?

Would to God, both for your sakes and ours, that an affirmative answer could be truthfully returned to these questions! Then would my task be light, and my burden easy and delightful.

But such is not the state of the case. I say it with a sad sense of the disparity between us. Your high independence only reveals the immeasurable distance between us. The rich inheritance of justice, liberty, prosperity, and independence, bequeathed by your fathers, is shared by you, not by me. The sunlight that brought light and healing to you, has brought stripes and death to me. This Fourth [of] July is yours, not mine. . . . To drag a man in fetters into the grand illuminated temple of liberty, and call upon him to join you in joyous anthems, were inhuman mockery and sacrilegious irony. Do you mean, citizens, to mock me, by asking me to speak today?

O! had I the ability, I would, today, pour out a fiery stream of biting ridicule, blasting reproach, withering sarcasm, and stern rebuke. For it is not light that is needed, but fire; it is not the gentle shower, but thunder. We need the storm, the whirlwind, and the earthquake. [T]he conscience of the nation must be roused; the propriety of the nation must be startled; the hypocrisy of the nation must be exposed; and its crimes against God and man must be proclaimed and denounced.

What, to the American slave, is your Fourth of July? I answer; a day that reveals to him, more than all other days in the year, the gross injustice and cruelty to which he is the constant victim. To him, your celebration is a sham; your boasted liberty, an unholy license; your national greatness, swelling vanity; your sounds of rejoicing, hollow mockery; your prayers and hymns are, to Him, mere bombast, fraud, deception, impiety, and hypocrisy — a thin veil to cover up crimes that would disgrace a nation of savages.

Go where you may, search where you will, roam through all the monarchies and despotisms of the Old World. There is not a nation on the earth guilty of practices more shocking and bloody than are the people of the United States, at this very hour. Search out every abuse, and when you have found the last, lay your facts by the side of the everyday practices of this nation, and you will say with me, that, for revolting barbarity and shameless hypocrisy, America reigns without a rival.

Sojourner Truth, "Ain't I a Woman?"
(1851)

The Black abolitionist Sojourner Truth, who was freed from slavery in 1827, spoke to a gathering of feminists in Akron in 1851, denouncing the religious arguments commonly made to justify the oppression of women. No exact transcript of the speech, which electrified its audience, exists, but the president of the Akron convention, Frances Gage, later recounted Truth's words.

—From *Voices of a People's History of the United States*,
edited by Howard Zinn and Anthony Arnove

WELL, CHILDREN, where there is so much racket there must be something out of kilter. I think that 'twixt the Negroes of the South and the women at the North, all talking about rights, the white men will be in a fix pretty soon. But what's all this here talking about?

That man over there says that women need to be helped into carriages, and lifted over ditches, and to have the best place everywhere. Nobody ever helps me into carriages, or over mud puddles, or gives me any best place! And ain't I a woman? Look at me! Look at my arm! I have ploughed and planted, and gathered into barns, and no man could head me! And ain't I a woman? I could work as much and eat as much as a man — when I could get it — and bear the lash as well! And ain't I a woman? I have borne 13 children, and seen most all sold off to slavery, and when I cried out with my mother's grief, none but Jesus heard me! And ain't I a woman?

Then they talk about this thing in the head; what's this they call it? [Member of audience whispers "intellect."] That's it, honey. What's that got to do with women's rights or Negroes' rights? If my cup won't hold but a pint, and yours holds a quart, wouldn't you be mean not to let me have my little half measure full?

Then that little man in black there, he says women can't have as much rights as men, 'cause Christ wasn't a woman! Where did your Christ come from? Where did your Christ come from? From God and a woman! Man had nothing to do with Him.

If the first woman God ever made was strong enough to turn the world upside down all alone, these women together ought to be able to turn it back, and get it right side up again! And now they is asking to do it, the men better let them.

John Brown, "John Brown's Last Speech" (Nov. 2, 1859)

On Oct. 16, 1859, John Brown and nearly two dozen comrades seized the armory at Harpers Ferry in Virginia, hoping to use its massive arsenal in the struggle to forcibly end slavery. Captured and brought to trial at nearby Charles Town, Brown was found guilty of treason. One month before his execution, John Brown addressed the courtroom, defending his role in the action at Harpers Ferry. Henry David Thoreau, although he himself did not favor violence, praised John Brown, and when the fiery preacher was sentenced to death, Ralph Waldo Emerson said: "He will make the gallows holy as the cross."

—From *Voices of a People's History of the United States*, edited by Howard Zinn and Anthony Arnove

I HAVE, may it please the Court, a few words to say.

In the first place, I deny everything but what I have all along admitted, the design on my part to free the slaves. I intended certainly to have made a clear thing of that matter, as I did last winter, when I went into Missouri and there took slaves without the snapping of a gun on either side, moved them through the country, and finally left them in Canada. I designed to have done the same thing again, on a larger scale. That was all I intended. I never did intend murder, or treason, or the destruction of property, or to excite or incite slaves to rebellion, or to make insurrection.

I have another objection; and that is, it is unjust that I should suffer such a penalty. Had I interfered in the manner that I admit, and which I admit has been fairly proved, had I so interfered in behalf of the rich, the powerful, the intelligent, the so-called great, or in behalf of any of their friends, either father, mother, brother, sister, wife, or children, or any of that class, and suffered and sacrificed what I have in this interference, it would have been all right; and every man in this Court would have deemed it an act worthy of reward rather than punishment.

This Court acknowledges, as I suppose, the validity of the law of God. I see a book kissed here that I suppose to be the Bible, or at least the New Testament. That teaches me that all things "whatsoever I would that men should do to me, I should do even so to them." It teaches me, further, to "remember them that are in bonds, as bound with them." I endeavored to act up to that instruction. I say, I am yet too young to understand that God is any respecter of persons. I believe that to have interfered as I have done, as I have always freely admitted I have done, in behalf of His despised poor, was not wrong, but right. Now, if it is deemed necessary that I should forfeit my life for the furtherance of the ends of justice, and mingle my blood further with the blood of my children and with the blood of millions in this slave country whose rights are disregarded by wicked, cruel, and unjust enactments, I submit; so let it be done!

Abolitionist Art

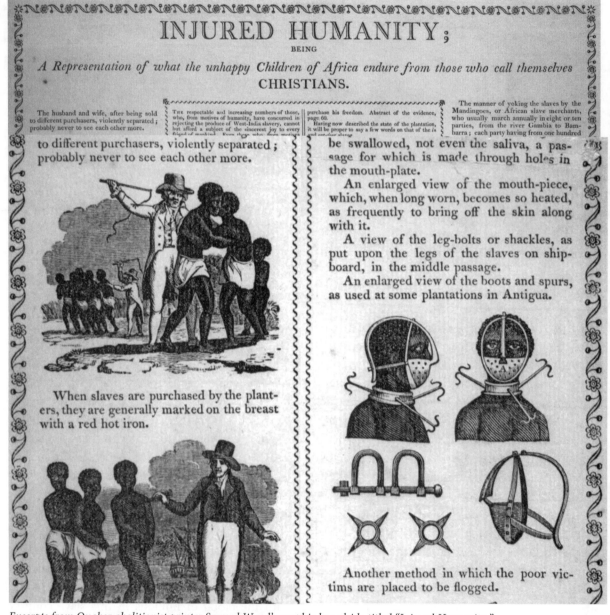

Excerpts from Quaker abolitionist printer Samuel Wood's graphic broadside titled "Injured Humanity."

Source: Wood, Samuel. "Injured Humanity; Being a Representation of What the Unhappy Children of Africa Endure from Those Who Call Themselves Christians." The Gilder Lehrman Institute of American History.

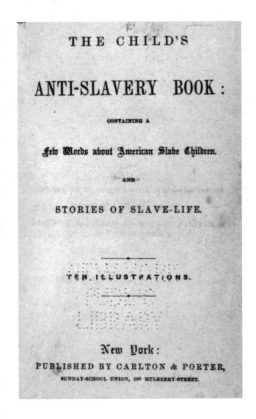

Excerpts from The Child's Anti-Slavery Book *that was distributed by the abolitionist Sunday School Union. The book uses real stories and vivid illustrations about enslaved children separated from their parents and mistreated by their "owners" to convince free children to be against slavery.*

Source: Sunday School Union. The Child's Anti-Slavery Book: Containing a Few Words About American Slave Children. And *Stories of Slave Life.* New York: Carlton & Porter. 1860. New York Public Library Digital Collections, Schomburg Manuscripts, Archives, and Rare Books Division.

"The Hunted Slaves," 1861, by English artist Richard Ansdell.

When the painting was first exhibited, the artist included a quotation in the catalogue from Henry Wadsworth Longfellow's 1842 antislavery poem "The Dismal Swamp":

> *In dark fens of the Dismal Swamp*
> *The hunted Negro lay;*
> *He saw the fire of the midnight camp,*
> *And heard at times a horse's tramp,*
> *And a bloodhound's distant bay.*
>
> *. . .*
>
> *Where hardly a human foot could pass,*
> *Or a human heart would dare,*
> *On the quaking turf of the green morass*
> *He crouched in the rank and tangled grass,*
> *Like a wild beast in his lair.*

Source: Ansdell, Richard. 1861. "The Hunted Slaves." The International Slavery Museum.

"Slaves Waiting for Sale: Richmond, Virginia," 1861, by Eyre Crowe

"After the Sale: Slaves Going South from Richmond," 1853, by Eyre Crowe

English Artist Eyre Crowe visited the United States in 1852–53 and traveled to many places with writer
William M. Thackeray, including Richmond, Virginia, where these scenes took place.
Source: EyreCrowe.com

A Colored Young Man in the City of New York," 1855, Engraving by Patrick H. Reason.

Engraver and lithographer Patrick Henry Reason was one of several African American artists who received support from the abolitionist movement. He is most famous for his engravings of chained, kneeling slaves, used widely in abolitionist publications. His lithographs and engravings were featured in the narrative of the abolitionist lecturer Henry Bibb, who had escaped slavery.

"Kneeling Slave," 1835, Engraving by Patrick H. Reason.

This engraving (right) of a chained enslaved female was often circulated with the caption "Am I not a woman and a sister?"

LESSON 6
Mapping the Slave Economy

BY BILL BIGELOW AND ADAM SANCHEZ

"To the Union of the States this nation owes its unprecedented increase in population, its surprising development of material resources, its rapid augmentation of wealth. . ."

—Republican Party Platform of 1860

"My paramount object in this struggle is to save the Union, and is not either to save or to destroy slavery. If I could save the Union without freeing any slave I would do it, and if I could save it by freeing all the slaves I would do it; and if I could save it by freeing some and leaving others alone I would also do that."

—Abraham Lincoln, Aug. 22, 1862,
Letter to Horace Greeley, editor of the New York Tribune

In 1860, cotton, picked by enslaved laborers, accounted for more than half of all U.S. exports.

As Abraham Lincoln made clear, at least initially, the Civil War was fought not to end slavery but to bring the rebellious Southern states back to the Union. Why was it so important to Lincoln that the states belong to one country? The Republican Party platform emphasizes that the United States owes its prosperity to the unity of the North and the South. How did this unity create prosperity? And prosperity for whom? In order to answer these questions, students need to have a basic understanding of the pre-Civil War economy.

The map activity, described below can be used to help students understand the economic connections that linked the North and the South in the lead-up to Lincoln's election. It's helpful background for students prior to participating in "Lesson 7: The Election of 1860 Role Play."

We are aware that the activity reduces hugely complicated economic relationships to their simplest terms. For example, for the purposes of this activity, the "Western farmers" category collapses farmers in different circumstances into one group. The new territories of Kansas and Nebraska, or any areas between there and Pacific states, included largely subsistence farmers. But in the stretch between Ohio and Iowa — generally what is now called the Midwest but was commonly called the "West" in the 1840s and '50s — most farmers grew wheat and corn for markets in the East and South. It's these latter farmers who grew for the market that we include as the "West" in this activity.

Also, in this lesson food crops are grown only in the West and exported to other regions. In reality, both the Northeast and the South purchased food from the West *and* grew their own food. The simulation simplifies the economies of these three regions to the commodities that were fundamental to their economic activity. Despite these simplifications, the activity helps students to get beyond some of the platitudes about the Civil War being a battle between good and evil, North and South, and lays a foundation for later activities that depend on students being able to think in terms of the economic stakes underlying the Civil War and Reconstruction.

Another caveat: This activity is not a role play. It's a demonstration, and is more teacher-directed than many Zinn Education Project activities. Nonetheless, it can be engaging, a kind of participatory and illustrated lecture. We've found this a helpful way for students to get a mental picture of some of the pre-Civil War economic tensions that would otherwise be difficult for them to grasp.

Materials Needed

- 2 bags of cotton balls
- 4 shirts
- 2 jars of grain or something representing food
- 2 stacks of fake money
- Copies of "Mapping the Pre-Civil War Economy"; on the reverse side, "Economic Tensions Contributing to Civil War" (Handout 6-A) for every student.
- Copies of "Complicity: How the North Promoted, Prolonged, and Profited from Slavery" (Handout 6–B) for every student.

Time Required

One class period.

Suggested Procedure

1. Prior to students arriving to class, tape off a large rectangle on the floor of the classroom. Tape off a section in the Northeast, a section in the South, and a section for all the land in the West. Tape off a section outside the rectangle, representing Great Britain. It should look roughly like this:

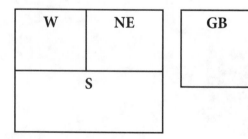

2. Explain to students that they will be participating in a map activity to help them understand in broad terms the economic relationships in the United States prior to the Civil War. Ask one or two students to represent each "station," and to go stand in their respective areas.

3. Distribute Handout 6–A to all students who remained seated. Ask other students to take notes on the information they learn during the activity, and to draw the connections between the regions on their maps as they learn details. Tell them that they will need these notes for a writing assignment on the tensions leading to Civil War.

4. Guide students through the activity by asking a series of questions that students answer out loud:

   a. **Q:** Where do you think the cotton comes from? **A:** The South.

      Hand the cotton to student(s) representing the South.

   b. **Q:** This cotton is pretty cheap. Why do you think that is? **A:** Stolen labor and knowledge of enslaved people.

   c. **Q:** These shirts represent goods that are made of cotton; they're not raw cotton, but manufactured cotton. Where would the shirts be produced? **A:** Northeast and Great Britain.

      Hand the shirts to student(s) representing the Northeast and Great Britain.

   d. **Q:** Who do you think grows the food crops? **A:** The West.

      Hand jars of food to the student(s) representing the West.

   e. **Q:** Why do you think that the landowners in the South would not choose to use most of that land to grow food crops? **A:** It is more profitable for them to produce cotton and buy food. Pause here to explain the difference between farms in the West and the South. In the West, there were mostly small farmers who produced food while in the South, the economy was dominated by

larger plantations producing cash crops. These included especially cotton, but also rice, tobacco, and sugarcane.

   f. **Q:** And lastly, where were most of the banks in the country? What city are most of the financial institutions located in today? **A:** Northeast/New York City.

      Hand one stack of money to student(s) representing the Northeast.

   g. **Q:** Before the Civil War there was a huge demand for cotton. This meant that the Southern plantation owners wanted more and more enslaved people and more and more farming equipment to produce more and more cotton, in order to make a big profit. But plantation owners in the South didn't always have the money to buy people and equipment. Where might they go to get a loan? **A:** The banks in the Northeast.

      Have student(s) representing the Northeast hand over their stack of money to the student(s) representing the South.

   h. **Q:** In the Northeast and Great Britain they produce manufactured goods, but what do they need to produce these goods? What is needed to produce these shirts? **A:** Raw materials, cotton.

      Have student(s) representing the South hand over one bag of cotton to the student(s) representing the Northeast and one to student(s) representing Great Britain.

   i. **Q:** So the South makes a bunch of money from selling their cotton. . .

   Teacher gives a second stack of money to student(s) in the South to represent the profit made.

   But because they had originally taken out a loan to produce that cotton, where would some of that money go to repay the loan?

   A: The Northeast. You might pause here to explain interest. Like any loans, these were expected to be repaid in full, *plus* interest.

Have the student representing the South give one stack of money back to the student(s) representing the Northeast (plus a little more if you want to represent interest).

j. **Q:** Also, there are very few factories in the South so from whom would they buy their clothes and other manufactured goods? **A:** The Northeast and Great Britain.

k. **Q:** But hold on a second. Who would be able to sell their shirts and other manufactured products more inexpensively? **A:** Here students generally suggest that the North would be able to sell more inexpensively, because the distance from North to South is shorter than from Great Britain to the South. Ask students: Are there any reasons why Great Britain might have a competitive advantage over the North? Who has more manufacturing experience? Where might labor costs be more expensive? (Again, this is all in broad strokes, but manufacturers in the North confronted the fact that workers were constantly tempted by the availability of land that had been stolen from Indigenous people in the West, and this would tend to inflate wages; there was no comparable "West" in Great Britain. Also, Great Britain had considerable manufacturing experience and had more experienced industrial workers.)

l. **Q:** Ask students: Let's imagine that the British can sell their manufactured products, including their cotton products, more inexpensively than the Northern manufacturers in the United States. If the manufacturers were powerful enough — if they had enough clout in making laws — is there any way that they could ensure that the British manufactured goods were more expensive than those made in the Northeast of the United States? **A:** Students may or may not come up with the answer, but one way the manufacturers in the United

States can protect their markets is through tariffs, taxes on imports, that would make British goods more expensive. You might give them an example, say a shirt coming from Great Britain costs a dollar and a shirt coming from the Northeast costs two dollars. How much of a tariff would you want there to be?

Have students representing the Northeast and Great Britain hand over one shirt to the student(s) representing the South. You may also want to physically block the British shirt from arriving in the South.

m. **Q (to student(s) representing the South):** What are your thoughts on this tariff on British manufactured goods? **A:** Make sure students realize that the South would not be happy about the tariff because it would mean they would ultimately be paying more for consumer goods.

n. **Q:** So where is this food from the West going? **A:** Northeast and South.

Have student(s) representing the West hand one jar of food to student(s) representing the Northeast and one to student(s) representing the South.

o. **Q:** What does the West need? **A:** Manufactured goods/clothing

p. **Q:** Where could they get these from? **A:** Northeast and Great Britain.

Have student(s) representing the Northeast and Great Britain give their remaining items to the West.

Although, here too, bring the tariff into play and ask Western farmers about their attitude on the tariff.

q. **Q:** Is the West getting anything from the South? **A:** No. (Although, of course, indirectly, they are getting cotton — produced by slave labor in the South — by buying manufactured goods from the Northeast.)

r. **Q (To the student(s) representing the West):** Out here in the West, if people in the South wanted to bring people they have enslaved and live nearby you, how would you feel as small farmers? Put aside how you might feel about this morally; think about how it could affect you economically. **A:** Western farms would have to compete with plantation owners who use enslaved workers — i.e., workers they pay nothing.

s. **Q (To the student(s) representing the West):** If plantation owners lived nearby and competed with you using enslaved workers, this would hurt you economically. How does slavery in the South affect you economically; does it hurt you? **A:** No, because you sell produce to the South, and indirectly benefit from manufactured products that use slave labor. This is important groundwork, as students will need to be able to see that there were many in the United States who opposed the expansion of slavery not on moral grounds but based on their own economic self-interest.

5. Ask your student volunteers to sit down. Tell students to flip over Handout 6–A to the side titled "Economic Tensions Contributing to Civil War" and ask students to answer the questions to reinforce what they just learned in the map activity. Note that students usually do not answer handout question #5 correctly. Because this activity deals with these issues strictly from an economic standpoint, many students expect Great Britain to support the South in the event of Civil War between the North and the South, and indeed, there were many in Great Britain who did favor the South. However, in Great Britain there had also been a powerful movement to abolish slavery in the British empire. A workers' movement in Great Britain also opposed slavery. Especially after the Emancipation Proclamation, when the war could be framed as a struggle between freedom and slavery, the British government could not side publicly with the South. Letting students answer question No. 5 incorrectly, and then discussing this history, can be an important example of how social movements can force

governments to act against the economic interests of powerful social classes.

Complicity: How the North Promoted, Prolonged, and Profited from Slavery

6. As a follow-up, assign the excerpt from *Complicity: How the North Promoted, Prolonged, and Profited from Slavery*, by Anne Farrow, Joel Land, and Jenifer Frank. It is included here as Handout 6–B.

7. Ask students to take notes while they complete the reading. Have them draw a line down the center of a piece of paper and list on one side quotes that detail how businesses, people, or governments in the North were complicit in slavery. On the other side, they should write their detailed reactions. Also encourage students to raise at least two questions that they would like to discuss with the rest of the class.

8. In addition to students' own questions, here are some questions for further discussion or writing:

- The authors state, "Only since the Civil Rights Movement have many historians themselves begun to recognize how central slavery was to our history." Why do you think that is? What does this say about how history is written and the importance of *who* is writing it?

- Why do you think the mayor of New York City called for the city to secede along with the Southern states? Use evidence from the text to explain your answer.

- What were the three most compelling facts in the reading that show the North's "complicity" with slavery?

- Did the reading change your view about the role the North played in slavery?

- Many well-known companies today, like the insurance company Aetna and JPMorgan Chase, one of the biggest financial services companies in the world, profited from slavery. What is the responsibility of companies that today are rich in part because human beings were enslaved?

Mapping the Pre-Civil War Economy

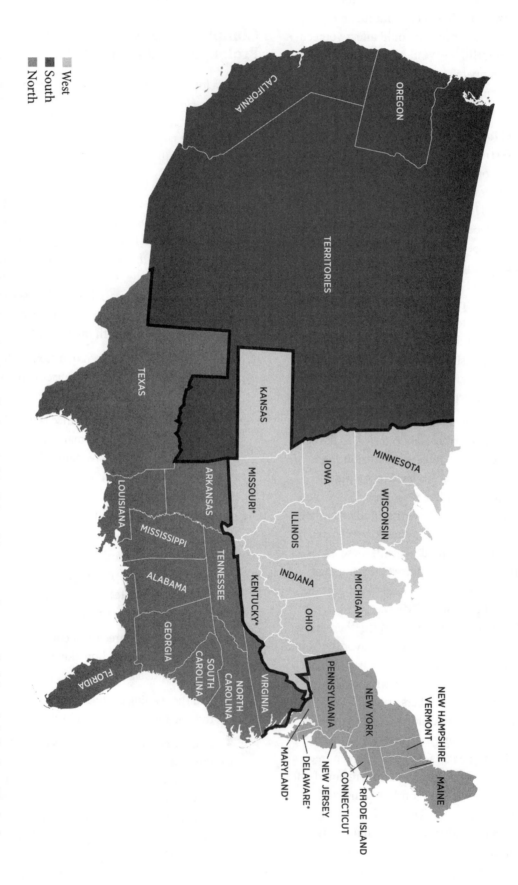

Legend:
- West
- South
- North

Missouri, Kentucky, Delaware, and Maryland are often referred to as "border states." In all four of these states slavery was legal, but only in Southern Maryland and Southwestern Kentucky did the economy resemble the large-scale cash crop production that dominated most Southern states. The area that became West Virginia during the Civil War is included here as part of the West.

States labeled on map:
CALIFORNIA, OREGON, TERRITORIES, TEXAS, KANSAS, MISSOURI*, IOWA, MINNESOTA, WISCONSIN, ARKANSAS, ILLINOIS, MICHIGAN, LOUISIANA, MISSISSIPPI, TENNESSEE, ALABAMA, KENTUCKY*, INDIANA, OHIO, GEORGIA, SOUTH CAROLINA, NORTH CAROLINA, VIRGINIA, FLORIDA, PENNSYLVANIA, NEW YORK, NEW HAMPSHIRE, VERMONT, MAINE, MARYLAND*, DELAWARE*, NEW JERSEY, CONNECTICUT, RHODE ISLAND, MASSACHUSETTS

Economic Tensions Contributing to Civil War

1   On the map draw lines showing the economic relationships between the different regions. In other words, draw lines clearly showing which products went where.

2. What region(s) stood to gain from tariffs? _____

    What region(s) stood to lose from tariffs? _____

3. If the South decided to secede from (leave) the United States, what region would be the big economic loser and why?

4. If the South seceded from the United States, would the West be more likely to join them in a separate country or to stay with the North in the United States? Why?

5. If the South seceded from the United States, who would the government of Great Britain be likely to support if there were a war: the North or the South? Why?

Complicity: How the North Promoted, Prolonged, and Profited from Slavery

By Anne Farrow, Joel Lang, and Jenifer Frank

FERNANDO WOOD thought his timing was perfect. Abraham Lincoln's election had sparked the exodus of 11 states from the Union. South Carolina was the first to secede. Within weeks, six more states had broken off from the United States, and by the end of May, the Confederacy was complete.

As the most profound crisis in our nation's history unfolded, Wood, the mayor of New York, America's most powerful city, made a stunning proposal: New York City should secede from the United States, too.

"With our aggrieved brethren of the Slave States, we have friendly relations and a common sympathy," Wood told the New York Common Council in his State of the City message on Jan. 7, 1861. "As a free city," he said, New York "would have the whole and united support of the Southern states, as well as all other states to whose interests and rights under the constitution she has always been true."

Wood's proposal illustrates a story that has been largely ignored when discussing the history of slavery: how the North helped create, strengthen, and

New York City had deep ties to slavery and the cotton trade. It was also home to an enormously profitable illegal slave trade.

prolong slavery in the United States. In the 18th century, even after the writing of the Declaration of Independence, tens of thousands of Black people lived as slaves in the North. Thousands of acres of Connecticut, New York, and tiny Rhode Island held plantations that used slave labor. And even after the abolition of slavery in the North, the Northern economy depended on the slaveholding South.

In 1860, the nearly 4 million enslaved people in the United States were valued at $3 billion, worth as much as all the country's factories, railroads, and livestock combined. Cotton was the single largest U.S. export, and New York City was the financial capital of the Cotton Kingdom. Cotton was more than just a profitable crop. It was the national currency, the product most responsible for United States' explosive growth in the decades before the Civil War.

The 10 major cotton states were producing 66 percent of the world's cotton, and raw cotton accounted for more than half of all U.S. exports. The numbers are almost impossible to grasp: In the season that ended in 1860, the United States produced close to 5 million bales of cotton, or roughly 2.3 billion pounds.

Lots of cotton could be produced because of the enslavement of lots of people [on land that had been seized from Native peoples through theft and massacres]. In 1850, some 2.3 million people were enslaved in the 10 cotton states; of these, nearly 2 million were involved in some aspect of cotton production.

From seed to cloth, Northern merchants, shippers, and financial institutions, many based in New York, controlled nearly every aspect of cotton production and trade.

Only large banks, generally located in Manhattan, could extend to plantation owners the credit they needed between planting and selling their crop. If a farmer wanted to expand his operations during those boom decades, he required the deep pockets of Northern banks to lend him

Cotton was the single largest U.S. export, and New York City was the financial capital of the Cotton Kingdom.

the money to buy additional equipment, as well as additional labor. Enslaved people were usually bought on credit.

Other Northerners made up the long chain of middlemen linking plantation owner and manufacturer. Northerners' influence and control infused nearly every phase of the trade. Most ships that carried the cotton from plantation to port to market were built in the North, and they were usually owned by Northerners. Northern companies sold the insurance to protect a farmer's crop and all of his property, including his slaves.

The power of the North over key aspects of cotton production was wide and deep, and involved many of the most important businessmen of the day.

Three brothers named Lehman were cotton brokers in Montgomery, Alabama, before they moved to New York and helped to establish the New York Cotton Exchange. Until it went bankrupt in 2008, Lehman Brothers was an internationally renowned investment firm.

Junius Morgan, father of J. Pierpont Morgan [of JPMorgan Chase], arranged for his son to study the cotton trade in the South as the future industrialist and banker was beginning his business career. Morgan Sr., a Massachusetts native who became a major banker and cotton broker in London, understood that knowledge of the cotton trade was essential to prospering in the commercial world of the 1850s.

Real estate and shipping magnate John Jacob Astor — one of America's first millionaires and namesake of the Waldorf Astoria Hotels and whole neighborhoods in New York City — made his fortune in furs and the China trade. But Astor's ships, like those of many successful merchant-shippers, also carried tons of cotton.

Scotsman Archibald Gracie immigrated to New York after training in Liverpool, Great Britain's great cotton port. Gracie became an international shipping magnate, a merchant prince. His son and grandson left the city to become cotton brokers in Mobile, Alabama, but their family's summer home, today called Gracie Mansion, is still the official residence of the mayor of New York.

And beyond New York, cotton created the basis for the wealth of textile manufacturers like Amos Adams Lawrence. By 1860, New England was home to 472 cotton mills. Just between 1830 and 1840, Northern mills consumed more than 100 million pounds of Southern cotton. And hundreds of Northern textile mills clothed enslaved people in the South, using coarse, simple material sometimes referred to as "negro cloth."

The cotton that didn't go to the mills of the North was exported to Great Britain's 2,650 cotton factories. And while it would have made more sense for Southern ports to trade directly with merchants and manufacturers across the Atlantic, doing so would have cut New York out of the loop, so the city's shipping community demanded that Southern cotton pass through New York City on its way to Great Britain.

For decades, Southern cotton was taken 200 miles north, where it was unloaded and then reloaded onto Britain-bound vessels. This added costs and jobs to the trade, allowing New York to cash in on a crop grown thousands of miles south. As early as 1822, cotton made up 40 percent of New York exports. Clinching New York's reliance on the South was the fact that, except for flour, which was largely a Northern product, tobacco and rice, grown with enslaved labor, were the other top exports. The South was providing New York with more than half of its exports.

The dependence of New York City's economy on the South and slavery influenced politicians to look the other way as the city became the hub

Slavery has long been identified as a Southern institution. The time to bury that myth is overdue. Slavery is a story about the United States, all of the United States. The nation's wealth, from the very beginning, depended upon the exploitation of Black people. Together, over the lives of millions of enslaved men and women, wealthy white Northerners and Southerners shook hands and made a country.

of an enormously profitable illegal slave trade. Manhattan shipyards built ships to carry captive Africans, the vessels often outfitted with crates of shackles and with the huge water tanks needed for their human cargo. A conservative estimate is that during the illegal trade's peak years, 1859 and 1860, at least two slave ships — each built to hold between 600 and 1,000 enslaved people — left lower Manhattan every month.

Southerners also helped fuel New York's tourism industry. As New York became the nation's commercial center, people were drawn there not only to conduct business but also to have fun. By the early 19th century, the city was an exciting place, offering theater and other cultural events. And it sure beat Alabama in August. Each summer, thousands of Southerners would leave their farms and plantations and head for the North — New York City; Newport, Rhode Island; and Saratoga, New York, were popular destinations — to escape the heat and diseases that were the scourge of the Southern summer. They couldn't have been more welcome. They filled the finest hotels in Northern cities, and Northern businesses aimed newspaper advertisements at Southern audiences.

The July 1859 issue of *De Bow's Review*, the most widely circulated Southern commercial journal during the antebellum era — a lifestyle magazine for slaveholders — carried ads for products to help a planter's business and every other aspect of his life. The journals were thick with notices, largely from New York, Pennsylvania, and Connecticut companies, for everything from cotton gins, made in Philadelphia, to fertilizer available through a Fulton Street firm in New York City. There were groceries from a company on Manhattan's Vesey Street, medicines from Boston, and iron railings ideal for verandas from a Philadelphia firm.

Three insurance companies advertised in the same issue of *De Bow's*, including Aetna of Hartford, already an "old established and leading Insurance Company." Two New York insurers listed as their agent William A. Bartlett at 81 Gravier Street in New Orleans. One life insurance ad read: "Insures the Lives of White Persons & Slaves."

Other Northern firms competed for the Southern dollar with fine china, fine furniture, and fine cutlery. Also: candles, soaps, French plate glass, pumps and fire hoses, pianos, pickles, liquors, and account room "weighing books," specifically for cotton, grain, sugar, and molasses.

Finally, any Southern planter who wanted to provide his daughter with "a solid education of the highest order" may have considered sending her to New York to study at the Rutgers Female Institute, located "in one of the most healthful, quiet, and moral neighborhoods in the city."

With fees and commissions, the manufacture of farm machinery, and the provision of everything else Southerners needed for a comfortable life — by some estimates the North took 40 cents of every dollar a planter earned from cotton.

So although Mayor Wood quickly backed away from his proposal that New York secede from the Union and join the Southern rebellion, it is little wonder that he and his party continued to talk sympathetically about the plight of the South and to condemn the "antislavery forces of the North."

As threatening as the regional differences over slavery were, the profits of the U.S. system of enforced servitude were hard for anyone at any level of government to dismiss. The truth is that slavery was a *national* phenomenon. The North shared in the wealth it created, and in the oppression it required.

Slavery has long been identified as a Southern institution. The time to bury that myth is overdue. Slavery is a story about the United States, all of the United States. The nation's wealth, from the very beginning, depended upon the exploitation of Black people. Together, over the lives of millions of enslaved men and women, wealthy white Northerners and Southerners shook hands and made a country.

Adapted from Anne Farrow, Joel Lang, and Jenifer Frank, Complicity: How the North Promoted, Prolonged, and Profited from Slavery *(New York: Ballantine Books, 2005).*

Anne Farrow *worked for New England newspapers for 30 years, and then helped build a website on Connecticut history. She lives in coastal Maine, where she volunteers in a soup kitchen and at a museum of maritime history.*

Joel Lang *worked at the* Hartford Courant *from 1968 to 2007. He now lives in Bridgeport, Connecticut, and writes occasionally about the arts.*

Jenifer Frank, *a Connecticut-based freelance writer, was a* Hartford Courant *editor for many years. She writes about health and inequity issues, and also tutors secondary school students in writing.*

The Election of 1860 Role Play

BY BILL BIGELOW

MOST OF MY STUDENTS share a cartoon-like version of the causes of the Civil War: Slavery was horrible; President Abraham Lincoln was a great man who hated slavery; so, to free the slaves, he fought a war against the South; the North won and the slaves were freed. This common but wildly inaccurate history reinforces at least two unfortunate myths: The United States fights wars only for high moral purposes; and African Americans owe their freedom to the efforts of a great white man. The activities in this lesson offer students a more complex and truthful historical picture of the social

forces that led to Lincoln's election and Southern secession, and thus help to puncture these myths.

Four political parties competed for the presidency in 1860. The outcome resulted in a social earthquake that permanently transformed the United States of America. This role play asks students to confront the actual issues addressed by the different parties in 1860. It gives students the tools to analyze some of the main causes of the Civil War, and helps them expel the simplistic notions of the war's aims that they may, perhaps unconsciously, carry around.

This 1860 campaign poster for the Lincoln/Hamlin ticket features planks in the Republican Party's platform.

Of course, to suggest that students are wrong to think that the Civil War was fought to end slavery does not mean that slavery was not the root cause of the Civil War. It was. The white planter class of the South pushed secession because planters felt that Lincoln's election threatened the preservation and extension of slavery. This role play will help students understand that. But it also helps them see the web of issues within which slavery was embedded.

Materials Needed

- Construction paper, crayons or colored markers, pins, scissors.

- Copies of "Election of 1860: Issues" (Handout 7–A) for every student.

- Copies of role play roles (Handout 7–B through 7–F), enough for every student to have one role.

- Copies of "Election of 1860: Ballot" (Handout 7–G) for every student.

Time Required

Two class periods. One to get into roles and meet other groups. Another to hear candidate speeches and debrief the role play.

Four political parties competed for the presidency in 1860. The outcome resulted in a social earthquake that permanently transformed the United States of America.

Suggested Procedure

1. The more background students have about the economic relations between different sections of the country the better. [See Lesson 6, "Mapping the Slave Economy."] Also useful, but not absolutely vital is knowledge about the Missouri Compromise, and its repeal in 1854; "Bloody Kansas"; the *Dred Scott* decision; John Brown's 1859 raid on the Harpers Ferry, Virginia, arsenal; and the historic dispossession of Native Americans from huge swaths of the United States that would be "homesteaded" and would become sites for the transcontinental railroad, both issues in the role play. On the board, list the four presidential candidates of 1860 and their political parties: Abraham Lincoln,

Republican; Stephen Douglas, Democrat (Northern); John Breckinridge, Democrat (Southern); and John Bell, Constitutional Union. Explain that for reasons that will become clear, the Democrats couldn't agree on one candidate in 1860 and the party split. Explain that the class will participate in a role play to understand the conflicting interests in that election, perhaps the most important in U.S. history, the results of which triggered events that led to the Civil War.

An historical note: In the election of 1860, there was also an abolitionist candidate Gerrit Smith, who ran on the Liberty Party ticket. Some abolitionists, particularly Black abolitionists, opted to support Smith. Ultimately, however, Smith received less than 0.01 percent of the popular vote and no electoral votes. For practical purposes, I limited the candidates to those receiving electoral votes.

And one more note: For the purposes of the role play, the Northern Workers, Northern Factory Owners and Merchants, and Western Farmers in the role play are all white, as the vast majority of voters in the 1860 election were white. However, prior to 1860 there were Black men who were voters in states like New York, Massachusetts, Ohio, and even in North Carolina.

2. Ask students to look at "Election of 1860: Issues" (Handout 7-A). Review each of the issues with students. It's vital that they understand the distinction between whether slavery should continue to be legal in states where it currently exists and whether slavery should

be legal in the territories. Each of their roles offers additional background on a number of the issues, and they'll be able to teach each other, but as you review these questions you should familiarize students with terms like homesteads and tariffs. There are a lot of issues included here, but in my experience, as they assume their respective roles, students quickly begin to see some of the implications of the various questions.

3. Divide students into five groups and assign each group a role. It's best if the Lincoln group includes people who are willing to assume leadership roles. The Lincolns will need to campaign among the different social groups and then give a speech outlining positions on the issues. Those students in "social" roles (i.e., farmers, manufacturers, planters, and workers) should begin by reading their roles and discussing and answering the questions posed in "Election of 1860: Issues." They may know very little about some of the issues. Assure them that later they will be able to meet with groups who may know more about these. Those in the Lincoln group should read the role and begin discussing campaign strategy, as indicated in the instructions following the description of Lincoln. [Obviously, this is not how it works in real life; a candidate doesn't campaign by circulating to different social groups trying to sniff out a winning coalition — although there is that dimension. You'll note from reading Lincoln's role that the only hard principle he begins with in the role play is opposition to slavery in the territories. The activity is not meant to portray Lincoln solely as a creature of political expediency, but aims to show students the electoral alliance he had to assemble in order to win the presidency.]

Distribute construction paper and markers to each group so that they can create placards indicating their social group. The Lincolns may want to make campaign buttons so that they will be easily recognizable when they travel among the other social groups.

4. As students discuss the issues, circulate to the different groups to answer their questions and raise points that students may not have considered. Make sure that students respond to the questions in ways that are consistent with their roles. There is, of course, some room for students to individualize their roles. A group needn't arrive at consensus on any particular issue, as later they'll be voting as individuals; nonetheless, they should do their best to try to reach agreement.

5. When you sense that each group has decided on tentative answers to the questions posed in "Election of 1860: Issues," explain the next step to them. Students should select half their group as traveling negotiators, while the rest stay seated at their table to meet with negotiators from other groups. All the Lincolns will be traveling campaigners. I tell my students something like the following: "During this session two things will happen at the same time. Those of you who are manufacturers, planters, workers, and farmers will be meeting with each other to discuss your agreements and disagreements on the various issues and to try to make alliances. Don't compromise on issues that you feel strongly about. But the more you're able to reach agreement with other groups, the more likely candidate Lincoln will need to pay attention. Second, the people in the Lincoln group will campaign by traveling to the different groups to listen to these groups' concerns, and also might offer ideas on the various issues. Because the Democrats have split in this election, there are four parties running. Lincoln has a pretty good chance of winning, so those of you in social groups want to convince Lincoln to support the issues that you feel most strongly about. Afterward, you'll hear speeches from Lincoln and all the candidates so you'll be able to decide who you want to cast your vote for." Does this sound complicated? Students rarely have a problem figuring out what to do once the session begins — especially if they've participated in similar role plays before.

6. Begin the campaign session. Tell students that travelers cannot talk to other travelers, only to those seated in groups. During this negotiation period I wander from group to group stirring the pot, playing devil's advocate, raising questions, and trying to discourage unrealistic alliances. But it's the students' show, and they listen to me or ignore me at their pleasure. Generally, I let the session run as long as the Lincolns want it to, so they can be sure of their stands on the various issues — perhaps 15 or 20 minutes.

7. After you've called a halt to the session, those in the Lincoln group will need to spend some time crafting their campaign speech. I invite my students-as-Lincoln to take their desks out in the hall to work. Encourage them to involve as many of their group in giving the speech as possible. The rest of the class does other work as the Lincolns prepare. I'll often ask the remaining students to write in character about what they hope or fear from the coming election or what their ideal candidate would stand for.

8. For what will likely be the next class session, seat students in rows facing a podium for the candidates' speeches. The order I use is Douglas, Lincoln, Bell, and Breckinridge. I give the speeches for the other three candidates in the election, unless I can rope in another teacher who has a prep period and is willing to play a John Bell or Stephen Douglas. Obviously, I don't read the actual campaign speeches delivered in 1860 as this would be tedious, but instead speak extemporaneously based on the candidates' positions. (In fact, in 1860, campaign speeches were not the tradition. Lincoln didn't give a single speech after his nomination, though Douglas broke with tradition and spoke widely.) Platforms for all four parties can be found in the 6th edition of *Documents of American History*, edited by Henry Steele Commager (Appleton-Century-Crofts, 1958: 363–66). In brief, here are the positions of the candidates on the issues students considered in the role play:

Douglas

1. **Slavery in the South.** Supported slavery where it existed.

2. **Slavery in the territories.** Douglas' platform reiterated agreement to support the Supreme Court's interpretation of the Constitution. Recently, the Supreme Court had been pro-slavery — in the *Dred Scott* decision, the court upheld an owner's right to take enslaved people wherever he wanted, and, in 1859, upheld the Fugitive Slave Law. Personally, Douglas believed the territories should be allowed to decide the question of slavery for themselves. Douglas' platform supported the acquisition of Cuba, then a Spanish colony with legal slavery. The platform also specifically supported the Fugitive Slave Law.

3. **Support for homesteads.** Douglas was in favor of homesteads, however the Democratic Party in recent years had successfully opposed them. Also Douglas' position of "popular sovereignty" raised doubt about whether homesteads would be granted solely to free farmers.

4. **Tariffs on manufactured goods.** Democrats in Congress had dramatically lowered tariffs in 1857. Douglas was not for increasing tariffs.

5. **Building of a transcontinental railroad.** The Democratic platform supported the construction of a railroad "between Atlantic and Pacific states."

Lincoln

1. **Slavery in the South.** Personally, Lincoln may have been opposed to slavery, but the Republican Party supported slavery in the states where it existed. The platform even went one step further and denounced "lawless invasion[s]" of slaveholding states, like those of John Brown, although without mentioning Brown by name.

2. **Slavery in the territories.** Lincoln and the Republican Party vehemently opposed the extension of slavery to the territories.

3. **Support for homesteads.** Strongly supported homesteads for free farmers.

4. **Tariffs on manufactured goods.** Lincoln had favored high tariffs as a congressman, and the Republicans played up support for tariffs in generally pro-tariff states like Pennsylvania and New Jersey. The Republican slogan in these states was "protection for American industry." Because the tariff was unpopular in farm states, Republicans sought to link the homesteads and tariffs with the slogan "Vote yourself a farm — vote yourself a tariff."

5. **Building of a transcontinental railroad.** The federal government should immediately aid in the construction of a railroad to the Pacific Ocean.

Bell

The platform of the Constitutional Union party was strictly concerned with preserving the Union. It had nothing to say about specific issues, such as slavery in the territories or tariffs. The party platform was brief, stating that adherents "*recognize* no political principle other than THE CONSTITUTION OF THE COUNTRY, THE UNION OF THE STATES, AND THE ENFORCEMENT OF THE LAWS. . ." [emphases in the original.]

Breckinridge

1. **Slavery in the South.** Breckinridge was from the slaveholding state of Kentucky, and was a supporter of slavery where it existed.

2. **Slavery in the territories.** According to the Democratic Party platform as amended by the Breckinridge faction in Richmond, Virginia, all slaveholders should be entitled to take their slaves into any territory. Further, Breckinridge Democrats held that the federal government should enact slave codes protecting the "rights" of slaveholders. Breckinridge also urged the annexation of Cuba, presumably to be divided in the future as slave states.

3. **Support for homesteads.** Southern Democrats had opposed homesteads in recent years.

4. **Tariffs on manufactured goods.** Did not support increasing tariffs.

5. **Building of a transcontinental railroad.** Supported the construction of a railroad from "the Mississippi River to the Pacific Ocean" — slightly, but significantly different wording from the Douglas Democrats who supported a railroad between "Atlantic and Pacific states."

9. I urge the students to take notes on the speeches as they will be voting for one of the candidates and, unlike in an actual election, they will need to offer detailed written reasons for their votes. After each speech, students (still in their roles) may pepper a candidate with questions or arguments. They have special fun with John Bell because of the Constitutional Union Party's silence on the specific issues students debated and built alliances on. When Linda Christensen and I taught together, Linda gave a wonderful Bell speech, waxing poetic about family values and the need to stay united at all costs.

10. After the speeches, I distribute ballots (Handout 7–G) to students that ask for name and social group, which candidate they are voting for and which candidates they are *not* voting for. The ballots provide space for students to say *why* they voted as they did. (Because Lincoln had the extra responsibility of writing and delivering a speech and because Lincoln is not "his" own social group, students in this group needn't complete this assignment. If you like, students in the Lincoln group might write predictions on who they think will win the election and offer thoughts on how much support each of the candidates will garner and from whom.)

11. We tally the ballots to see who won. Obviously, the deck is stacked in Lincoln's favor, although a couple of classes have elected a President Douglas in past years. Some of the issues and questions to raise in the post-role play discussion:

- Ask how the Southern planters feel about the outcome of the election. Remaining in character, what angers or frightens them about the election results? How might they respond?

- Why will a number of Southern states secede from (leave) the Union before Lincoln even takes office?

- How do other groups feel about the election results? How will they respond?

- Was "compromise" possible in the election of 1860? Was it even desirable?

- Using a map of the 1860 election results, ask students to review the regional strength of the four parties.

- How will Lincoln respond to the secession of Southern states? What arguments might Southern states have given to support their right to secede? What arguments might Lincoln and others have made denying a

---

Who benefited economically from the South and North belonging to the same country? Who didn't benefit?

---

state's right to leave the Union? What does the Constitution say about a state's obligation to remain in, or right to leave, the Union?

- Why should Lincoln care if the Southern states secede? Why not just say, "Good riddance," and get on with the business of running what's left of the United States?

- Part of the Republican Party platform for 1860 reads: "to the Union of the States this nation owes its unprecedented increase in population, its surprising development of material resources, its rapid augmentation of wealth. . ." In other words, the United States is prosperous — at least some people are — because the states belong to one country. How did the unity of North and South create prosperity? Who benefited economically from the South and North belonging to the same country? Who did not benefit?

- Describe to students the drama unfolding at Fort Sumter in South Carolina in the weeks after Lincoln takes office. Ask: If necessary, should Lincoln resupply the fort by force? From their point of view, should leaders of the new Confederacy attack and seize the fort?

- Which social groups would be willing to fight a war to keep the Union together? Why?

Election of 1860: Issues

Each group: You must come to a position on the following issues. Answer not from your personal beliefs, but based on how you think people in your social group would respond.

1. Should slavery be allowed in the Southern states where it currently exists? Why or why not?

2. Should slavery be allowed in the Western territories? Why or why not?

3. Should the U.S. government begin giving "homesteads" to people who are willing to work the land themselves? Why or why not?

4. Should tariffs on imported goods be increased? Why or why not?

5. Should the United States government use tax money to support the building of railroads across the country?

6. List the issues that your group feels most strongly about.

Abraham Lincoln

YOU ARE THE REPUBLICAN candidate for president of the United States in 1860. Most of your life you've been a politician. In fact, you were only 23 years old when you first ran for office. The only time you weren't in politics was a few years back when, because your party was too weak, you left political life to work as a lawyer. Your friends say that you are very ambitious and that what you want most in the world is to be president.

It's never easy to run for president, but these days it is especially difficult with the country deeply divided. Historically, you have been politically cautious and have not taken unpopular stands on issues. For example, in private you tell people how much you dislike slavery. But publicly, you have never said that slavery should be abolished where it currently exists. In fact, in public you never even spoke out against the Fugitive Slave Law, which required Northerners in free states to help capture people who escaped from slavery. In private, you wrote: "I confess I hate to see the poor creatures hunted down . . . but I bite my lips and keep quiet." You are no abolitionist and have strongly condemned those abolitionists, like John Brown, who broke the law and used violence in their efforts to stop slavery. However, you have always said that slavery should not be spread to any new states or territories.

You believe that what makes this a great country is the opportunity it provides its free citizens. If you work hard, you can rise and succeed. Look at you: Your parents were not rich and now you may become president.

Right now, what you want most is to be elected. That will require you to convince people who have very different interests and ideas to compromise and to see that your positions are the best. You will be able to please some of the people on some of the issues, but not all the people on all the issues. Good luck.

In the "Campaign" period, you will meet with as many of the groups as you can. Listen to their concerns and test out some of your positions. They will also be talking to each other to try to build alliances so that they can urge you to adopt their positions on various issues. Hint: In order to win, you will probably need a majority of at least three of the four groups.

1. Read over the questions included in "Election of 1860: Issues." Come up with tentative positions on each of these issues. Don't feel that you need to be sure at this stage. Remember that you'll be meeting with each group and will be able to change positions afterward.

2. Decide among yourselves which of you will campaign with which groups. There are four other groups: Northern workers, Western farmers, Southern planters, and Northern manufacturers.

3. Decide what questions you will ask the different social groups in the upcoming campaign session.

Western Farmers

YOU LIVE IN WESTERN and Midwestern states and territories — places like Illinois, Ohio, Nebraska, and Kansas. Your family owns a farm and you work it yourselves. You are white, but you don't own other human beings as slaves, like the plantation owners in the South. Some of you were born in the United States, but many of you come from other countries like Germany and Great Britain.

Like farmers everywhere, you want the best land you can get. Those of you in states like Ohio and Illinois think about moving someday to Western territories like Kansas and Nebraska where there is plentiful, rich land and good amounts of rainfall. For all of you, perhaps your biggest worry is that Southerners will move into the territories and bring their slaves with them. You hate slavery. Not because you believe that all people are created equal, but because slave labor would cheapen *your* labor. Any crop grown by slaves can be sold more cheaply. How can you compete against people who work for free? Let the slave owners keep their slaves in the South where they've always been. But every year, these white plantation owners get bolder. In 1854 Congress repealed the Missouri Compromise that outlawed slavery in Kansas and Nebraska. In the 1857 *Dred Scott* decision, the Supreme Court ruled that a slave owner can take slaves wherever he wants, and Congress can't say anything about it. You want these slave owners to keep away from free farmers like you.

For a long time, there has been talk of the government giving good land in the West to farmers who will work it themselves. Congress passed a "homestead" act recently, but President Buchanan, a Democrat, vetoed it. Maybe you'd move and maybe you wouldn't, but you sure would like the choice. Perhaps you could sell your farm for a profit and move farther west onto better land.

Another concern of yours these days is transportation. Travel is slow. There's no way to get way out west to California or Oregon except by wagon. And if you move farther west, how would you get manufactured goods like guns, stoves, and tools from the east? And you'd need some quick and safe way to get your products to market in the east.

Northern Factory Owners and Merchants

YOU ARE A POWERFUL CLASS growing more powerful. You manufacture and sell products like cotton cloth and machinery. You depend on a government that will not interfere with your right to make profits. However, this isn't to say you want a "do-nothing" government. Not at all. You have a number of concerns that require a strong and sympathetic government. You are still worried about products from other countries, especially from Great Britain and her colonies, being sold here more cheaply than your products. To make sure that people buy from you, you want the government to tax imported goods from other countries. These import taxes are called tariffs. For example, as recently as the early 1840s, cotton cloth made in the United States sold for just under 7 cents a yard. The tariff for foreign cloth was 7 and a half cents — more than 100 percent! This was great because it made foreign cloth more expensive than your cloth so people bought your products. Of course, *some* people support low tariffs because with low tariffs goods are cheaper to buy. In 1857, Congress lowered the tariff to 24 percent. This hurt your industry and, in fact, you think this contributed to the terrible depression of 1857, which still hurts business.

To keep growing, you need more and more places to sell your products. Transportation is a problem. If there were more railroads to the Western states and territories you'd be able to sell a great deal more than you do now. You could get cheap food and whiskey from the Western regions, and could sell them cloth, guns, tools, stoves, and the like. You'd also be able to invest in the railroads and make even more money.

Here's a problem: Many workers and farmers want the government to allow them to "homestead" (farm on free land) in the Western territories. You worry about your workers leaving to become farmers. Then who'd do all the work? As it is, because of labor shortages, you pay between a third and a half more in wages than do factory owners in Great Britain. Cheaper labor gives them an unfair advantage. The only thing that helps out the labor shortage here is the steady supply of immigrants coming to the United States from Europe. The more workers available, the lower the wages you have to pay. You don't like homesteads — and you want a president who opposes homesteads — but you might be willing to put up with a homestead law if you could get the president and Congress to support higher tariffs on foreign goods.

Your major political rivals are the Southern slave owners, almost all of whom are Democrats. Just about everything you support, they oppose. You need the cheap cotton, grown with slave labor, that they send north and you need them to buy your products. But you don't need them to get any stronger in Congress. Frankly, you benefit from slavery in the South, but you don't need it to spread. Because that would increase the power of your biggest rivals: the Southern plantation owners.

Southern Plantation Owners

IT SEEMS THAT EVERYONE who is not a Southerner wants to destroy your way of life. Just last year, that lunatic criminal John Brown tried to start a slave uprising in Virginia. It failed miserably. But you know there are lots more crazy abolitionists where he came from. Brown even got financial support from church people in the North.

The coming election of 1860 is perhaps the most important election in the short history of this country. Here is your situation. As you know, your livelihood depends on growing crops like tobacco, rice, sugar, and especially cotton. A plantation requires a great deal of labor — slave labor. Above all, you want the South to remain open to slavery. However, you believe that in a free country you should also have the right to bring your slaves to wherever you choose to live. Fortunately, the Supreme Court seems to agree with you. In the 1857 *Dred Scott* decision, the court decided that if a slave were taken to a "free" state, it didn't mean the slave got his freedom. To you, the logical conclusion is that you should be able to own land in Western territories like Kansas and Nebraska and bring your slaves to work that land. However, there are many in the North and West who want to outlaw slavery in the territories — in direct violation of the Constitution. These people must be defeated at all costs. (For that matter, many in the South would like to take over Cuba and Nicaragua to open up more territory for the expansion of slavery. To them you have one thing to say: Good.)

To make matters worse, many in the North and West propose to give "free" farmers homesteads in the territories — excellent land they can move onto. Nobody says anything about giving *you* free land and allowing you to bring your slaves. Why not? Because they are afraid that they won't be able to compete. So they demand unfair government protection. As long as homesteads go only to "free" farmers, then you oppose them. They are just an unfair giveaway.

The rich owners in the North are happy to take your cheap cotton grown with slave labor, but their representatives in Congress have always voted for high tariffs — a tax on imports — so that they don't have to compete with cheaper goods from Great Britain and her colonies. They make cotton shirts for less in India, but they cost more here because of the tariffs. In 1857, Congress lowered the tariffs to 24 percent. At one point they'd been more than 100 percent. You want to keep them low — even lower than 24 percent.

The government also wants to take your tax money and give it to people who will build a railroad across the Northern United States, all the way to California. This will cost tens of millions of dollars. The railroad might help Northerners sell cloth and iron tools in Kansas and California. But you have good rivers in the South. A Northern railroad won't help you, although you would support a railroad from the Mississippi River to the Pacific.

Northern Workers

YOU WORK IN A FACTORY that produces cloth from cotton. As you know, the United States is becoming more "industrialized." Factories are springing up everywhere. Recently you read that in just the last 20 years, the value of manufactured goods produced by workers like you quadrupled. You are white. Many of you are native-born, and some of you left your farms for work in the cities. Others of you are from different countries, especially Ireland. Currently, you face a number of problems.

In 1857 a major depression hit the country and, at least temporarily, some of you lost your jobs. This taught you that even though more and more things are produced by machines in factories, you don't have a guaranteed job. The factory owners try to convince you that the depression was caused by the Democrats in Congress who lowered the tariffs on imported manufactured goods in 1857. The owners say that because foreign owners can find cheaper workers, the United States needs high tariffs — which make foreign goods more expensive. Otherwise, American products can't compete. Or so they say. The owners say that we should elect politicians who support high tariffs to protect American industries and American jobs.

Because of your job insecurity, and because factory jobs aren't so great, many of you dream of owning your own farm out west. It would be expensive to pull up and move, but there is one proposal that would make it a lot cheaper. Some politicians support the idea of giving "homesteads" — free land out west — to people who will work a plot of land with their families. This would be great. However, some people think that slave owners should be able to take advantage of the homesteads and bring in their slaves to work the land. With free workers, these Southerners could sell their crops for almost nothing. How could you and other *free* farmers compete with that?

Something else that would make it easier to move west is if there were railroads to take you there. You might want to go all the way to California or Oregon. But to do that now, it takes months of difficult and dangerous travel by wagon. For years, politicians have talked about building a railroad across the entire country, but so far they haven't done anything about it. The owners support railroads because they say they'll sell more products and that will make your jobs more secure. Of course, the owners say lots of things.

Election of 1860: Ballot

Your Name: _____   Your Social Group: _____

Candidate You Are Voting For: _____

Reasons Why: _____
_____
_____
_____
_____
_____

Candidate You Are **Not** Voting For: _____

Reasons Why Not: _____
_____
_____
_____
_____
_____

Candidate You Are **Not** Voting For: _____

Reasons Why Not: _____
_____
_____
_____
_____
_____

Candidate You Are **Not** Voting For: _____

Reasons Why Not: _____
_____
_____
_____
_____

A War to Free the Slaves?

BY BILL BIGELOW

FEW DOCUMENTS IN U.S. HISTORY share the hallowed reputation of the Emancipation Proclamation. Many, perhaps most, of my students have heard of it. They know — at least vaguely — that it pronounced freedom for enslaved African Americans, and earned President Abraham Lincoln the title of Great Emancipator. They know what it says, but no one has read it. Every U.S. history textbook mentions it, but I've never seen a single textbook that actually includes its full text.

Here, students examine excerpts from Lincoln's first inaugural address, the rarely mentioned original 13th Amendment to the Constitution that Lincoln promised to support, and the Emancipation Proclamation. This lesson asks students to think about what these documents reveal about Lincoln's war aims. Was it a "war to free the slaves"? Lincoln never said it was. Most textbooks don't even say it was. And yet the myth persists: It was the "war to free the slaves."

A group of African American Union soldiers and their white officer in a portrait sketched in 1862.

Bettmann/CORBIS

This lesson's intent is important but narrow. Although Lincoln did not begin his presidency with the intent to abolish slavery, that doesn't mean that the Confederacy did not secede with the intent to maintain slavery. And, of course, the seceding states *did* believe that it was Lincoln's intention to end slavery. As South Carolina delegates wrote in their "Declaration of the Immediate Causes Which Induce and Justify the Secession of South Carolina from the Federal Union," "A geographical line has been drawn across the Union, and all the States north of that line have united in the election of a man to the high office of President of the United States, whose opinions and purposes are hostile to slavery."

This lesson introduces students to documents that puncture the myth that Lincoln waged the war to "free the slaves." It concludes by asking them to reflect on why Lincoln and the Republicans would wage war, if it was not to end slavery.

One caveat: As Eric Foner demonstrates well in his book *The Fiery Trial: Abraham Lincoln and American Slavery*, Lincoln's views shifted as the war progressed. Were you to want to expand this lesson, you might read with students Lincoln's full second inaugural address (much shorter than the first), delivered while the war was still on. By March of 1865, Lincoln was not promising slaveholders that they could keep their slaves, as he did in 1861; nor is he the careful author of the 1863 Emancipation Proclamation, which indicates county by county where slavery is not to be abolished. By 1865, Lincoln strikes a weary but unambiguously antislavery stance: "Fondly do we hope, fervently do we pray, that this mighty scourge of war may speedily pass away. Yet, if God wills that it continue until all the wealth piled by the bondsman's 250 years of unrequited toil shall be sunk, and until every drop of blood drawn with the lash shall be paid by another drawn with the sword, as was said 3,000 years ago, so still it must be said 'the judgments of the Lord are true and righteous altogether.'" Attitudes of many whites, including Abraham Lincoln, about slavery shifted dramatically during the war. This transformation is not the subject of this lesson, but is important.

Materials Needed

- Copies of Handout 8–A (which includes excerpts from Lincoln's first inaugural address; on the reverse side, the original 13th Amendment and reading questions) for every student.

- Copies of the "Emancipation Proclamation" (Handout 8–B) for every student.

Time Required

One class period.

Suggested Procedure:

1. Ask students: If you were to go up to most people on the street and ask them, "Why did Lincoln and the North fight the Civil War?" what do you think they'd say? Some students will respond that people would just say, "I don't know." But, in my experience, most students will say that people would tell them that the North was in the Civil War to "free the slaves." Write this on the board: LINCOLN AND THE NORTH FOUGHT THE CIVIL WAR TO FREE THE SLAVES. Tell students that by analyzing some key documents, you want to test out this statement, and with them, propose some other possible explanations for the war. We're speaking here of real, underlying reasons for the war, not why particular individuals fought. As we know, many individuals did fight to free the slaves; indeed, that was the only reason some people fought. Like many teachers, I use the film *Glory* to explore the role of Black soldiers, some of them formerly enslaved, in making it a "war to free the slaves." But this activity, focusing on Lincoln's 1861 inaugural address and the Emancipation Proclamation, highlights official U.S. government aims, not the aims of the abolition movement or of particular individuals.

[The above instruction probably deserves an asterisk. My 30 years of teaching high school history was spent in Oregon. This lesson is based on addressing the myths that I found my students had absorbed about the causes of the Civil War — at least about the war aims of Lincoln and the North. If one were to ask this question in a more open-ended manner — for example, "Why was the Civil War fought?" — "states' rights" would be a frequent student answer, as it would be were we to ask "Why did Southern states secede and fight in the Civil War?" It would be a different lesson, but depending on where you teach, and the particular myths you feel are the most important to examine, rewording this question so that it asks about the war's aims from the standpoint of the Confederate states might be a provocative opening to a lesson examining secession documents. As the South Carolina quote above indicates, "states' rights" is as historically inaccurate a myth as "to free the slaves." The virulent Southern support for the 1850 Fugitive Slave Act, which was a frontal attack on "states' rights," is another piece of evidence that punctures this myth.]

2. Next, ask students: If you were to ask "*Who freed the slaves?*" what would most people answer?" Again, there might be a few outliers, but the general answer students will give is Lincoln. Now ask students, "Given that most people believe that Abraham Lincoln was the Great Emancipator, what would you expect to find in his first speech as president?" In my experience, students have many ideas about what Lincoln might say, but almost always the comments center around slavery being an immoral, unjust evil that must be stopped. List students' ideas on the board.

3. Ask students to read "From Lincoln's First Inaugural Address" (Handout 8-A). Depending on the skill level of the group, and how easily frustrated they become, ask them to pair up and answer the questions following the reading.

4. Some further questions for discussion:

    •   Why does Lincoln say that the Southern states shouldn't worry about the Republicans endangering slavery?

    •   What reasons does Lincoln offer for why he will not interfere with slavery?

    •   What laws might Lincoln be referring to when he says that he will enforce the laws and offer protection "as cheerfully to one section as to another. . ."?

    •   What does Lincoln promise the leaders of slaveholding states in the second excerpt?

    •   If Lincoln was against slavery, why would he promise to make the protection of slavery "irrevocable" — permanent? In what sense was Lincoln against slavery?

    •   How might U.S. history have turned out differently had the Southern states accepted Lincoln's offer to support the original 13th Amendment to the U.S. Constitution, guaranteeing slavery forever, and returned to the Union?

"Abe's Proclamation," an 1865 engraving by J. L. Magee, casts Lincoln as the liberator of both Black and white Americans through the Emancipation Proclamation and his leadership in the Civil War.

5. Return to the list students generated about what they thought Lincoln would say in his inaugural speech. Ideas on this often stand in sharp contrast to Lincoln's actual remarks. Ask students to consider: Why is there such a difference between the popular image of Lincoln, and the Lincoln of 1861?

6. Ask students to turn to the "Emancipation Proclamation" (Handout 8–B). With students, define the document's title word by word. Collect their knowledge: What have they heard about the Emancipation Proclamation? Have they ever read it? Who told them about it? Again, ask students to pair up or to form small groups to read and analyze the document together. Ask them to look for "Who did the Emancipation Proclamation emancipate? Who did it not emancipate?" Some additional discussion questions:

   • The Emancipation Proclamation was issued more than three months (Sept. 22, 1862) from the date it was to take effect (Jan. 1, 1863). What was the significance of the proclamation not taking effect immediately?

   • Based on how the document is worded, could someone who owned slaves in, say, Alabama keep his slaves, if sometime in December 1862 Alabama had rejoined the Union?

   • Why doesn't the Emancipation Proclamation simply declare immediate freedom for all people enslaved anywhere in the United States?

   • Why does Lincoln say he is issuing this proclamation? [Notice that in only two places does he offer any explanation. He writes that it is an action required because of "actual armed rebellion against the authority and government of the United States, and as a fit and necessary war measure for suppressing said rebellion. . ." Later in the document he says that he issues the proclamation "upon military necessity." He offers no critique of slavery here.]

   • What advice does Lincoln offer to the people who may eventually be freed by the proclamation?

   • Lincoln says that the Emancipation Proclamation is a war measure, but he doesn't urge people freed from slavery to stop working on Southern plantations or to attack the Confederacy and their former masters. Why not?

   • In the document, President Lincoln lists numerous counties and Louisiana parishes. Why? What's so special about these places?

   • One written criticism of the Emancipation Proclamation, from the Democrat-controlled Illinois Legislature, warned that "The proclamation invites servile insurrection. . ." — slave revolts. Do you agree?

   • Even though Lincoln's Emancipation Proclamation holds out the promise that slavery may be maintained in many regions of the United States, how might African Americans, both free and enslaved, have worked to make the Civil War into an antislavery crusade?

7. Finally, ask students to suggest some alternative theories for why Lincoln and the Republicans in power (and many Democrats) were willing to wage war to keep the Union together. List these on the board. Ask students how one might test these theories. If students don't suggest it themselves, I offer one theory: that powerful interests in the North were desperate to maintain the Union because they benefited materially from the raw materials, especially cotton, grown by cheap (enslaved) workers in the South; and benefited from the Southern markets for Northern manufactured goods. You might ask students to make columns of different theories and in the columns to list evidence that supports or refutes the theories.

From Lincoln's First Inaugural Address

March 4, 1861

Excerpt #1

Apprehension seems to exist among the people of the Southern States that by the accession of a Republican administration their property and their peace and personal security are to be endangered. There has never been any reasonable cause for such apprehension. Indeed, the most ample evidence to the contrary has all the while existed and been open to their inspection. It is found in nearly all the published speeches of him who now addresses you. I do but quote from one of those speeches when I declare that "I have no purpose, directly or indirectly, to interfere with the institution of slavery in the States where it exists. I believe I have no lawful right to do so, and I have no inclination to do so." . . .

I now reiterate these sentiments; and, in doing so, I only press upon the public attention the most conclusive evidence of which the case is susceptible, that the property, peace, and security of no section are to be in any wise endangered by the now incoming administration. I add, too, that all the protection which, consistently with the Constitution and the laws, can be given, will be cheerfully given to all the States when lawfully demanded, for whatever cause — as cheerfully to one section as to another.

Excerpt #2

I understand a proposed amendment to the constitution — which amendment, however, I have not seen — has passed Congress, to the effect that the Federal Government shall never interfere with the domestic institutions of the States, including that of persons held to service. To avoid misconstruction of what I have said, I depart from my purpose not to speak of particular amendments so far as to say that, holding such a provision to now be implied constitutional law, I have no objection to its being made express and irrevocable.

From Commager, Henry Steele, ed. *Documents of American History*, Sixth Edition (New York: Appleton-Century-Crofts, 1958): 385, 388.

Original Proposed 13th Amendment to the Constitution

No AMENDMENT shall be made to the Constitution which will authorize or give to Congress the power to abolish or interfere, within any State, with the domestic institutions thereof, including that of persons held to labor or service by the laws of said State.

Questions:

1. In your own words, summarize what Lincoln is saying in these two excerpts from his first inaugural address. What is he promising?

2. Which part or parts of the country do you think Lincoln is mainly speaking to in these excerpts?

3. Put the original 13th Amendment in your own words.

4. By the time Abraham Lincoln gave this inaugural address in March 1861, seven states had already seceded from the Union. Why do you think these Southern states did not accept his offer and return to the Union?

Emancipation Proclamation

Jan. 1, 1863

A PROCLAMATION

Whereas on the 22nd day of September, A.D. 1862, a proclamation was issued by the President of the United States, containing, among other things, the following, to wit:

"That on the 1st day of January, A.D. 1863, all persons held as slaves within any State or designated part of a State the people whereof shall then be in rebellion against the United States shall be then, thenceforward, and forever free; and the executive government of the United States, including the military and naval authority thereof, will recognize and maintain the freedom of such persons and will do no act or acts to repress such persons, or any of them, in any efforts they may make for their actual freedom.

"That the executive will on the 1st day of January aforesaid, by proclamation, designate the States and parts of States, if any, in which the people thereof, respectively, shall then be in rebellion against the United States; and the fact that any State or the people thereof shall on that day be in good faith represented in the Congress of the United States by members chosen thereto at elections wherein a majority of the qualified voters of such States shall have participated, shall, in the absence of strong countervailing testimony, be deemed conclusive evidence that such State and the people thereof are not then in rebellion against the United States."

Now, therefore, I, Abraham Lincoln, President of the United States, by virtue of the power in me vested as Commander-In-Chief of the Army and Navy of the United States in time of actual armed rebellion against the authority and government of the United States, and as a fit and necessary war measure for suppressing said rebellion, do, on this 1st day of January, A.D. 1863, and in accordance with my purpose so to do, publicly proclaimed for the full period of one hundred days from the first day above mentioned, order and designate as the States and parts of States wherein the people thereof, respectively, are this day in rebellion against the United States the following, to wit:

Arkansas, Texas, Louisiana (except the parishes of St. Bernard, Plaquemines, Jefferson, St. John, St. Charles, St. James, Ascension, Assumption, Terrebonne, Lafourche, St. Mary, St. Martin, and Orleans, including the city of New Orleans), Mississippi, Alabama, Florida, Georgia, South Carolina, North Carolina, and Virginia (except the forty-eight counties designated as West Virginia, and also the counties of Berkeley, Accomac, Northhampton, Elizabeth City, York, Princess Anne, and Norfolk, including the cities of Norfolk and Portsmouth), and which excepted parts are for the present left precisely as if this proclamation were not issued.

And by virtue of the power and for the purpose aforesaid, I do order and declare that all persons held as slaves within said designated States and parts of States are, and henceforward shall be, free; and that the Executive Government of the United States, including the military and naval authorities thereof, will recognize and maintain the freedom of said persons.

And I hereby enjoin upon the people so declared to be free to abstain from all violence, unless in necessary self-defense; and I recommend to them that, in all case when allowed, they labor faithfully for reasonable wages.

And I further declare and make known that such persons of suitable condition will be received into the armed service of the United States to garrison forts, positions, stations, and other places, and to man vessels of all sorts in said service.

And upon this act, sincerely believed to be an act of justice, warranted by the Constitution upon military necessity, I invoke the considerate judgment of mankind and the gracious favor of Almighty God.

In witness whereof, I have hereunto set my hand and caused the seal of the United States to be affixed.

Done at the City of Washington, this first day of January, in the year of our Lord one thousand eight hundred and sixty-three, and of the Independence of the United States of America the eighty-seventh.

By the President: ABRAHAM LINCOLN

WILLIAM H. SEWARD, Secretary of State.

LESSON 9

"Who Freed the Slaves?" Civil War Jigsaw

By Adam Sanchez

PROBABLY THE MOST crucial period to examine in order to answer "who freed the slaves?" is the Civil War. As students have learned from previous lessons, although for the South the war was clearly about maintaining and expanding slavery, for Lincoln, at least initially, it was a war to preserve the union, not to end slavery. As we saw in Lesson 8, in his first inaugural address, Lincoln promised the South he would not interfere with slavery where it existed and offered to support a constitutional amendment that would have forbidden the federal government from ever doing so.

But nearly two and a half years into the war, the North was losing and Lincoln changed course. He issued the Emancipation Proclamation, freeing enslaved people in the states "under rebellion." By his second inaugural address, Lincoln had completely changed his position, arguing that it was God's will that "all the wealth piled by the bondsman's 250 years of unrequited toil shall be sunk," and adding that "every drop of blood drawn with

Black soldiers played a crucial role in transforming the Civil War.

Collection of the Gettysburg National Military Park Museum

the lash shall be paid by another drawn with the sword." In fact, Lincoln spent his last days trying to ensure the passage of the 13th Amendment to guarantee that emancipation would outlast his administration. And while never embracing full equality, in a letter to the Louisiana governor in 1864 Lincoln suggested that "some of the colored people . . . for instance, the very intelligent, and especially those who have fought gallantly in our ranks" should be given the right to vote. So, what pushed Lincoln to make the end of slavery a key goal of the Civil War and eventually move toward Black suffrage?

For one, the abolitionists continued agitating — with a growing audience in the North — making the argument that the war could only be won if the abolition of slavery was its objective. Enslaved people freed themselves as soon as Lincoln's army came near, creating a political crisis about their status behind the Union Army lines. After the Emancipation Proclamation opened the Union Army to them, Blacks, many formerly enslaved, increasingly joined the front lines. As Howard Zinn wrote, "The more Blacks entered the war, the more it appeared a war for their liberation." It became particularly difficult to deny Black soldiers basic rights of citizenship after they played such a key role in the Union victory.

Through a series of short readings, this jigsaw activity helps students engage with the various historical actors who transformed the Civil War into a war of liberation. In particular, this activity can help students gather evidence from a variety of secondary sources for an essay on "Who freed the slaves?"

Materials Needed

- "Civil War Jigsaw Worksheet"; on the reverse side, "Civil War Jigsaw: Teach Out" (Handout 9–A), enough for every student in the class.

- Readings: "Enslaved People and the Civil War" (Handout 9–B), "Abolitionists and the Civil War" (Handout 9–C), "Black Soldiers and the Civil War" (Handout 9–D), and "Lincoln and the Civil War," View One and Two (Handout 9–E) — enough for each student to have one of the readings.

Time Required

One or two class periods.

Suggested Procedure

1. Divide students into expert groups. Give each student the Civil War Jigsaw Worksheet and each group one of the readings: "Enslaved People and the Civil War" (Handout 9–B), "Abolitionists and the Civil War" (Handout 9–C), "Black Soldiers and the Civil War" (Handout 9–D), and "Lincoln and the Civil War," View One and Two (Handout 9–E). [Note: "Lincoln and the Civil War" contains two different readings with different opinions about Lincoln's role. The two readings on Lincoln are slightly over half the length of the other readings in the jigsaw. Depending on the reading level of your students, you may want to assign both views on Lincoln to one expert group of strong readers, or you might assign each shorter view on Lincoln to different groups of emerging/less proficient readers.]

2. Explain that students will be participating in an activity examining the Civil War from

multiple perspectives. The Civil War led to the passage of the 13th Amendment and the emancipation of enslaved people in the United States, but historians still debate the question of "who freed the slaves?" Each group will get a short reading on which to become an expert. Each reading in some way argues a position on "who freed the slaves." One reading explains abolitionist efforts to make liberation the primary purpose of the war, another discusses the role of Black soldiers, another looks at the actions of enslaved people during the war, and the final readings give two opposing views on Lincoln's efforts.

3. Explain how each group will become an expert on their reading — by reading it out loud at least once and deciding together: 1) what the author's main arguments are; and 2) the most important passages that support the author's arguments. They should record their answers on "Civil War Jigsaw Worksheet" (Handout 9–A). Make sure students know that all students in the group should be able to explain their portion of the worksheet to others. If time permits, it's helpful to have students in these expert groups rehearse the presentation that they will give to others. If you choose to give both Lincoln readings to one group, have them record two main arguments and one piece of evidence from each reading.

4. When all of the expert groups seem finished, have students within each group number off and move their desks into "jigsaw" groups. Each group should have at least one student who read "Enslaved People and the Civil War," one who read "Abolitionists and the Civil War," one who read "Black Soldiers and the Civil

War," and one who read "Lincoln and the Civil War" (View One and Two). If there is an odd number of students, there may be a few larger groups. Note: Depending on how mobile your classroom furniture is, it can be helpful to start in these groups at the beginning of the lesson so students have a clear understanding that they will be responsible for explaining their reading to their jigsaw group.

5. Explain that each student should present the article they read to the others in their group. While they are presenting, the other students should write the information on the back of "Civil War Jigsaw: Teach Out" (Handout 9-A).

6. After the activity, it is helpful to debrief as a whole class. Here are a few questions you might use to debrief the activity:

   - You read arguments about the role four groups played in ending slavery: enslaved people, abolitionists, Black soldiers, and the Lincoln administration. If you had to pick one of these groups most responsible for ending slavery, which group would it be? Why?

   - Do you think any of these groups deserve no credit at all? Why?

   - What arguments from the readings did you find most convincing? Why?

   - Was there anything in the readings that you found new or surprising?

   - Given that most people would answer the question "Who freed the slaves?" by saying Abraham Lincoln, why do you think they leave out some of the groups you read about?

   - In thinking about the group or groups most responsible for ending slavery, does it matter which groups were first to oppose slavery and which opposed slavery later?

   - What power did each of these different groups have that others did not? Does power matter?

   - How much credit should Lincoln get for freeing the slaves? What evidence would you use from the readings to support this?

   - Do you agree more with James McPherson's or Lerone Bennett Jr.'s view on Lincoln? Why?

   - Slavery is over. Does it matter who we credit with ending slavery? Why?

   - What questions are you left with?

Civil War Jigsaw Worksheet

Reading: _____

Author: _____

What are the main arguments the author is making? (Try to provide 2–4 reasons the author gives to back up their argument.)	Find at least two quotes from the reading that you might use to argue who freed the slaves.	Analyze the quotes you chose. What does it say about who freed the slaves?
• • • •		

Civil War Jigsaw: Teach Out

Directions: As you listen to your groupmates share out about their readings answer the questions below.

Enslaved People and the Civil War
Adapted from *There Is a River: The Black Struggle for Freedom in America* by Vincent Harding

1. What are two pieces of evidence to show that formerly enslaved people freed themselves?

Abolitionists and the Civil War
Adapted from "Architects of Their Own Liberation: African Americans, Emancipation, and the Civil War" by Manisha Sinha

2. What are two pieces of evidence that you could use to show that the abolitionists helped to transform the purpose of the war?

Black Soldiers and the Civil War
Adapted from *Black Reconstruction in America* by W. E. B. Du Bois

3. In what ways did Black soldiers help the North win the war? Why is this important in answering "who freed the slaves?"

Lincoln and the Civil War (View One)
Adapted from "Who Freed the Slaves?" by James M. McPherson

4. What is one piece of evidence you might use to argue that Lincoln was responsible for freeing the slaves?

Lincoln and the Civil War (View Two)
Adapted from "Was Abe Lincoln a White Supremacist?" by Lerone Bennett Jr.

5. What is the most important piece of evidence you might use to argue Lincoln did not free the slaves?

Enslaved People and the Civil War

IN MANY PARTS OF THE NATION and the world there had been predictions that the Civil War would lead to a massive Black insurrection and drown the South in blood. Yet most enslaved people realized that this path to freedom would surely unite the white North and the South more quickly than any other single development, making Black men, women, and children the enemy. Therefore, instead of mass insurrection, the Civil War created the context for self-emancipation through steadily increasing the number of runaways.

As the guns sounded across the South, the movement of Black folk out of slavery began to build. One day in Virginia in the spring of 1861, a Black runaway appeared at the Union-held Fortress Monroe. Two days later eight more arrived, the next day more than 50, soon hundreds. The word spread throughout the area: There was a "freedom fort," and within a short time thousands were flooding toward it.

Similarly, in Louisiana two families traveled six miles across a swamp, "spending two days and nights in mud and water to their waists, their children clinging to their backs, and with nothing to eat." In Georgia, a woman with her 22 children and grandchildren floated down the river on a flatboat until she made contact with Union armies. In South Carolina, Black folk floated to freedom on "basket boats made out of reeds." As W. E. B. Du Bois said of the Black surge toward freedom in those first two years of the war, "Many thousands of Blacks of all ages, ragged, with no possessions, except the bundles which they carried, had assembled at Norfolk, Hampton, Alexandria, and Washington. Others . . . in multitudes . . . flocked north from Tennessee, Kentucky, Arkansas, and Missouri."

This was the Black struggle in the South as the guns roared, coming out of loyal and disloyal states, creating their own liberty. This was the Black movement toward a new history, a new life, a new beginning. Every day they came into the Northern lines, in every condition, in every season of the year, in every state of health. Children came wandering, set in the right direction by dying parents. Women came, stumbling and screaming, their wombs bursting with the promise of new and free Black life. Old folks who had lost track of their age, also came, some blind, some deaf, yet no less eager to taste a bit of that long-anticipated freedom. No more auction block, no more driver's lash. This was the river of Black struggle in the South, waiting for no one to declare freedom for them.

As a *New York Times* correspondent stated in February 1862: "Everywhere I find the same state of things existing; everywhere the Blacks hurry in droves to our lines; they crowd in small boats around our ships; they swarm upon our decks; they hurry to our officers from the cotton houses of their masters, in an hour or two after our guns are fired." When they heard the guns, they were ready, grasping freedom with their own hands, walking to it, swimming to it, sailing to it — determined that it should be theirs. By all these ways defying masters, patrols, Confederate soldiers, slowly, surely, they pressed themselves into the central reality of the war.

The rapid flow of Black runaways was a critical part of the challenge to the embattled white rulers of the South; by leaving, they denied slavery's power and its profit. But much of their movement out of slavery carried them into the camps of the Union troops, bringing them harshly against the reality of the white North. The Black community soon discovered the cruelties and racism of the Union camps, yet another set of obstacles to their freedom. In many places the runaways were mistreated, abused, or chased away by Union soldiers. In some cases, soldiers returned runaways to their owners. Still, the Black flood did not slow. By the end of the spring of 1862, tens of thousands were camped out in whatever areas the Northern armies had occupied, thereby making themselves an unavoidable military and political issue.

In Washington, D.C., Lincoln had developed no serious plan for channeling the Black river. Instead, he was still trapped in his own obsession with saving the white Union — maintaining his allies in the "loyal" slave states of Delaware, Maryland, Kentucky, and Missouri — at all costs, even the cost of continued Black slavery. Consequently, his generals in the field made and carried out their own plans. They were badly strapped for manpower, and the Black runaways provided some answers to whatever prayers generals pray. They could serve as spies, scouts, and messengers in the countryside they knew so well. They could work the familiar land, growing crops for the food and profit of the Union armies. And as the war dragged on, many Union commanders saw the Black men among them as potential soldiers. Many of the Black men were eager to fight, but Lincoln was still not prepared to go that far.

Some Union commanders began issuing their own emancipation proclamations. First General John C. Frémont in Missouri and later General David Hunter farther South had their emancipation orders reversed by Lincoln. But reports were pouring into Washington that told not only of the flood of runaways, but also of Black unrest everywhere. Black men were literally fighting their way past local police forces to get themselves and their families into the Union encampments. There was word of agricultural workers killing or otherwise getting rid of their overseers, and taking over entire plantations. The dark presence at the center of the national conflict could no longer be denied. Lincoln's armies were in the midst of a surging movement of Black people who were in effect freeing themselves from slavery. His generals were desperate and convinced that only through military discipline could this revolutionary Black element be contained.

In Washington, Congress was discussing its own plans for emancipation, primarily as a weapon against the South. Meanwhile, Lincoln was being constantly attacked in the North for his conduct of the war. In September 1862, Abraham Lincoln, in a double-minded attempt both to bargain with and weaken the South while replying to the pressures of the North, finally made public his proposed Emancipation Proclamation.

The proclamation excluded the "loyal" slave states and other "loyal" areas. Legally, then, nearly 1 million Black people whose masters were "loyal" to the Union had no part of the emancipation offered. In effect, Lincoln was announcing freedom to the captives over whom he had the least control, while allowing those in states clearly under the rule of his government to remain in slavery. However, Lincoln was justifying his armies' use of the Confederates' Black "property," and preparing the way for an even more extensive use of Black power through the military. Once the Emancipation Proclamation went into effect, the tens of thousands of Black people who were creating their own freedom could be used by the North to win the war.

Yet out of the celebrations of the Emancipation Proclamation was born the mythology of Abraham Lincoln the Emancipator. The heart of the matter is this: While concrete historical realities of the time testified to the costly, daring, courageous activities of hundreds of thousands of Black people breaking loose from slavery and setting themselves free, the myth gave the credit to a white Republican president, unable to see beyond the limits of his own race, class, and time.

Adapted from Vincent Harding, *There Is a River: The Black Struggle for Freedom in America* (New York: Harcourt Brace, 1981).

Abolitionists and the Civil War

ABRAHAM LINCOLN WAS NOT originally an advocate of abolition. His journey to what he called "the central act of my administration, and the great event of the 19th century" was a relatively slow one. Behind this "great event" lies a complex process that involved many historical actors. Yet too often forgotten in the history of emancipation are Black and white abolitionists who played a crucial part in turning the Civil War into an abolition war. Emancipation was not just a singular event made possible by the stroke of a pen. It had long roots. Abolitionists had agitated for an end to slavery for 30 years prior to the Civil War. To reduce emancipation to an event triggered by military crisis is to miss the long history of resistance to slavery. The simultaneous radicalization of the abolitionist movement and the emergence of antislavery electoral politics set the stage for war and emancipation.

During the war, abolitionists and their Radical Republican allies in Congress pushed the Lincoln administration from non-extension (the position that slavery should be prohibited where it does not yet exist) to abolition to Black rights. When elected president, Lincoln, a moderate antislavery Republican, was committed only to the non-extension of slavery. Lincoln presented himself as an antislavery man who would do nothing to interfere with Southern slavery. Lincoln had long recommended the colonizing of all free Blacks outside of the country. In the first year of the war, the Lincoln administration, concerned with retaining the loyalty of the border slave states and Northern conservatives, made the preservation of the Union rather than abolition its war aim.

Black and white abolitionists argued early on that the Civil War was a revolutionary struggle against slavery, not just a war for the Union. No longer political outsiders, the abolitionist movement gained a new respectability in the eyes of the Northern public during the Civil War. The abolitionists revived their earlier tactics from the 1830s in this new context. William Lloyd Garrison formed the Emancipation League in Boston in 1861 to pressure Lincoln to abolish slavery and criticize him for advocating colonization. Making similar criticisms, Wendell Phillips, now one of the North's most sought-after public speakers, went on a lecture tour speaking to large audiences. Women's rights activists such as Susan B. Anthony formed the Women's National Loyal League, flooding Congress with petitions for abolition. The crucial difference this time was that their petitions were read with respect rather than gagged as incendiary documents.

For Black abolitionists, as much as their white counterparts, a Republican presidency meant having for the first time the political opportunity to pressure the federal government to act on abolition. Perhaps no other Black abolitionist leader was more influential in this regard than Frederick Douglass, who used his monthly magazine and speeches to vent his views on abolition, Black rights, and military service. When Lincoln met Douglass, he acknowledged having read his criticisms of Lincoln's slowness to act on emancipation. African Americans who struggled to have their voices heard had gained the president's ear.

As abolitionist criticism mounted, Lincoln began to move. When the enslaved began fleeing to the Union Army it presented a new dilemma for the Lincoln administration. Should the federal government enforce the Fugitive Slave Law and return runaways to the Confederacy? Abolitionists answered with a resounding no.

Soon "contraband camps" became a common part of Union encampments as thousands of enslaved people fled to the Union Army. Many Black women abolitionists, some of them former slaves like Harriet Jacobs and Sojourner Truth, were especially active in providing relief for the runaways. Harriet Tubman joined runaways who were put to work performing menial chores such as doing the soldiers' laundry. Using the skills acquired as a "conductor" in the Underground Railroad, Tubman later acted as a scout for the Union Army in South Carolina and led the Combahee River Raid, freeing more than 700 enslaved men, women, and children.

As the war dragged on and the need for manpower increased, emancipation became sound military strategy. The abolitionists had argued since the beginning of the war that Lincoln should use his war powers to strike against slavery. Toward the end of 1862, Lincoln embraced this position when the border slaveholders refused to adopt the president's proposals for gradual, compensated emancipation, and the war reached a stalemate amid heavy Union losses. Douglass and Phillips in particular were vocal in the failure of the federal government to enlist Black men into the Union Army. Tubman argued that God would not let Lincoln win the war unless he did the right thing and abolished slavery.

While Black abolitionists formed one part of the chorus of voices that pressured Lincoln to act on emancipation, they were the most important in opposing his ideas on colonization. When in August 1862, Lincoln invited five African Americans to the White House, hoping to persuade them to support his plans for colonizing Black Americans outside of the United States, the reaction among Black abolitionists was swift and hostile. The failure of Lincoln's colonization schemes, along with strong African American and abolitionist protest, finally convinced Lincoln to abandon colonization as a viable option for Black Americans after emancipation.

On Jan. 1, 1863, when Lincoln issued the Emancipation Proclamation, he had come to abolitionist ground. By this time, Lincoln came to share the abolitionist and African American view of the Civil War as a revolutionary event that would not only end slavery, but also redeem the American republic and its founding principles. The Emancipation Proclamation allied Black freedom with the powers of the federal government and the Union cause.

Responding both to abolitionist criticisms and the need for more troops as the conflict dragged on, the proclamation opened the Union Army to African Americans, including slaves, and granted freedom to those who served and their families. Black military service also became a powerful argument for African American citizenship and equality. Abolitionists like Massachusetts Governor John Andrew and the wealthy George L. Stearns, a proponent of Black military service, hired prominent African American abolitionists like Frederick Douglass, William Wells Brown, and Henry Highland Garnet as recruiting agents. Frederick Douglass issued the pamphlet *Men of Color, to Arms!*, which encouraged potential Black soldiers with the thought that "liberty won by white men would lack half its luster. [They] who would free themselves must strike the blow." By the end of the war, nearly 200,000 Black Americans had served in the Union Army and Navy.

Lincoln soon came to sympathize with the abolitionist argument that one could not possibly deny citizenship rights to Black soldiers who had fought on behalf of the Union. In a letter to Louisiana Governor Michael Hahn, he suggested that "the very intelligent, and especially those who have fought gallantly in our ranks," should be given the right to vote.

By the time of his death, Lincoln's views on slavery and racial equality had evolved greatly. Abolitionists challenged him to abandon colonization and accept both abolition and Black rights. Emancipation gave meaning and purpose to the Civil War that a war for the Union never could. Modestly, toward the end of his life Lincoln claimed he had been "only an instrument" of emancipation, adding, "The logic and moral power of Garrison and the antislavery people of the country and the army, have done all."

Adapted from Manisha Sinha, "Architects of Their Own Liberation: African Americans, Emancipation, and the Civil War," *OAH Magazine of History* 27 (April 2013).

Black Soldiers and the Civil War

IN THE NORTH, the Emancipation Proclamation meant the Black soldier, and the Black soldier meant the end of the war. "We have come to set you free!" cried the Black cavalrymen who rode at the head of the Union Army as it entered Richmond in 1864.

At first, this was to be a white man's war. First, because the North did not want to affront (insult) the South, and the war was going to be short; and secondly, if Negroes fought in the war, how could it help being a war for their emancipation? And for this the North would not fight. Yet scarcely a year after the war started, the Negroes were fighting, although unrecognized as soldiers; in two years they were free and in the army.

In 1862 came Gen. [David] Hunter's Black regiment in South Carolina. Gen. Hunter had fewer than 11,000 men under his command, and had to hold the whole seacoast of Georgia, South Carolina, and Florida. He appealed often and in vain to Washington for reinforcements. [With] no reinforcements to be had from the North [and] the enemy continually increasing . . . Gen. Hunter announced his intention of "forming a Negro regiment, and compelling every able-bodied Black man in the department to fight for the freedom that could not but be the issue of our war."

Reports of the organization of the first Black regiment were forwarded to headquarters in Washington, and the War Department took no notice. Nothing was said, nor was any authority given to pay the men. [Eventually, the War Department simply sent] a demand for information in regard to the Negro regiment.

Hunter declared: "The experiment of arming the Blacks, so far as I have made it, has been a complete and even marvelous success. They are sober, docile, attentive, and enthusiastic; displaying great natural capacities in acquiring the duties of the soldier. They are now eager beyond all things to take the field and be led into action; and it is the unanimous opinion of officers who have had charge of them that . . . they will prove invaluable." When the reply was read in the House of Representatives: "Its effects were magical."

[Next came Louisiana under Gen. Butler.] The use of Negro troops was precipitated by the attack on Aug. 5, 1862, on Baton Rouge. Butler had to have troops to defend New Orleans, and had applied to Washington, but none could be sent. Therefore, by proclamation, Butler "called on Africa," accepted a free Negro regiment that had previously offered its services, and proceeded to organize other Negro troops. Thousands of volunteers under Butler's appeal appeared. In 14 days, a regiment was organized with colored line officers and white field officers. More than half of the privates were fugitive slaves.

On Jan. 6, 1863, five days after the Emancipation Proclamation, the secretary of war authorized the governor of Massachusetts to raise two Negro regiments for three years' service. These were the celebrated 54th and 55th Negro regiments — the first regularly authorized Negro regiments of the war. One thousand Negroes responded within two weeks.

It would not have been America, however, not to have maintained some color discrimination. First, there was the matter of pay. The pay of soldiers at the beginning of the war was $13 a month. Negro soldiers were allowed $10 a month, and $3 of this was deducted for clothing. Many of the [Black] regiments refused to receive the reduced pay. The 54th Massachusetts Infantry refused pay for a whole year until they were treated equally.

There was at first a very great distaste on the part of white men for serving in colored regiments.

Later, when the Black troops made their reputation in battle, the chance to command them was eagerly sought.

Abraham Lincoln, under a fire of criticism, warmly defended the enlistment of Negro troops: "The slightest knowledge of arithmetic will prove to any man that the rebel armies cannot be destroyed with Democratic strategy. It would sacrifice all the white men of the North to do it. There are now in the service of the United States near 200,000 able-bodied colored men, most of them under arms, defending and acquiring Union territory. . .

My enemies pretend I am now carrying on this war for the sole purpose of abolition. So long as I am president, it shall be carried on for the sole purpose of restoring the Union. But no human power can subdue this rebellion without the use of the emancipation policy, and every other policy calculated to weaken the moral and physical forces of the rebellion. Freedom has given us 200,000 men raised on Southern soil. It will give us more yet. Just so much it has subtracted from the enemy."

When the draft law was passed in 1863, it meant that the war could no longer be carried on with volunteers; that [white] soldiers were going to be compelled to fight, and these soldiers were going to be poor men who could not buy exemption. The result throughout the country was widespread disaffection that went often as far as rioting. [The riots] showed the North that unless they could replace unwilling white soldiers with Black soldiers, who had a vital stake in the outcome of the war, the war could not be won.

This was the proof of manhood required of Black men. He might labor for the nation's wealth, and the nation took the results without thanks, and handed him next to nothing in return. But when he rose and fought and killed, the whole nation with one voice proclaimed him a man and a brother. Nothing else made emancipation possible in the United States. Nothing else made Negro citizenship conceivable, but the record of the Negro soldier as a fighter.

The military aid of the Negroes began as laborers and as spies. All through the war and after, Blacks were indispensable as informers. Negro military labor had been indispensable to the Union armies. There were 200,000 Negroes in the camps and employ of the Union armies, as servants, teamsters [animal driver], cooks, and laborers. Of the actual fighting of Negroes, Union General Morgan, says, "History has not yet done justice to the share borne by colored soldiers in the war for the Union." Black men were repeatedly and deliberately used as shock troops, when there was little or no hope of success.

Official figures say that there were in all 186,017 Negro troops, and that the losses during the war were 68,178. They took part in 198 battles and skirmishes. Without doubt, including servants, laborers, and spies, between 300,000 and 400,000 Negroes helped as regular soldiers or laborers in winning the Civil War.

Of the effect of Negro soldiers in the Northern Army, there can be no doubt. John C. Underwood, resident of Virginia for 20 years, said before the Committee on Reconstruction: "[T]he enlistment of Negro troops by the United States was the turning point of the rebellion; that it was the heaviest blow [the Confederate Army] ever received. . . . When the Negroes deserted their masters, and join[ed] the forces of the United States, intelligent men everywhere saw that the matter was ended."

Adapted from W. E. B. Du Bois, *Black Reconstruction in America* (New York: The Free Press, 1998).

Lincoln and the Civil War
(View One)

THE TRADITIONAL ANSWER TO "who freed the slaves?" is "Abraham Lincoln." In recent years though, this answer has been challenged as an example of focusing only on the actions of great white males. But what if the traditional answer is right?

First, one must ask what was the one thing without which emancipation would not have happened. The clear answer is: the Civil War. Without the war, no slave would have been freed. So what brought the war? The secession of the Southern states and the refusal of the United States government to recognize its legitimacy. In these matters Abraham Lincoln moves to center stage.

From 1854 until nominated for president in 1860, the dominant, unifying theme of Lincoln's career was opposition to the expansion of slavery as the first step toward getting rid of it. Lincoln denounced slavery repeatedly as a "monstrous injustice" and "an unqualified evil." Southerners read Lincoln's speeches and his election in 1860 was a sign that they had lost control of the national government. It was not merely Lincoln's election, but his election as a principled opponent of slavery on moral grounds that caused the South to secede.

It is quite true that once the war started, Lincoln moved more slowly toward making it a war for freedom than Black leaders, abolitionists, radical Republicans, and the slaves themselves wanted him to move. But ultimately the fate of the institution of slavery depended on the outcome of the war. If the North won, slavery would be weakened if not destroyed; if the Confederacy won, slavery would survive and perhaps even grow stronger.

Lincoln's chief concern of 1861 was to maintain a united coalition including Republicans, loyal Democrats and border state Unionists. To do this he considered it essential to define the war as being waged solely for Union between North and South, because that, not slavery, is what united this coalition. The four border slave states of Missouri, Kentucky, Maryland, and Delaware had remained in the Union and all except Delaware had a strong pro-confederate faction. Any rash action by Northern governments against slavery therefore might push three more states into the Confederacy.

Moreover, in the North itself nearly half of the voters were Democrats, who supported a war for the Union but might oppose a war against slavery. In 1864 Lincoln told a visiting delegation of abolitionists that two years earlier "many of my strongest supporters urged emancipation before I thought it indispensable, and, I may say, before I thought the country ready for it. It is my conviction that, had the [Emancipation Proclamation] been issued even six months earlier than it was, public sentiment would not have sustained it." Lincoln could actually have made a case that the country was not ready for the Emancipation Proclamation even when it was issued. Democratic gains in Northern congressional elections in the fall of 1862 resulted in part from a voter backlash against the preliminary proclamation. Without question, this issue bitterly divided the Northern people and threatened fatally to erode support for the war effort. Even in the summer of 1864, Northern morale again plummeted and many white Northerners criticized Lincoln for refusing to abandon emancipation as a precondition for negotiations with the South. But Lincoln stood firm.

The Emancipation Proclamation turned the Union Army into an army of liberation. Most slaves were liberated by Union armies. And who was the commander in chief who called these armies into being, appointed their generals, and gave them direction and purpose?

By pronouncing slavery a moral evil that must come to an end and winning the presidency in 1860, by refusing to compromise on the issue of slavery's expansion, by careful leadership and timing that kept a fragile Unionist coalition together, by refusing to compromise on the policy of emancipation once he had adopted it, and by prosecuting the war to unconditional victory as commander in chief of an army of liberation, Abraham Lincoln freed the slaves.

Adapted from James McPherson, "Who Freed the Slaves?" *Proceedings of the American Philosophical Society* 139 (1995).

Lincoln and the Civil War
(View Two)

ABRAHAM LINCOLN WAS NOT the Great Emancipator. He said repeatedly, in public and in private, that he was a firm believer in white supremacy. Lincoln believed that Black people and white people would be much better off separated.

Lincoln was not opposed to slavery; he was opposed to the extension of slavery. More than that Lincoln was opposed to the extension of slavery out of devotion to the interests of white people, not out of compassion for suffering Blacks. He did say from time to time that slavery was "a monstrous injustice." But he also said, repeatedly, that he was not prepared to do anything to remove that injustice where it existed. On the contrary, he said that it was his duty to tolerate and, if necessary, to give practical support to an evil supported by the U.S. Constitution.

While other white Northerners were fighting the Fugitive Slave Law, Lincoln publicly supported it. In a private letter, he said: "I confess I hate to see the poor creatures hunted down . . . but I bite my lip and keep quiet."

In 1858, during a series of debates with Stephen Douglas, Lincoln said:

I will say, then, that I am not, nor ever have been, in favor of bringing about in any way the social and political equality of the white and black races (applause); that I am not, nor ever have been, in favor of making voters or jurors of negroes, nor of qualifying them to hold office, nor to intermarry with white people . . . there is a physical difference between the white and black races which I believe will forever forbid the two races living together on terms of social and political equality. And . . . while they do remain together there must be the position of superior and inferior, and

I as much as any other man am in favor of having the superior position assigned to the white race.

Lincoln grew during the war — but he didn't grow much. He spent the first 18 months of his administration in a desperate attempt to save slavery where it existed. He began his presidential career by saying that he had neither the power nor the desire to interfere with slavery. The War Department refused to accept Black troops and some generals returned fugitive slaves to rebel owners. Union officers like Gen. John Frémont, who refused to go along with the "soft-on-slavery" policy, were replaced.

Insofar as it can be said that Lincoln had an emancipation policy, it was to rid America of Black people. On Aug. 14, 1862, Lincoln called a hand-picked group of Black men to the White House and proposed a Black exodus. Lincoln told the Black men that it was their duty to leave America. "It is better for us both," he said, "to be separated."

When Lincoln eventually adopted a new policy, he did so from necessity, not conviction. In July of 1862, the Union war effort was failing. "Things," he said later, "had gone from bad to worse, till I felt we had reached the end of the rope." Lincoln said he was driven to the "alternative of either surrendering the Union, and with it, the Constitution, or of laying a strong hand upon the colored element."

Lincoln issued the Emancipation Proclamation and warned the South that he would free their slaves in 100 days if the rebellion had not ended by that time. Yet the document did not apply to slaves in the border states and areas under federal control in the South. In other words, Lincoln "freed" slaves where he had no power and left them in chains where he had power.

After a period of vacillation and doubt, Lincoln did help win passage of the 13th Amendment, which made the paper freedom of the proclamation real. But Lincoln never recognized Black people as deserving of fair and equal treatment.

In the final analysis, Lincoln must be seen as the embodiment of the American tradition, which is a racist tradition. Lincoln holds up a flawed mirror to the American soul.

Adapted from Lerone Bennett Jr., "Was Lincoln a White Supremacist?" *Ebony* (February 1968).

Arguing Abolition: Essay with an Attitude

By Adam Sanchez

I'VE FOUND THAT in history classes, some teachers assign rather than teach essay writing. By high school, the thinking goes, students should know how to write an essay, and if they don't, that's what English class is for. I've found that no matter how much experience students have with writing essays, when they enter my class they often struggle with articulating their ideas and putting them on paper. Furthermore, I've found that history essays particularly suffer from formulaic, rigid paragraph and essay structures that suffocate student writing and lack passion.

As Rethinking Schools editor Linda Christensen reminds us in *Reading, Writing, and Rising Up*, "Student essays don't have to be boring. They can be playful, personal, and provocative as poetry and stories; they can raise their fists and shout, 'Injustice!' or shake us with laughter." Rather than the "dull approach," Christensen asks her students to write an "essay with an attitude." What follows are several ways, many inspired by Christensen's work, to help students begin writing an essay answering the question "Who freed the slaves?"

Building an Evidence Wall

One method I use in my classroom throughout the unit is an Evidence Wall. At the very beginning of the unit, I let students know that when we finish, I expect them to write an essay answering "Who freed the slaves?" As we progress through the lessons in the unit, I regularly ask students to think about what they learned and add both potential answers to the essay question and evidence for those answers to the wall. The "Evidence Wall" can be an actual wall or a bulletin board — basically any space in the classroom that you label and section off for students.

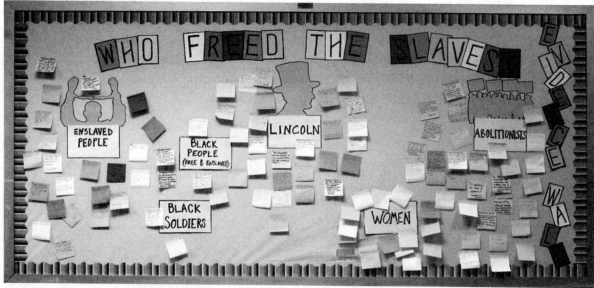

"Who Freed the Slaves?" Evidence Wall

Throughout the unit, as we read sources and debrief lessons, I encourage students to add to the Evidence Wall. For example, as we read Lincoln's first inaugural address, I place a piece of paper labeled "Lincoln" on the wall. I encourage students to pull out evidence on whether Lincoln did or did not free the slaves and write that evidence down on Post-Its. As they read, I ask students to stick their Post-Its near the paper on the wall labeled "Lincoln." Many students rush to be the first to add his quote "I have no purpose, directly or indirectly, to interfere with the institution of slavery in the states where it exists. I believe I have no lawful right to do so, and I have no inclination to do so." Other students add that "Lincoln was not against slavery in the South when elected president," or other nuggets they glean from his speech. When putting up quotes, I encourage students to put the author and the source for the quote below it, so later on they can easily reference the quote in their essays.

When I assign readings for homework, during the warm-up to get students re-engaged in the content of the unit I ask students to pull out evidence to discuss and put on the Evidence Wall. The Evidence Wall can also be a closing activity. For example, after "Lesson 4: Who Fought to End Slavery?" I might add a paper to the wall labeled "Abolitionists" and ask students to think about the different actions taken by abolitionists they met during the mixer that they could use as evidence to argue the abolition movement freed the slaves. Students might add "gathered signatures and sent antislavery petitions to Congress" and "helped escaped slaves through the Underground Railroad" under the label "Abolitionists."

Throughout the unit — but especially after Lesson 9, which introduces students to various arguments historians have made when answering "Who freed the slaves?" — I encourage students to brainstorm their own answers to the essay question. "Who has a potential answer?" I ask. Max shouts out, "The slaves freed themselves!" I respond by asking, "What evidence can help Max write his essay?" And we spend several minutes reviewing the Evidence Wall and adding to it. Many students choose to write about Lincoln, abolitionists, or the actions of the enslaved themselves; sometimes they will come up with less common answers like Black soldiers or the South's intransigence.

Thinking through different potential answers and visually mapping the evidence for those answers can be a good way to help students identify whether there is enough evidence to justify their argument. It can also be a particularly great spark for students who struggle getting started. Students will often stand by the wall or take a photo of it for inspiration. Furthermore, using an Evidence Wall makes knowledge creation a social and collective process rather than an individual one.

Discussing the Essay Question

In addition to using an Evidence Wall, before jumping into writing the essay, it's helpful to have a few lessons that get students thinking and talking further about the essay topic. If students can articulate their argument out loud, it becomes easier for them to get it down on paper. And for students who aren't sure what they want to write about, hearing their peers express positions can help stimulate their own thinking. I rarely have enough time for all of the classroom activities listed below, but I pick and choose from the various end-of-unit essay preparation ideas that follow, depending on my students and their needs.

I've found that one of the best ways to get students to prepare for their essay is to hold a student-led discussion on the essay question "Who freed the slaves?"

I usually assign part of Howard Zinn's *A People's History of the United States* chapter "Slavery Without Submission, Emancipation Without Freedom," excerpted in Handout 10-A. This chapter gives a good overview of the content we covered in the entire unit, so serves well as both review and preparation for the discussion and essay. If you've gone through the entire unit, the chapter will repeat much of what students have already learned but this can be helpful for students in recalling information they learned early on. If I have time to go through the chapter in class, we listen to it on audiobook. I ask students to follow along, annotate their copy in the margins and look for evidence they can use in their essay. Periodically, I pause the audiobook and ask students to discuss the quotes they highlighted in small groups. If I don't have time to read the chapter in class, I have them read it for homework and come up with questions they want to ask other students based on the reading.

The next day I seat students in a circle (or multiple circles depending on my class size) and let students' questions guide the discussion. I encourage students to discuss what they think they want to argue in their essay and the evidence they think they have or need. But I also urge them to debate differences to strengthen their arguments. Usually students have no problem leading off the discussion with their own questions, but if they struggle I start them with a particularly juicy one: "Should Lincoln get any credit for freeing the enslaved?" I tell students to pay attention to who dominates the discussion and who hasn't spoken and try to bring as many voices into the conversation as possible. I also encourage students to refer to specific evidence as much as possible. Although the main text they utilize is the Zinn chapter, students bring in evidence from other readings and lessons throughout the unit.

Another less time-intensive way to get students discussing their ideas is to assign "The Civil War and the Death of Slavery Timeline" (Handout 10–B). Ask students to read the timeline and pick two or three events that they think most directly addresses the question "Who freed the slaves?" Then have students in pairs share with each other events they chose and why. Note that this timeline focuses exclusively on the Civil War, so you might also ask students to think about other factors and historical actors that led to the Civil War and how those should be weighed when answering the essay question.

Sparking Student Passion

Another way for students to find their voice is to return to the "Lincoln freed the slaves" narrative. Now that they have a more complex view about how slavery ended, students can be articulate about what's wrong with the simple story many of them previously held. I present students with children's books, songs, and textbook excerpts that perpetuate the idea that Lincoln freed the slaves with a stroke of his pen. Asking students to "talk back" to these texts can be empowering.

Although many textbooks now acknowledge the role enslaved people played in transforming the Civil War's direction and putting emancipation on the table, in a few accounts this history is still absent. Some textbooks discuss abolitionists before the war, but in most, the abolitionist movement disappears when the war begins. While the textbooks vary in their clarity about Lincoln's positions on slavery, he is almost always portrayed in a positive light and more critical perspectives like Lerone Bennett Jr.'s (see Lesson 9, Handout 9–E) are nonexistent.

One description ripe for student criticism can be found in *History Alive! The United States*. After a section titled "Abraham Lincoln versus Jefferson Davis" that focuses on the politicians' heights, personality traits, and upbringing (not their politics), the textbook gives us a description of emancipation that acknowledges Lincoln's shift and some of the limitations of the Emancipation Proclamation, but removes the enslaved or abolitionists from playing any role. In class, we read the excerpt and ask students to "talk back" to it by commenting in the margins:

While neither side won at the battle of Antietam, it was enough of a victory for Lincoln to take his first steps toward ending slavery. When the Civil War began Lincoln had resisted pleas from abolitionists to make emancipation, or the freeing of slaves, a reason for fighting the Confederacy. He himself opposed slavery. But the purpose of the war, he said, "is to save the Union, and is not either to save or destroy slavery."

As the war dragged on, Lincoln changed his mind. Declaring an end to slavery, he realized, would discourage Europeans who opposed slavery from assisting the Confederacy. Freeing slaves could also deprive the Confederacy of a large part of its workforce.

On Jan. 1, 1863, President Lincoln issued the Emancipation Proclamation. The proclamation, or formal order, declared slaves in all Confederate states to be free. This announcement had little immediate effect on slavery. The Confederate states simply ignored the document. Slaves living in states loyal to the Union were not affected by the proclamation.

Still, the Emancipation Proclamation changed the war from a fight to save the Union into a crusade for freedom. "The time came," Lincoln said later, "when I felt that slavery must die [so] that the nation might live."

I ask students to critique what is left out of the textbook account, which can provide important fodder for their essay. My students ask, "Where are the enslaved people running to the Union Army? And where are the abolitionists pressuring the president to change his mind?"

Elementary school lesson plans, songs, and children's books can be even clearer in their hero worship. One lesson plan published by Scholastic asks children to make and wear stovepipe hats and cardboard beards and "perform Lincoln's actions" as they sing:

President Lincoln, I've been thinkin'
Back to when you wrote the E—
Mancipation Proclamation,
So the slaves could all be free.

President Lincoln, I've been thinkin'
How you bravely led the land.
Once divided, now united,
You made sure our house would stand!

When I look at this lesson plan with my high school students they are quick to point out that it provokes a deep sympathy with Lincoln rather than abolitionists or enslaved people.

Children's books such as *Climbing Lincoln's Steps* by Suzanne Slade (Albert Whitman & Company, 2010) and *Abraham* by former Oklahoma Republican Governor Frank Keating (Simon & Schuster, 2017) similarly provoke reverence for Lincoln, and minimize or exclude the role played by abolitionists or the enslaved. Lines such as "I liberated the slaves" and "Abraham had to find a way to end slavery and unite the country he loved" can provoke passionate indignation from students armed with the complex history of Lincoln's presidency.

Lastly, simply showing students a picture of the Emancipation Memorial, built in 1876 in Washington, D.C., can elicit compelling critique. The memorial depicts Lincoln, proclamation in one hand while the other is outstretched toward a kneeling Black man in chains. The message of who emancipated who is crystal clear. It can also be powerful to share with students excerpts from Frederick Douglass' speech when the memorial was unveiled. While Douglass acknowledged that Lincoln was "a great public man whose example is likely to be commended for honor and imitation," he also stated that "Truth compels me to admit, even here in the presence of the monument we have erected to his memory, Abraham Lincoln was not, in the fullest sense of the word, either our man or our model. In his interests, in his associations, in his habits of thought, and in his prejudices, he was a white man. He was preeminently the white man's president, entirely devoted to the welfare of white men. He was ready and willing at any time during the first years of his administration to deny, postpone, and sacrifice the rights of humanity in the colored people to promote the welfare of the white people of this country. In all his education and feeling he was an American of the Americans."

These examples can help students find creative ways to introduce their essays, or in some cases, students may even decide to write their essay in the form of a letter to the textbook company or children's book author.

Adam Sanchez helps a student writing her essay.

Writing the Essay

Eventually, students need to start writing. For more in-depth instructions on teaching the writing process, see "Writing Wild Essays from Hard Ground" in *Teaching for Joy and Justice* and "Essays with an Attitude" in the second edition of *Reading, Writing, and Rising Up*, two essays in two essential books by Linda Christensen.

Here are some insights from Christensen's work:

- Start with questions and have students list their answers: Why does it matter "who freed the slaves?" What do most people get wrong when answering this question? What is the most important thing that most people leave out? What makes you angry about this topic? What gets under your skin? What do you want others to know?

- Begin by gathering evidence. Once students have an idea of what they want to write about, give students time to gather evidence and make sure they have enough to prove their point. If they don't have enough, you might encourage them to add some complexity to their answer by choosing an additional factor to discuss that led to the destruction of slavery.

- Use student examples. A close reading of model student essays can help students understand what their essay should include. Use highlighters to highlight the different elements of an essay: thesis statement, evidence, analysis, transitions, etc. This brings to life the criteria sheet (Handout 10–C).

- Create a wall of thesis statements. Have students anonymously write their thesis statements on sentence strips and put them around the room. Have students circulate, reading the statements, and then conduct a discussion highlighting what makes a strong thesis.

- Use model introductions to help develop student creativity. Show students different ways of writing an introduction by using quotes, anecdotes, questions, or powerful one-liners. Introductions can be a major place where student writing comes alive.

- Build in time for students to revise. Any good writer goes through multiple drafts, and students need to learn the art of revision. Conference with students, especially those who struggle to get started. During the writing process, draw out their ideas, push them to clarify their thinking, and find more evidence to better make their argument. Don't mark every error but diagnose the major problems that students need to learn in order to produce a better second draft.

- Encourage students to take their writing beyond the school walls. As mentioned above, some students might want to write their essay in the form of a letter to a textbook company or children's book author. Others might want to submit their work to the school newspaper or neighborhood publications. Encourage students to submit their writing to magazines that publish teen voices or a local newspaper.

I've found that given the time, student papers on this topic can be complex, humorous, fiery, devastating, measured, and hopeful. Some students are able to draw out important lessons for today. As my student Jada Vazquez concluded her essay, "The abolitionists fought for what they believed in and didn't stop until they got what they wanted. . . . When people learn that Lincoln freed the slaves instead of the abolitionists, they probably think they don't have a voice that can change history. People are going to believe that you can only change things if you hold a position of power, but that's not true. The history of the abolitionist movement teaches us that we have the power to bring the change we wish to see."

Slavery Without Submission, Emancipation Without Freedom

By Howard Zinn

SLAVE REVOLTS IN THE UNITED STATES were not as frequent or as large scale as those in the Caribbean islands or in South America. Probably the largest slave revolt in the United States took place near New Orleans in 1811. Four hundred to 500 slaves gathered after a rising at the plantation of a Major Andry. Armed with cane knives, axes, and clubs, they wounded Andry, killed his son, and began marching from plantation to plantation, their numbers growing. They were attacked by U.S. Army and militia forces; 66 were killed on the spot, and 16 were tried and shot by a firing squad.

The conspiracy of Denmark Vesey, himself a free Negro, was thwarted before it could be carried out in 1822. The plan was to burn Charleston, South Carolina, then the sixth-largest city in the nation, and to initiate a general revolt of slaves in the area. Several witnesses said thousands of Blacks were implicated in one way or another. Blacks had made about 250 pike heads and bayonets and more than 300 daggers, according to Herbert Aptheker's account. But the plan was betrayed, and 35 Blacks, including Vesey, were hanged. The trial record itself, published in Charleston, was ordered

During slavery, extended kinship networks were created to maintain Black families and community.

Library of Congress

destroyed soon after publication, as too dangerous for slaves to see.

In Southampton County, Virginia, in the summer of 1831, a slave named Nat Turner, claiming religious visions, gathered about 70 slaves who went on a rampage from plantation to plantation, murdering at least 55 men, women, and children. They gathered supporters, but were captured as their ammunition ran out. Turner and perhaps 18 others were hanged.

This threw the slaveholding South into a panic, and then into a determined effort to bolster the security of the slave system. After that, Virginia kept a militia force of 101,000, almost 10 percent of its total population. Rebellion, though rare, was a constant fear among slave owners.

Eugene Genovese, in his comprehensive study of slavery, *Roll, Jordan, Roll*, sees a record of "simultaneous accommodation and resistance to slavery." The resistance included stealing property, sabotage and slowness, killing overseers and masters, burning down plantation buildings, running away. Even the accommodation "breathed a critical spirit and disguised subversive actions."

Running away was much more realistic than armed insurrection. During the 1850s about 1,000 slaves a year escaped into the North, Canada, and Mexico. Thousands ran away for short periods. And this despite the terror facing the runaway. The dogs used in tracking fugitives "bit, tore, mutilated, and if not pulled off in time, killed their prey," Genovese says.

Harriet Tubman, born into slavery, her head injured by an overseer when she was 15, made her way to freedom alone as a young woman, then became the most famous conductor on the Underground Railroad. She made 19 dangerous trips back and forth, often disguised, escorting more than 300 slaves to freedom, always carrying a pistol, telling the fugitives, "You'll be free or die." She expressed her philosophy: "There was one of two things I had a right to, liberty or death; if I could not have one, I would have the other; for no man should take me alive. . ."

One form of resistance was not to work so hard. W. E. B. Du Bois wrote, in *The Gift of Black Folk*:

As a tropical product with a sensuous receptivity to the beauty of the world, he was not as easily reduced to be the mechanical draft horse that the Northern European laborer became. . . . [T]hus he was easily accused of laziness and driven as a slave when in truth he brought to modern manual labor a renewed valuation of life.

The instances where poor whites helped slaves were not frequent, but sufficient to show the need for setting one group against the other. Genovese says:

The slaveholders . . . suspected that non-slaveholders would encourage slave disobedience and even rebellion, not so much out of sympathy for the Blacks as out of hatred for the rich planters and resentment of their own poverty. White men sometimes were linked to slave insurrectionary plots, and each such incident rekindled fears.

This helps explain the stern police measures against whites who fraternized with Blacks. In return, Blacks helped whites in need. One Black runaway told of a slave woman who had received 50 lashes of the whip for giving food to a white neighbor who was poor and sick.

When the Brunswick Canal was built in Georgia, the Black slaves and white Irish workers were segregated, the excuse being that they would do violence against one another. That may well have been true, but Fanny Kemble, the famous actress and wife of a planter, wrote in her journal:

But the Irish are not only quarrelers, and rioters, and fighters, and drinkers, and despisers of niggers — they are a passionate, impulsive, warm-hearted, generous people. . . . [T]hey might actually take to sympathy with the slaves, and I leave you to judge of the possible consequences. You perceive, I am sure, that they can by no means be allowed to work together on the Brunswick Canal.

The need for slave control led to an ingenious device, paying poor whites — themselves so troublesome for 200 years of Southern history — to be overseers of Black labor and therefore buffers for Black hatred.

Religion was used by plantation owners for control.

As for Black preachers, as Genovese puts it, "they had to speak a language defiant enough to hold the high-spirited among their flock but neither so inflammatory as to rouse them to battles they could not win nor so ominous as to arouse the ire of ruling powers." Practicality decided: "The slave communities counseled a strategy of patience, of acceptance of what could not be helped, of a dogged effort to keep the Black community alive and healthy. . ."

It was once thought that slavery had destroyed the Black family. But interviews with ex-slaves, done in the 1930s by the Federal Writers' Project of the New Deal for the Library of Congress, told a different story, which George Rawick summarizes (*From Sundown to Sunup*): "The slave community acted like a generalized extended kinship system in which all adults looked after all children and there was little division between 'my children for whom I'm responsible' and 'your children for whom you're responsible.' . . . It was part and parcel, as we shall see, of the social process out of which came Black pride, Black identity, Black culture, the Black community, and Black rebellion in America."

Old letters and records dug out by historian Herbert Gutman (*The Black Family in Slavery and Freedom*) show the stubborn resistance of the slave family to pressures of disintegration. A woman wrote to her son from whom she had been separated for 20 years: "I long to see you in my old age. . . . Now my dear son I pray you to come and see your dear old Mother. . . . I love you Cato you love your Mother — You are my only son. . ."

And a man wrote to his wife, sold away from him with their children: "Send me some of the children's hair in a separate paper with their names on the paper. . . . I had rather anything to had happened to me most than ever to have been parted from you and the children. . . . Laura I do love you the same. . ."

Also insisting on the strength of Blacks even under slavery, Lawrence Levine (*Black Culture and Black Consciousness*) gives a picture of a rich culture among slaves, a complex mixture of adaptation and rebellion, through the creativity of stories and songs:

We raise de wheat,
Dey gib us de corn;
We bake de bread,
Dey gib us de crust,
We sif de meal,
Dey gib us de huss;
We peel de meat,
Dey gib us de skin;
And dat's de way
Dey take us in. . .

The slave community acted like a generalized extended kinship system . . . out of which came Black pride, Black identity, Black culture, the Black community, and Black rebellion in America.

Spirituals often had double meanings. The lyrics "O Canaan, sweet Canaan, I am bound for the land of Canaan" often meant that slaves meant to get to the North, their Canaan. During the Civil War, slaves began to make up new spirituals with bolder messages: "Before I'd be a slave, I'd be buried in my grave, and go home to my Lord and be saved." And the spiritual "Many Thousand Go":

No more peck o' corn for me, no more, no more,
No more driver's lash for me, no more, no more. . .

While Southern slaves held on, free Blacks in the North (there were about 130,000 in 1830, about 200,000 in 1850) agitated for the abolition of slavery. In 1829, David Walker, son of a slave, but born free in North Carolina, moved to Boston, where he sold old clothes. The pamphlet he wrote and printed, *Walker's Appeal*, became widely known. It infuriated Southern slaveholders; Georgia offered a reward of $10,000 to anyone who would deliver Walker alive, and $1,000 to anyone who would kill him. It is not hard to understand why when you read his *Appeal*. Blacks must fight for their freedom, he said:

Let our enemies go on with their butcheries, and at once fill up their cup. Never make an attempt to gain our freedom or natural . . . until you see your way clear when that hour arrives and you move, be not afraid or dismayed. . . . God has been pleased to give us two eyes, two hands, two feet, and some sense in our heads as well as they. They have no more right to hold us in slavery than we have to hold them. . . . "Every dog must have its day," the American's is coming to an end.

One summer day in 1830, David Walker was found dead near the doorway of his shop in Boston.

Some born in slavery acted out the unfulfilled desire of millions. Frederick Douglass, a slave sent to Baltimore to work as a servant and as a laborer in the shipyard, somehow learned to read and write, and at 21, in the year 1838, escaped to the North, where he became the most famous Black man of his time, as lecturer, newspaper editor, writer. In his autobiography, *Narrative of the Life of Frederick Douglass*, he recalled his first childhood thoughts about his condition:

> Why am I a slave? Why are some people slaves, and others masters? Was there ever a time when this was not so? How did the relation commence?
>
> Once, however, engaged in the inquiry, I was not very long in finding out the true solution of the matter. It was not color, but crime, not God, but man, that afforded the true explanation of the existence of slavery; nor was I long in finding out another important truth, viz: what man can make, man can unmake. . .
>
> I distinctly remember being, even then, most strongly impressed with the idea of being a free man someday. This cheering assurance was an inborn dream of my human nature — a constant menace to slavery — and one that all the powers of slavery were unable to silence or extinguish.

The Fugitive Slave Act passed in 1850 was a concession to the Southern states in return for the admission of the Mexican War territories (California, especially) into the Union as nonslave states. The act made it easy for slave owners to recapture ex-slaves or simply to pick up blacks they claimed had run away. Northern Blacks organized resistance to the Fugitive Slave Act, denouncing President Fillmore, who signed it, and Senator Daniel Webster, who supported it. One of these was Jermain W. Loguen, son of a slave mother and her white owner. He had escaped to freedom on his master's horse, gone to college, and was now a minister in Syracuse, New York. He spoke to a meeting in that city in 1850:

> The time has come to change the tones of submission into tones of defiance — and to tell Mr. Fillmore and Mr. Webster, if they propose to execute this measure upon us, to send on their bloodhounds. . . . I received my freedom from Heaven, and with it came the command to defend my title to it. . . . I don't respect this law — I don't fear it — I won't obey it! It outlaws me, and I outlaw it. . .

The following year, in Syracuse, a runaway slave named Jerry was captured and put on trial. A crowd used crowbars and a battering ram to break into the courthouse, defying marshals with drawn guns, and set Jerry free.

Loguen made his home in Syracuse a major station on the Underground Railroad. It was said that he helped 1,500 slaves on their way to Canada. His memoir of slavery came to the attention of his former owner, and she wrote to him, asking him either to return or to send her $1,000 in compensation. Loguen's reply to her was printed in the abolitionist newspaper the *Liberator*:

> Mrs. Sarah Logue . . . . You say you have offers to buy me, and that you shall sell me if I do not send you $1,000, and in the same breath and almost in the same sentence, you say, "You know we raised you as we did our own children." Woman, did you raise your own children for the market? Did you raise them for the whipping post? Did you raise them to be driven off, bound to a coffle in chains? . . . Shame on you! . . .
>
> Have you got to learn that human rights are mutual and reciprocal, and if you take my liberty and life, you forfeit your own liberty and life? Before God and high heaven, is there a law for one man which is not a law for every other man?
>
> If you or any other speculator on my body and rights, wish to know how I regard my rights, they need but come here, and lay their hands on me to enslave me. . .
> Yours, etc. J. W. Loguen

Frederick Douglass knew that the shame of slavery was not just the South's, that the whole nation was complicit in it. On the Fourth of July, 1852, he gave an Independence Day address:

Fellow Citizens: What to the American slave is your Fourth of July? I answer, a day that reveals to him more than all other days of the year, the gross injustice and cruelty to which he is the constant victim. 'To him your celebration is a sham; your boasted liberty an unholy license; your national greatness, swelling vanity; your sounds of rejoicing are empty and heartless; your denunciation of tyrants, brass-fronted impudence; your shouts of liberty and equality, hollow mockery; your prayers and hymns, your sermons and thanksgivings, with all your religious parade and solemnity, are to him mere bombast, fraud, deception, impiety, and hypocrisy — a thin veil to cover up crimes that would disgrace a nation of savages. There is not a nation of the earth guilty of practices more shocking and bloody than are the people of these United States at this very hour.

Ten years after Nat Turner's rebellion, there was no sign of Black insurrection in the South. But that year, 1841, one incident took place that kept alive the idea of rebellion. Slaves being transported on a ship, the *Creole*, overpowered the crew, killed one of them, and sailed into the British West Indies (where slavery had been abolished in 1833). England refused to return the slaves (there was much agitation in England against American slavery), and this led to angry talk in Congress of war with England, encouraged by Secretary of State Daniel Webster. The *Colored Peoples Press* denounced Webster's "bullying position," and, recalling the Revolutionary War and the War of 1812, wrote: "If war be declared . . . will we fight in defense of a government that denies us the most precious right of citizenship? . . ."

As the tension grew, North and South, Blacks became more militant. Frederick Douglass spoke in 1853:

David Walker's Appeal *terrified slave-holders and encouraged abolitionists.*

Let me give you a word of the philosophy of reforms. The whole history of the progress of human liberty shows that all concessions yet made to her august claims have been born of struggle. . . . If there is no struggle there is no progress. . . . Power concedes nothing without a demand. It never did and it never will. . .

How ever-present was slavery in the minds of Northern Negroes in the decades before the Civil War is shown by Black children in a Cincinnati school, a private school financed by Negroes. The children were responding to the question "What do you think most about?" Only five answers remain in the records, and all refer to slavery. A 7-year-old child wrote: "I am sorrow to hear that the boat . . . went down with 200 poor slaves from up the river. Oh how sorrow I am to hear that, it grieves my heart so that I could faint in one minute."

White abolitionists did courageous and pioneering work, on the lecture platform in newspapers, in the Underground Railroad. Black abolitionists, less publicized, were the backbone of the antislavery movement. Before William Lloyd Garrison published his famous *Liberator* in Boston in 1831, the first national convention of Negroes had been held, David Walker had already written his *Appeal*, and the Black abolitionist magazine named *Freedom's Journal* had appeared. Of *The Liberator's* first 25 subscribers, most were Black.

Blacks had to struggle constantly with the unconscious racism of white abolitionists. They also had to insist on their own independent voice. Douglass wrote for the *Liberator*, but in 1847 started his own newspaper in Rochester, the *North Star*, which led to a break with Garrison. In 1854, a conference of Negroes declared: ". . . it is emphatically our battle; no one else can fight it for us. . . . Our relations to the antislavery movement must be and are changed. Instead of depending upon it we must lead it."

Certain Black women faced the triple hurdle — of being abolitionists in a slave society, of being Black among white reformers, and of being women in a reform movement dominated by men. When Sojourner Truth rose to speak in 1853 in New York City at the Fourth National Women's Rights Convention, it all came together. There was a hostile mob in the hall shouting, jeering, threatening. She said: "I know that it feels a kind o' hissin' and ticklin' like to see a colored woman get up and tell you about things, and Woman's Rights. . . . I am sittin' among you to watch; and every once and awhile I will come out and tell you what time of night it is. . ."

After Nat Turner's violent uprising and Virginia's bloody repression, the security system inside the South became tighter. Perhaps only an outsider could hope to launch a rebellion. It was such a person, a white man of ferocious courage and determination, John Brown, whose wild scheme it was to seize the federal arsenal at Harpers Ferry, Virginia, and then set off a revolt of slaves through the South.

Harriet Tubman, 5 feet tall, a veteran of countless secret missions piloting Blacks out of slavery, was involved with John Brown and his plans. But sickness prevented her from joining him. Frederick Douglass too had met with Brown. He argued against the plan from the standpoint of its chances of success, but he admired the ailing man of 60, tall, gaunt, white-haired.

Douglass was right: The plan would not work. The local militia, joined by 100 marines under the command of Robert E. Lee, surrounded the insurgents. Although his men were dead or captured, John Brown refused to surrender: He barricaded himself in a small brick building near the gate of the armory. The troops battered down a door; a marine lieutenant moved in and struck Brown with his sword. Wounded, sick, he was interrogated. W. E. B. Du Bois, in his book *John Brown*, writes:

Osborne Anderson, the only surviving African American member of John Brown's raid on Harpers Ferry.

Picture the situation: An old and blood-bespattered man, half-dead from the wounds inflicted but a few hours before; a man lying in the cold and dirt, without sleep for 55 nerve-wrecking hours, without food for nearly as long, with the dead bodies of his two sons almost before his eyes, the piled corpses of his seven slain comrades near and afar, a wife and a bereaved family listening in vain, and a Lost Cause, the dream of a lifetime, lying dead in his heart. . .

Lying there, interrogated by the governor of Virginia, Brown said: "You had better — all you people at the South — prepare yourselves for a settlement of this question. . . . You may dispose of me very easily — I am nearly disposed of now, but this question is still to be settled — this Negro question, I mean; the end of that is not yet."

Ralph Waldo Emerson, not an activist himself, said of the execution of John Brown: "He will make the gallows holy as the cross."

Of the 22 men in John Brown's striking force, five were Black. Two of these were killed on the spot, one escaped, and two were hanged by the authorities. Before his execution, John Copeland wrote to his parents: "Remember that if I must die I die in trying to liberate a few of my poor and oppressed people from my condition of servitude that God in his Holy Writ has hurled his most bitter denunciations against. . . . I am not terrified by the gallows."

John Brown was executed by the state of Virginia with the approval of the national government. It was the national government that, while weakly enforcing the law ending the slave trade, sternly enforced the laws providing for the return of fugitives to slavery. It was the national government that, in Andrew Jackson's administration, collaborated with the South to keep abolitionist literature out of the mails in the Southern states. It was the Supreme Court of the United States that declared in 1857 that the slave Dred Scott could not sue for his freedom because he was not a person, but property.

Such a government would never accept an end to slavery by rebellion. It would end slavery only under conditions controlled by whites, and only when required by the political and economic needs of the business elite of the North. It was Abraham Lincoln who combined perfectly the needs of business, the political ambition of the new Republican Party, and the rhetoric of humanitarianism. He would keep the abolition of slavery not at the top of his list of priorities, but close enough to the top so it could be pushed there temporarily by abolitionist pressures and by practical political advantage.

Lincoln could skillfully blend the interests of the very rich and the interests of the Black at a moment in history when these interests met. And he could link these two with a growing section of Americans, the white, up-and-coming, economically ambitious, politically active middle class. As Richard Hofstadter puts it:

> Thoroughly middle class in his ideas, he spoke for those millions of Americans who had begun their lives as hired workers — as farmhands, clerks, teachers, mechanics, flatboat men, and rail-splitters — and had passed into the ranks of landed farmers, prosperous grocers, lawyers, merchants, physicians, and politicians.

Lincoln could argue with lucidity and passion against slavery on moral grounds, while acting cautiously in practical politics. He believed "that the institution of slavery is founded on injustice and bad policy, but that the promulgation of abolition doctrines tends to increase rather than abate its evils."

Lincoln refused to denounce the Fugitive Slave Law publicly. He wrote to a friend: "I confess I hate to see the poor creatures hunted down . . . but I bite my lips and keep quiet." And when he did propose in 1849, as a congressman, a resolution to abolish slavery in the District of Columbia, he accompanied this with a section requiring local authorities to arrest and return fugitive slaves coming into Washington. (This led Wendell Phillips, the Boston abolitionist, to refer to him years later as "that slavehound from Illinois.") He opposed slavery, but could not see Blacks as equals, so a constant theme in his approach was to free the slaves and to send them back to Africa.

Lincoln refused to denounce the Fugitive Slave Law publicly. He wrote to a friend: "I confess I hate to see the poor creatures hunted down . . . but I bite my lips and keep quiet."

In his 1858 campaign in Illinois for the Senate against Stephen Douglas, Lincoln spoke differently depending on the views of his listeners (and also perhaps depending on how close it was to the election). Speaking in northern Illinois in July (in Chicago), he said:

> Let us discard all this quibbling about this man and the other man, this race and that race and the other race being inferior, and therefore they must be placed in an inferior position. Let us discard all these things, and unite as one people throughout this land, until we shall once more stand up declaring that all men are created equal.

Two months later in Charleston, in southern Illinois, Lincoln told his audience:

> I will say, then, that I am not, nor ever have been, in favor of bringing about in any way the social and political equality of the white and Black races (applause); that I am not, nor ever have been, in favor of making voters or jurors of Negroes, nor of qualifying them to hold office, nor to intermarry with white people. . .
>
> And inasmuch as they cannot so live, while they do remain together there must be the position of superior and inferior, and I as much as any other man am in favor of having the superior position assigned to the white race.

Behind the secession of the South from the Union, after Lincoln was elected president in the fall of 1860 as candidate of the new Republican Party, was a long series of policy clashes between South and North. The Northern elite wanted economic expansion — free land, free labor, a free market, a high protective tariff for manufacturers, a bank of the United States. The slave interests opposed all that; they saw Lincoln and the Republicans as making continuation of their pleasant and prosperous way of life impossible in the future.

So, when Lincoln was elected, seven Southern states seceded from the Union. Lincoln initiated hostilities by trying to repossess the federal base at Fort Sumter, South Carolina, and four more states seceded. The Confederacy was formed; the Civil War was on.

Lincoln's first inaugural address, in March 1861, was conciliatory: "I have no purpose, directly or indirectly, to interfere with the institution of slavery in the states where it exists. I believe I have no lawful right to do so, and I have no inclination to do so." And with the war four months on, when General John C. Frémont in Missouri declared martial law and said slaves of owners resisting the United States were to be free, Lincoln countermanded this order. He was anxious to hold in the Union the slave states of Maryland, Kentucky, Missouri, and Delaware.

It was only as the war grew more bitter, the casualties mounted, desperation to win heightened, and the criticism of the abolitionists threatened to unravel the tattered coalition behind Lincoln that he began to act against slavery. Hofstadter puts it this way: "Like a delicate barometer, he recorded the trend of pressures, and as the Radical pressure increased he moved toward the left."

Racism in the North was as entrenched as slavery in the South, and it would take the war to shake both. New York Blacks could not vote unless they owned $250 in property (a qualification not applied to whites). A proposal to abolish this, put on the ballot in 1860, was defeated two to one.

Wendell Phillips, with all his criticism of Lincoln, recognized the possibilities in his election. Speaking at the Tremont Temple in Boston the day after the election, Phillips said:

> If the telegraph speaks truth, for the first time in our history the slave has chosen a president of the United States. . . . Not an abolitionist, hardly an antislavery man, Mr. Lincoln consents to represent an antislavery idea. A pawn on the political chessboard, his value is in his position; with fair effort, we may soon change him for knight, bishop, or queen, and sweep the board. [Applause.]

The spirit of Congress, even after the war began, was shown in a resolution it passed in the summer of 1861, with only a few dissenting votes: ". . . this war is not waged . . . for any purpose of . . . overthrowing or interfering with the rights of established institutions of those states, but . . . to preserve the Union."

The abolitionists stepped up their campaign. Emancipation petitions poured into Congress in 1861 and 1862. In May of that year, Phillips said: "Abraham Lincoln may not wish it; he cannot prevent it. . . . [T]he Negro is the pebble in the cog-wheel, and the machine cannot go on until you get him out."

In July of 1862 Congress passed a Confiscation Act, which enabled the freeing of slaves of those fighting the Union. But this was not enforced by the Union generals, and Lincoln ignored the nonenforcement. Horace Greeley, editor of the *New York Tribune*, wrote an open letter to Lincoln warning him that his supporters were "sorely disappointed and deeply pained. . . . We require of you, as the first servant of the Republic, charged especially and preeminently with this duty, that you EXECUTE THE LAWS. . . . We think you are strangely and disastrously remiss . . . with regard to the emancipating provisions of the new Confiscation Act. . . . We think you are unduly influenced by the councils . . . of certain politicians hailing from the border slave states."

Greeley appealed to the practical need of winning the war. "We must have scouts,

Susie King Taylor, the first Black Army nurse. Black women played a crucial role during the Civil War.

guides, spies, cooks, teamsters, diggers, and choppers from the Blacks of the South, whether we allow them to fight for us or not. . . . I entreat you to render a hearty and unequivocal obedience to the law of the land."

Lincoln replied to Greeley:

Dear Sir: . . . I have not meant to leave any one in doubt. . . . My paramount object in this struggle is to save the Union, and is not either to save or destroy slavery. If I could save the Union without freeing any slave, I would do it; and if I could save it by freeing all the slaves, I would do it. . . . I have here stated my purpose according to my view of official duty, and I intend no modification of my oft-expressed personal wish that all men, everywhere, could be free.

When in September 1862 Lincoln issued his preliminary Emancipation Proclamation, it was a military move, giving the South four months to stop rebelling, threatening to emancipate their slaves if they continued to fight, promising to leave slavery untouched in states that came over to the North.

Thus, when the Emancipation Proclamation was issued Jan. 1, 1863, it declared slaves free in those areas still fighting against the Union (which it listed very carefully), and said nothing about slaves behind Union lines.

Limited as it was, the Emancipation Proclamation spurred antislavery forces. By the summer of

1864, 400,000 signatures asking legislation to end slavery had been gathered and sent to Congress, something unprecedented in the history of the country. That April, the Senate had adopted the 13th Amendment, declaring an end to slavery, and in January 1865, the House of Representatives followed.

With the proclamation, the Union Army was open to Blacks. And the more Blacks entered the war, the more it appeared a war for their liberation. The more whites had to sacrifice, the more resentment there was, particularly among poor whites in the North, who were drafted by a law that allowed the rich to buy their way out of the draft for $300. And so the draft riots of 1863 took place, uprisings of angry whites in Northern cities, their targets not the rich, far away, but the Blacks, near at hand.

It was an orgy of death and violence. A Black man in Detroit described what he saw: a mob, with kegs of beer on wagons, armed with clubs and bricks, marching through the city, attacking Black men, women, children. He heard one man say: "If we are got to be killed up for Negroes then we will kill everyone in this town."

The Civil War was one of the bloodiest in human history up to that time: 600,000 dead on both sides, in a population of 30 million — the equivalent, in the United States of 1990, with a population of 250 million, of 5 million dead. As the battles became more intense, as the bodies piled up, as war fatigue grew, and hundreds of thousands of slaves were deserting the plantations, 4 million Blacks in the South became a great potential force for whichever side would use them.

Du Bois, in *Black Reconstruction*, pointed this out: "It was this plain alternative that brought Lee's sudden surrender. Either the South must make terms with its slaves, free them, use them to fight the North . . . or they could surrender to the North with the assumption that the North after the war must help them to defend slavery, as it had before." Black women played an important part in the war, especially toward the end. Sojourner Truth became recruiter of black troops for the Union Army, as did Josephine St. Pierre Ruffin of Boston. Harriet Tubman raided plantations, leading Black and white troops, and in one expedition freed 750 slaves.

It has been said that Black acceptance of slavery is proved by the fact that during the Civil War, when there were opportunities for escape, most slaves stayed on the plantation. In fact, half a million ran away — about one in five, a high proportion when one considers that there was great difficulty in knowing where to go and how to live.

In 1865, a South Carolina planter wrote to the *New York Tribune*:

> . . . the conduct of the Negro in the late crisis of our affairs has convinced me that we were all laboring under a delusion. . . . I believed that these people were content, happy, and attached to their masters. But events and reflection have caused me to change these positions. . . . If they were content, happy, and attached to their masters, why did they desert him in the moment of his need and flock to an enemy, whom they did not know; and thus left their perhaps really good masters whom they did know from infancy?

In parts of Mississippi, Arkansas, and Kentucky, slaves destroyed plantations or took them over. Two hundred thousand Blacks joined the Army and Navy, and 38,000 were killed. Historian James McPherson says: "Without their help, the North could not have won the war as soon as it did, and perhaps it could not have won at all."

Howard Zinn is author of *A People's History of the United States.*

Used by permission of Howard Zinn. This reading is excerpted from A People's History of the United States *(abridged teaching edition), by Howard Zinn (New York: The New Press, 1997).*

The Civil War and the Death of Slavery Timeline

January 1861: Just two months after Lincoln is elected president, most Southern states secede. They take with them the labor of about 3.5 million enslaved Black people. Blacks form the backbone of the Southern economy: cotton, rice, sugar, dockwork, etc. Southern crops are also crucial to the Northern economy.

March 1861: Lincoln's inaugural address: If the Southern states return to the Union, President Lincoln promises to support a constitutional amendment guaranteeing that slavery will never be abolished in states where it currently exists.

April 1861: Lincoln expects a short war to reunify the nation; he calls for 75,000 volunteers for three months.

May 1861: Major General Benjamin Butler refuses to return fugitive slaves who fled to Fort Monroe in Virginia to seek refuge with the Union Army. Butler declares the runaways "contraband of war" — property that can be seized because of its military value to the enemy. Thousands of fugitives begin arriving at Fort Monroe.

June 1861: Baltimore. Northern General Burnside returns two enslaved Black people to their supposed master because they had tried to escape to Union lines.

July 4, 1861: Colonel Tyler of the North declares to residents in Virginia: "I desire to assure you that the relation of master and servant as recognized in your state shall be respected. Your authority over that species of property shall not in the least be interfered with. To this end, I assure you that those under my command have orders to take up and hold any Negroes found running about the camp without passes from their masters."

Aug. 6, 1861: Congress passes the First Confiscation Act, which nullifies slave owners' claims to fugitive slaves who had been employed in the Confederate war effort.

Aug. 30, 1861: Union General Frémont in Missouri issues a proclamation freeing people enslaved by enemy plantation owners. President Lincoln orders him to rescind the proclamation. When Frémont refuses, Lincoln dismisses him.

October 1861: Major General Dix of the Union Army seizes two Virginia counties. He orders that slavery is not to be interfered with, and that enslaved people are not to be given freedom by the Union Army. One Union general promises to put down any attempted slave insurrection "with an iron hand."

1861 and most of 1862: Free Blacks in the North are not allowed to volunteer to fight with the Union Army. The abolitionist Frederick Douglass criticizes this policy: "[T]his is no time to fight with one hand when both are needed; . . . this is no time to fight only with your white hand, and allow your black hand to remain tied."

By the beginning of 1862: By the thousands, people are escaping from slavery and finding their way to the invading Union armies. Some generals decide to return enslaved people, others decide to put them to work for the Union cause.

April 1862: Union General Hunter, with only 10,000 men, must hold the coasts of Georgia, South Carolina, and Florida. He pleads with Washington for more troops. The War Department replies: "You must get along as best you can. Not a man from the North can be spared."

Against orders, Hunter begins using runaway slaves as soldiers. He writes: "They are now eager beyond all things to take the field and be led into action. . . . They are displaying great natural capacities in acquiring the duties of the soldier."

May 9, 1862: Gen. Hunter declares all enslaved people free in South Carolina, Georgia, and Florida. Lincoln quickly issues a proclamation revoking Hunter's abolition order and urges the border states to adopt gradual, compensated emancipation.

May 12, 1862: Robert Smalls, with seven other enslaved people, steals the *CSS Planter*, a Confederate military ship, and sails it out of the Charleston Harbor in South Carolina. Smalls surrenders the ship to the Union forces, freeing himself and the others on the ship.

July 17, 1862: Congress passes the Second Confiscation Act and the Militia Act. Enslaved people "belonging" to disloyal slaveholders are declared "forever free" and Black men are allowed and encouraged to join the military for the first time. Congress also authorizes Lincoln to colonize all Blacks willing to immigrate to "some tropical country" and provides $600,000 to deport them.

Aug. 22, 1862: Lincoln realizes that whatever he does, enslaved people are freeing themselves simply by running to the Union armies by the thousands. However, in a letter to Horace Greeley, editor of the *New York Tribune*, he still maintains that "My paramount object in this struggle is to save the Union and is not either to save or destroy slavery. If I could save the Union without freeing any slaves, I would do it; and if I could save it by freeing all the slaves, I would do that. What I do about slavery and the colored race, I do because I believe it would help to save the Union." He worries, in part, that if he freed the slaves, the 20,000 Kentuckians fighting for the Union might go over to the Confederacy. In addition to Kentucky, the slave states of Missouri, Maryland, and Delaware also did not secede.

1862: The North is having great trouble winning the war. If France and England were to support the South, the North may be defeated. Lincoln finds it increasingly hard to get new recruits to fight.

September 1862: Lincoln announces the Emancipation Proclamation, which will take effect Jan. 1, 1863. It will free all enslaved people in the states and portions of states "under rebellion," but will not free enslaved people in the areas under Union control such as the border states of Kentucky, Maryland, Delaware, and Missouri, or in the western counties of Virginia that split off from Virginia and stayed in the Union — later becoming the state of West Virginia. Thus, if states or parts of states were to return to the Union between September and January, slave owners would be able to keep their slaves.

Dec. 1, 1862: In his message to Congress, Lincoln proposes a peace plan that would amend the Constitution to compensate loyal slave owners for any slaves they "lost" as a result of the war and allow rebelling slave owners to keep their slaves for another 40 years — until 1900 — if they lay down their arms.

January 1863: The Emancipation Proclamation takes effect, freeing enslaved people in states under rebellion, but not in the border states or in areas controlled by Union armies, such as New Orleans and other parts of Louisiana. Lincoln changes course; he allows active recruitment of free Blacks into the Union Army. In the South, slave resistance continues to grow. Enslaved people sabotage plantations, stop work, flee to Union lines, and volunteer to fight their former masters.

Spring 1863: The Emancipation Proclamation swings English and French public opinion to the side of the Union.

June 2, 1863: Just a few weeks after the War Department approves the creation of Union Army regiments composed of African Americans, abolitionist Harriet Tubman leads 150 Black soldiers in the Combahee River Raid. The raid freed more than 700 enslaved men, women, and children — the largest liberation of enslaved people in U.S. history.

July 1863: Lincoln begins a draft to get enough soldiers to continue the war. Only white males — no free Blacks — are to be drafted. The Irish workers in New York City stage massive and violent protests. Riots kill more than 100 people, and injure more than 1,000, mostly African Americans. Workers and poor whites protest the draft and the provision of the law that allows wealthy people to hire substitutes or to buy their way out for $300. One slogan is: "It's a rich man's war and a poor man's fight."

July 1863: The 54th Regiment Massachusetts Volunteer Infantry, a Black regiment under the command of Colonel Robert Gould Shaw, leads the attack on the Confederate Fort Wagner in Charleston, South Carolina. They fight courageously. More than half the regiment dies in battle.

June 1864: An officer under General Ulysses S. Grant, commenting on the performance of the 20,000 Black soldiers under his command in Virginia, says, "The problem [of finding troops to fight] is solved. The Negro is a man, a soldier, a hero."

1864: The largest petition drive ever before in the nation's history is spearheaded by Susan B. Anthony and Elizabeth Cady Stanton of the Women's Loyal National League. Abolitionists gather 400,000 signatures to abolish slavery.

Jan. 31, 1865: Congress passes the 13th Amendment, abolishing slavery and involuntary servitude "except as a punishment for crime."

March 17, 1865: In an act of desperation, Confederate President Jefferson Davis calls for forming a Black army to fight for the South. The Confederate Congress approves drafting 300,000 Black slaves for combat, and implies that those who volunteer will gain their freedom.

April 9, 1865: General Robert E. Lee surrenders.

During the Civil War, nearly 500,000 enslaved people escaped to the Union Army lines. More than 186,000 Black soldiers fought, having formed 154 regiments. At least 68,000 Blacks died in combat. Eight out of every 10 Black soldiers who served were either liberated or escaped slaves.

—compiled by Bill Bigelow and Adam Sanchez

"Who Freed the Slaves?"
Essay Criteria Sheet

Write an essay on the following topic: Who or what freed the slaves? Use essay format. Include evidence from the history you've learned in class as well as any outside sources you researched. Think broadly. There is no one right answer. Depending on your evidence, many answers could be "correct." **Your essay must have a thesis statement, an introduction, supporting details/evidence, and a conclusion. Use quotes from the readings.**

Criteria Sheet:

___1. **THESIS**

Is the essay's main point clear about who or what freed the slaves? A thesis can be stated plainly or it can be implied, but it needs to be clear to your reader. Note that you don't have to say *one* person or group, there might be many factors.

___2. **INTRODUCTION**

Is the introduction engaging? Does it make your reader want to read further? Use a quote, question, story, or simply a dramatic thesis statement.

___3. **EVIDENCE**

Does your evidence support the essay's thesis? You should use clear historical evidence from a variety of sources. Include dates, names of historical figures, laws, and quotes that support your thesis.

___4. **ANALYSIS OF DATA**

Do you discuss your evidence? Say clearly how your evidence supports your thesis.

___5. **CONCLUSION**

Do you have an effective conclusion? The conclusion might summarize, restate, or emphasize the importance of the thesis. It might circle back to the essay's introduction. It might make a connection to something going on today or raise further questions to think about.

___6. **ORGANIZATION AND TRANSITIONS**

Do you make connections between paragraphs? Are transitions smooth? Did you check and correct grammar, punctuation, and spelling?

___7. **(Optional) COUNTERCLAIM**

Present, analyze, and critique someone who answers "Who freed the slaves?" differently from you. What is legitimate about their argument and what do you think is wrong? What are they emphasizing? What are they leaving out?

AFTERWORD

From the Civil War to Reconstruction

By Adam Sanchez

IT'S IMPOSSIBLE TO EXPLAIN the explosive era following the Civil War without understanding how the actions of thousands of abolitionists and enslaved people led to emancipation. The revolutionary process that destroyed slavery continued as formerly enslaved people defined and redefined freedom during Reconstruction. The immediate and uncompensated emancipation of 4 million enslaved people, something that only a few years earlier seemed utterly impossible, and the apparent success of the abolitionists who were previously considered dangerous radicals, unleashed hope for millions that a new world based on equality and justice was possible. Therefore, a people's history of abolition and the Civil War lays a crucial foundation for a people's history of Reconstruction.

Reconstruction was a moment in which people who had been enslaved became congressmen. It was a moment where a Black-majority South Carolina Legislature could tax the rich to pay for

THE FIRST COLORED SENATOR AND REPRESENTATIVES.
In the 41ˢᵗ and 42ⁿᵈ Congress of the United States.

More than 1,500 African Americans were elected to state and local offices during Reconstruction.

163

public schools. It was a moment that spawned the first experiments in Black self-determination in the Georgia Sea Islands, where 400 freedmen and women divided up land, planted crops, started schools, and created a democratic system with their own constitution, congress, supreme court, and armed militia. It was a moment where thousands of Blacks and poor whites organized together across the South in the Union Leagues, engaging in strikes, boycotts, demonstrations, and educational campaigns. And it was a moment where other social movements — in particular, the labor movement and the feminist movement — drew strength from the inspiring actions of African Americans to secure and define their own freedom. In sum, the Reconstruction era was a moment when Black lives, Black actions, and Black ideas mattered.

Yet too often, the violent white supremacist backlash overshadows the possibilities and achievements of this era. Too often in classrooms across the country, teachers skip or rush through the story of this grand experiment in interracial democracy. This reflects the textbook treatment of the era. For example, in the chapter on Reconstruction in *History Alive! The United States*, the only time the textbook explicitly discusses the monumental accomplishments of Black Americans is in one paragraph titled "African Americans in Office." Yet *History Alive!* devotes two paragraphs to "White Terrorism" and *five pages* — nearly half the entire chapter — to Reconstruction's demise. Although it is crucial to teach the counter-revolution that led to the establishment of Jim Crow, it's also important that teachers don't make the backlash the only story — once again putting whites at the center of U.S. history. To ignore or minimize the successes of Reconstruction reinforces the narrative of slow American racial progress — a historical myth in which our country gradually evolved from slavery to Jim Crow to a post-racial society. This is a fable that ignores the actions of millions of people who fought to end systems of white supremacy and prevent new ones from taking hold.

The story of Reconstruction, told in nearly every major U.S. history textbook, highlights the ideas and actions of those at the top — the debates between the president and Congress. For example, the popular textbook *The American Journey* spends about 15 of the 21 pages devoted to Reconstruction explaining the actions of Congress and the president. The book dedicates most of the remaining pages to white resistance to Reconstruction in the South. The message communicated through textbooks like *The American Journey* is clear: It's the actions of those at the top that matter most. Yet, as Howard Zinn wrote:

> *An education that focuses on elites, ignores an important part of the historical record. . . . As a result of omitting, or downplaying, the importance of social movements of the people in our history . . . a fundamental principle of democracy is undermined: the principle that it is the citizenry, rather than the government, that is the ultimate source of power and the locomotive that pulls the train of government in the direction of equality and justice.*

The Reconstruction era is precisely one where the actions of citizens — many of whom had only recently won that designation — pulled the government "in the direction of equality and justice."

Furthermore, the backlash against Reconstruction was about much more than white terrorism. It was about taking back the Southern governments from the interracial coalition of poor people that for a brief time gained real political power. Once power was firmly in the hands of white elites, it was used to bury the real history of the Civil War and Reconstruction under a sea of Confederate monuments and memorials to the "Lost Cause" that still dot the landscape. As historian Eric Foner wrote in *The New York Times*, "Historical monuments are, among other things, an expression of power — an indication of who has the power to choose how history is remembered

Once power was firmly in the hands of white elites, it was used to bury the real history of the Civil War and Reconstruction under a sea of Confederate monuments and memorials to the "Lost Cause" that still dot the landscape.

in public places." We want teachers and students to feel empowered to reclaim the history of their community and their country.

That's why, in addition to publishing this collection, the Zinn Education Project has launched our Teach Reconstruction campaign. Today — in a moment where activists are struggling to make Black lives matter — every student should probe the relevance of Reconstruction. If anything, the Reconstruction period teaches us that when it comes to justice and equality, what may seem impossible is indeed possible — but depends on us, not simply the president or Congress.

We've included one Reconstruction lesson immediately following this afterword and encourage teachers to download others that we continue to add at the Zinn Education Project website. While the textbooks emphasize what was done to or for newly freed people, the role play that follows asks students to imagine themselves as people who were formerly enslaved and to wrestle with a number of issues about what they needed to ensure genuine freedom. Together, students discuss who should own the plantation land — and what that land would be used for; the fate of Confederate leaders; voting rights; self-defense; and conditions placed on the former Confederate states prior to being allowed to return to the Union. By having students confront the questions that shaped the Reconstruction era from the perspective of freedmen and women, the role play mirrors the sense of power and historical possibility of the era.

If anything, the Reconstruction period teaches us that when it comes to justice and equality, what may seem impossible is indeed possible — but depends on us, not simply the president or Congress.

As the late historian Lerone Bennett Jr. concludes in his indispensable book *Black Power U.S.A.: The Human Side of Reconstruction 1867–1877*, although the dream of interracial democracy may have died with the white supremacist counter-revolution that began in the 1870s, "the reconstruction of that dream, when it comes, if it comes, must go back . . . to the fundamental principles of that first Reconstruction — Economic Security, Political Liberty, and Light for all the bondsmen of America, Black and white."

Reconstructing the South: A Role Play

By Bill Bigelow

WHAT KIND OF COUNTRY is this going to be? This was the urgent question posed in the period immediately following the U.S. Civil War. When students learn about Reconstruction, if they learn about this period at all, too often they learn how the presidents and Congress battled over the answer to this question. Textbooks and curricula emphasize what was done *to* or *for* newly freed people, but usually not how they acted to define their own freedom. This role play asks students to imagine themselves as people who were formerly enslaved and to wrestle with a number of issues about what they needed to ensure genuine "freedom": ownership of land—and what the land would be used for; the fate of Confederate leaders; voting rights; self-defense; and conditions placed on the former Confederate states prior to being allowed to return to the Union. The role play's premise is that the end of the war presented people in our country with a key turning point, that there existed at this moment an opportunity to create a society with much greater equality and justice.

A sketch by Jas. E. Taylor of a farmer plowing in South Carolina, published in Frank Leslie's Illustrated Newspaper, *Oct. 20, 1866.*

Library of Congress

The students' role begins: "And now the war is over. This is a joyous time. The horrors of slavery have ended. In millions of gestures, large and small, Black people in America resisted slavery from its very beginning in 1619. You won your freedom and the 13th Amendment to the Constitution ended slavery once and for all. All through the summer of 1865 there have been parades and celebrations. It's a time of unbelievable excitement, but also apprehension. What exactly does freedom mean? What kind of lives will you have now?"

Knowing how deeply segregated and unequal our country is today can make it seem that this was our destiny. As Howard Zinn often said, when we look only at what happened, it can make history seem inevitable. But history is full of choice points; there are always alternatives. Looking carefully at Reconstruction can alert students to some of the most significant could-have-beens in our country's history.

Materials Needed

- Copies of "Freedmen and Women" role for every student.
- Copies of "Reconstructing the South: Problems" for every student.

Suggested Procedure

1. Of course, the more background on slavery and the Civil War students have, the better. Ask students, "Now that the Civil War is over and the Confederate leaders have surrendered, and the 13th Amendment has ended slavery, what do you think will happen to the people who had until just recently been enslaved?" Pause for students to think about and respond to this question, but don't turn this into a full discussion, as it's meant simply to get them thinking about the issues they will explore in more depth in the role play.

2. Distribute the "Freedmen and Women" role to every student in the class. Read it aloud with the class, pausing to make sure everyone understands the circumstances in which people find themselves. Depending on how much writing on slavery students have already done, one way to help students enter their role is by asking them to create a persona as a formerly enslaved individual and to write an interior monologue from this person's perspective. (See "Promoting Social Imagination Through Interior Monologues" at the Zinn Education Project for examples of how to help students write interior monologues.) If you choose to do this, brainstorm possible interior

monologue perspectives with students and list these for students to see. Allow students to write for 10 minutes or so. The aim is not to complete a finished piece, but to get them to quickly enter another persona and to imagine this individual's hopes and concerns. Once students have finished writing — and it's fine if they stop mid-thought — ask students to pair up and to read their monologues to one another. Afterward, ask for volunteers to share a few interior monologues aloud with the rest of the class. Ask students to comment on what they appreciate about these pieces, and about which themes emerge from students' writing.

3. Distribute a copy to all students of "Reconstructing the South: Problems." Over the years, I have handled this in a number of different ways. If students are accustomed to doing homework, you can give these questions to students in advance of the class period where they will be discussed, and ask students to read and decide what they think is best, keeping in mind that they are attempting to consider these as people who were recently enslaved. Another option is to put students into small groups and have them attempt to reach agreement on each of the questions, and then to meet as a large group to talk through these problems. This has the advantage of students having thought about and discussed these prior to the large-group meeting. The small-group work makes it more likely that once the large group convenes, every student will have something to say. The disadvantage is that it makes this a longer activity, and may feel repetitive, as

each question gets discussed twice, once in the small group and once in the large. I've also simply given these questions to the full class to discuss and decide. Instructions from here on out presume this last option.

4. The structure of this role play is simple. All students are in the same role — attempting to represent people who have been recently freed from slavery. The premise of the role play is described in the student handout: "You are part of a delegation of African Americans who, up until recently, were enslaved. You are traveling to Washington, D.C., to demand legislation that will make sure that freedmen and women become truly free and are able to advance socially, politically, educationally, and economically. Before you leave, there are a number of key questions that you must agree upon. These are difficult questions, and your answers to them could determine whether your future is one of progress or misery."

Tell students that you will not be leading them in this activity — that, just as in the real historical moment, it was the people themselves, newly freed from slavery, who had to confront these difficult choices. Students will need not only to figure out what they think are the best answers to the questions posed in the handout, but they will also need to decide *how* they will discuss and resolve these. Review with students some of the ways that they might handle their conversations about these issues. They might choose one student to chair the entire proceedings. They might choose one student per question to chair the discussion. They might decide to have a system where one student raises a hand to speak and then calls on the next student who calls on the next student. Through the years, this last choice has been the one that has seemed to work best with a whole-group role play like this, but I still remember one class several years ago that selected a trusted student to call on people and lead the deliberations, and this student was magnificent. The important thing is that students feel that the process belongs to them. At the outset, I emphasize

that they should discuss and decide on a process for decision-making prior to beginning their conversations. On occasion, these can become chaotic when students have not agreed on the process. Also, remind them to speak in the "I" or "we" voice, as people formerly held in slavery.

As students deliberate, my job is to take notes on their conversations. I will be able to review these to plan teaching from this point forward but also I use these to read excerpts aloud to students so that they can appreciate themselves as intellectuals, struggling with big ideas. The first question focuses on the ownership of land. It's key, of course. Here's a sampling from one year's 2nd-period class at Franklin High School in Portland, Oregon:

Alex: *We did all the work. We worked so everyone else could live.*

Eron: *We need a new beginning. Somehow we need to grow as people. I think that we should own all the plantations. Well, not all. But it would bring a new wave of power to us.*

Ilantha: *We should be given the plantations. What would whites do with them? Where else would we live if we didn't have the plantations?*

Allen: *I don't think we should get the land. They've owned the land a long time. If there are 50 of us on a plantation, which one gets it. We should work for wages.*

Britany: *It's their land. They owned it. During the time they held us as slaves, it was legal. They didn't do anything illegal.*

Karli: *They paid for them in money, but we paid for them in work. We took care of them. We bought that land with our labor. It ought to be ours.*

Wendi: *I think we should think about what we would do if the roles were reversed. Think about what happened to the Indians, getting kicked off their land. Do we want to do that to the plantation owners? We have to think about this from their point of view.*

Ultimately, in an 18 to 11 vote, this class decided not to demand ownership of the plantations. It's not the conclusion that I had hoped they would arrive at, but that's not the point. No matter what decisions students reach, their discussions — and sometimes heated arguments — lend themselves to rich follow-up, exploring fundamental questions about legality, ownership, justice, and race. And students' comments allow me to see where there are misunderstandings, as in Wendi's false equivalence of taking land from Native Americans and from plantation owners. [*Freedom's Unfinished Revolution* (American Social History Project, 1996) includes an excellent chapter exploring landownership following the Civil War that is available on the Zinn Education Project website.]

5. Depending on how students' conversation goes for the six questions, you might simply let them continue these until they have finished. Another alternative is to pause after each question to discuss students' arguments and to draw them back to their charge to demand policies that will advance them "socially, politically, educationally, and economically."

6. Following their deliberations, I ask students to choose at least three of the issues they discussed and to write about what they think happened in real life and why. I also ask students to reflect on the process of making decisions together: What difficulties did you have making decisions that freedmen and women might also have? When were you

successful in overcoming these difficulties? Kelly concluded her response paper: "These questions were hard to answer according to our role. You felt like you had to be realistic and honest about what could happen, but at the same time you wanted to think big, and stand up for your full rights. I'll be interested to find out what really happened. . . . [The role play] gave us a better understanding for other people and a sense of empathy."

And that's where we want to leave students with this activity: eager to learn about "what really happened," how the actual human beings resolved these questions. I return to my notes on students' conversations about the six questions to plan my follow-up discussion on the role play. There are always gems, deserving to be explored further, like Eron's comment while discussing the fifth question that asks "How will the Black freedmen and women be protected from the revenge of the defeated soldiers and from the plantation owners?" Eron said: "We need to fight the system of our country. If we can't change that then there is no way to protect ourselves — we have to completely change the South."

Through engaging students in some of the essential questions that confronted people freed from slavery, students can begin to grasp how these questions are interrelated. It gives them a framework to evaluate different proposals for how the South would be "reconstructed" after the war. And as the "opening act" in students' study of Reconstruction, it establishes that the interests of freedmen and women should be seen as paramount.

Freedmen and Women

1865/1866: And now the war is over. This is a joyous time. The horrors of slavery have ended. In millions of gestures, large and small, Black people in America resisted slavery from its very beginning in 1619. You won your freedom and the 13th Amendment to the Constitution ended slavery once and for all. All through the summer of 1865 there have been parades and celebrations. It's a time of unbelievable excitement, but also apprehension. What exactly does freedom mean? What kind of lives will you have now? True, you are free to leave the plantation. You are free to go North. Free to travel. Free to seek out lost family members who had been sold off. But you're also free to starve, free to be attacked by angry whites seeking revenge, free to be kicked out of your homes by defeated plantation owners.

Consider all the problems you face: Even though you have lived your entire lives in the South working to make white people rich, you yourselves own nothing. The shack you live in is owned by your former owner. Same with all the tools, work animals, and seed. Even the clothes you have on are owned by your ex-master. Most important, you own no land. For the last 250 years, enslaved Black people were robbed of their labor and their knowledge in order to make white people rich and now in "freedom" you own absolutely nothing. Without land you will always be dependent, always forced to serve the property owners. You want to farm your own land, and grow food for your family.

And there are other problems: At least 90% of you are illiterate. Under slavery it was a crime to teach a slave to read or write. Some learned anyway, but most had no opportunity. Most of you own no guns. Almost all firearms are owned by your former masters and the whites who fought for the Confederacy. (Remember, however, that the Union Army still occupies much of the South, and some Union soldiers used to be held in slavery, like you.) Also you have no political rights: You can't vote or hold office.

Long ago, your people were kidnapped in Africa, stuffed into the bellies of stinking slave ships, stripped of your language, dumped in a strange land, punished for practicing your religion, frequently separated from your family members, and forced to labor with a whip at your back. The wealth of this country, both South and North, is because of *your* labor, *your* skills, *your* knowledge. You've suffered too much — and whites have profited too much — for you to be forced to wander the countryside as beggars. This is not your idea of freedom.

Freed African Americans heading into Newbern, North Carolina. Harper's Weekly, *Feb. 21, 1863.*

Reconstructing the South: Problems

YOU ARE PART OF A DELEGATION of African Americans who, up until recently, were enslaved. You are traveling to Washington, D.C., to demand legislation that will make sure that freedmen and women become truly free and are able to advance socially, politically, educationally, and economically. Before you leave, there are a number of key questions that you must agree upon. These are difficult questions, and your answers to them could determine whether your future is one of progress or misery.

1. **SITUATION:** Right now, almost no ex-slaves in the South own any land. Legally, most of you don't even own the clothes you are wearing. All your lives you have lived and worked on plantations owned by wealthy whites. Some people argue that the legitimate owners of the Southern plantations are you, the freed slaves. They say that for almost 250 years, your people are the ones who did all the work and made the plantations profitable — and that because of your sacrifices, rightfully the plantations should belong to you. And, remember, these white plantation owners are traitors. They began a war that killed more than 600,000 people. Why should they get to keep the land that *you* worked on all those years? Others say that this might be the moral thing to demand, but it would be politically unwise. Ultimately, it will be Northern politicians who will be deciding your fate. Remember, like Abraham Lincoln, most of these people were never abolitionists. And now that you are free, they will be reluctant to take away the property of other white people to give it to Black people. For one thing, they may worry that this would set an example for poor whites in the North to take over the property of rich whites. They, too, could say that the factories were built with their labor and they should own them. Northern politicians may also worry that if you owned the land, you might want to grow food instead of cotton, and this could have a negative impact on the Northern economy.

   QUESTION: Now that the war is ended, who should own and control these plantations?

2. **QUESTION:** Would you be willing to promise the Northern politicians that if they gave you land, that you would continue to grow cotton?

   ARGUMENTS: Some of you argue that, of course, you have to give politicians this assurance, otherwise you'll get nothing from them. They argue: Look, we may not want to grow cotton, and we may not want to make promises to anyone, but we have to be realistic; these people care about Northern industries maintaining their supply of cheap cotton more than they care about your desires. It's better to get something than to get nothing. Others of you argue that to offer this promise is just to trade in one kind of slavery for another. What kind of freedom is it when you are forced to grow a crop you don't want to grow? Cotton is a "sorrow" crop, associated with slavery. You can't eat cotton and growing it makes you dependent on cotton dealers — all white — to market your product. And it makes you vulnerable to prices of cotton going up and down, something you have no control over. If it's your land, you should be able to grow what you want.

3. **SITUATION:** There are still lots of Confederate (Southern) military officers and political leaders at large in the South. True, the war is over. But these are the people who actively led the slave owners' fight to keep slavery.

    QUESTION: What do you propose should happen to these Confederate leaders?

    ARGUMENTS: Some of you argue that the top leaders should be executed or at least imprisoned for the rest of their lives. They argue that these ex-Confederate leaders are guilty of mass murder because they led an illegal war — a war that killed more than 600,000 human beings and caused great suffering. These people also argue that not only do Confederate leaders deserve to be executed because of their role in the war, but more importantly they also pose the greatest danger to your freedom. These are the people who will be desperate to return to slavery days and they have the money and leadership capabilities to organize secret armies to push you back into slavery. Others argue that if you appear to want revenge, and go after the most popular white leaders in the South that it will poison relations between Blacks and whites, and damage the long-term possibility for racial harmony. They argue that the best way to get white Southerners to rise up against you is to kill or imprison their leaders. They say that we need to put the war behind us, and that so long as you have rights and resources, you don't need to hurt anyone else.

4. **SITUATION:** Before the war, enslaved Blacks counted as 3/5 of a person in determining how many U.S. representatives a state was entitled to — even though, of course, Blacks held in slavery had no vote. Now that slavery has ended, Blacks will be counted as full people whether or not they are allowed to vote. Ironically, if former slaves *don't* vote, this could mean that the white-controlled South could become even more powerful.

    QUESTION: Who should be allowed to vote in the new South? Everyone? Only former slaves? Only those who were loyal to the United States during the war? Women?

    ARGUMENTS: This is a controversial and complicated issue: Some people say only those with land should vote, because they are the ones who have the most stake in society and they are the most stable people. Some argue that only people who can read should be able to vote, because otherwise people will not vote intelligently. Others say this sounds good, but if landownership or literacy were qualifications for voters, then people who would be able to vote would be mostly rich white people with educations. Some argue that any Southerner who picked up arms against the U.S. government should not be allowed to vote — that these people proved that they were disloyal to the United States and should not now be rewarded with the vote. Besides, anyone who supported the Confederacy and slavery will now use their vote to work against your freedom. Others believe that if you try to deny the vote to all those who supported the Confederacy that would mean taking it away from most white Southerners, and this would make it seem like you were trying to impose a Black government on the South. Denied the vote, whites might turn to rebellion or terrorism and begin murdering Blacks. As you know, many of those who made up the abolition movement in the North were white women. They argue that now is the time to demand a Constitutional amendment that would give everyone the vote: white men, white women, Black men, Black women. Freedom and democracy is in the air, and this is the time to create a whole new society based on equality. Others say that if you demand the right for women to vote, this will make you look radical and foolish and no one will take you seriously. It will be seen as radical enough just demanding the vote for Black men, but to add women to the mix will doom your movement.

5. **SITUATION:** Most of the guns in the South are owned by whites. Many people who fought with the Confederacy still have their weapons from the war. Temporarily, the South is occupied by the Union Army. Many white Southerners, probably most of them, would like nothing better than to return Blacks to slavery. There has been talk of a new organization, called the Ku Klux Klan, designed to terrorize Blacks and their white supporters, and to return the South to slavery.

QUESTION: How will the Black freedmen and women be protected from the revenge of the defeated soldiers and from the plantation owners?

ARGUMENTS: One proposal would be to keep the Union Army in the South, and perhaps to even bring in more troops. Some people argue that the Confederate Army might not have been able to defeat the Union Army, but it *would* be able to defeat the newly freed Black people. Therefore the Union Army will be needed for years. Others argue that the presence of Union soldiers will continue to anger white Southerners and some other solution must be found. Some argue that no Confederates should be allowed to own guns. Others counter that this would not be a solution and would continue to anger white Southerners. Some suggest that the Union Army should arm Blacks, so that they can defend themselves from possible attacks from whites. Others say that more guns in the South will just lead to more violence.

6. **QUESTION:** What conditions should be put on the Southern states before they are allowed to return to the Union?

ARGUMENTS: Some Northerners say that the Southern states never actually left the Union, so these states should be allowed back into the United States immediately. After all, didn't Lincoln wage the war based on the belief that secession was illegal? Others say this is ridiculous, the Southern states would just re-elect the rich racists who led the country to Civil War—the Southern states left the Union and organized a separate country, with a new constitution and president. The 13th Amendment to the U.S. Constitution ended slavery forever. However, if the South is allowed to re-enter the Union without any changes, what would stop them from passing laws that would bring back slavery under a different name? Here are some possibilities you might consider: Southern states can rejoin the Union after they ratify (approve) the 13th Amendment abolishing slavery. Others say this isn't enough, that the Southern states need to create new state governments that are democratically elected by the people, including now-freed Black people. Others say that this is not the business of the federal (U.S.) government, that it's up to each state to decide who gets to vote or not. Some Northerners say that the South should be ruled as conquered territory for several more years. It's too early to even raise the question of allowing the former Confederate states back into the Union. What do you think?

About the Authors

Adam Sanchez teaches social studies at Harvest Collegiate High School in New York City. He is on the editorial board of *Rethinking Schools* magazine and is a frequent contributor. Adam is also a Zinn Education Project Teacher Leader. During the 2017–2018 school year, he served as the Zinn Education Project Organizer/Curriculum Writer, focusing on Abolition, Civil War, and Reconstruction. In addition to writing for Rethinking Schools and the Zinn Education Project's "If We Knew Our History" column, Adam's writing has been featured in *The Nation*, *Teen Vogue*, *Newsela*, *History News Network*, *Common Dreams*, the *Huffington Post*, *Alternet*, *Socialist Worker*, and *Jacobin*. He lives in Astoria, Queens, with his wife Madelynn and their daughter Yemaya.

Bill Bigelow taught high school social studies in Portland, Oregon, for almost 30 years. He is the curriculum editor for *Rethinking Schools* magazine and co-directs the Zinn Education Project. He has authored or co-edited numerous books on teaching, including *Strangers in Their Own Country: A Curriculum on South Africa*, *The Power in Our Hands: A Curriculum on the History of Work and Workers in the United States*, *Rethinking Columbus*, *Rethinking Our Classrooms* (volumes 1 and 2), *Rethinking Globalization*, *The Line Between Us: Teaching About the Border and Mexican Immigration*, and most recently, *A People's Curriculum for the Earth: Teaching Climate Change and the Environmental Crisis*. He lives in Portland with his wife Linda Christensen.

Index

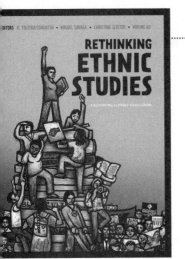

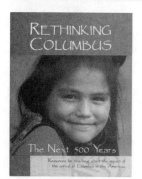

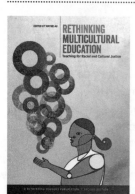

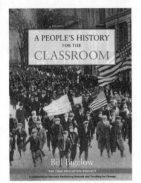

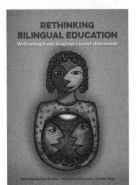